P9-DNG-009

Burnt Toast

Makes You Sing Good

Also by Kathleen Flinn

The Kitchen Counter Cooking School
The Sharper Your Knife, the Less You Cry

Flinn family—rejected Christmas card photo, 1971

Burnt Toast
Makes You Sing Good

A Memoir of Food and Love
from an American Midwest Family

Kathleen Flinn

Viking

VIKING
Published by the Penguin Group
Penguin Group (USA) LLC
375 Hudson Street
New York, New York 10014

USA I Canada I UK I Ireland I Australia I New Zealand I India I South Africa I China
penguin.com
A Penguin Random House Company

First published by Viking Penguin, a member of Penguin Group (USA) LLC, 2014

Photographs courtesy of Irene Flinn

Montreal steak seasoning recipe from *Field Guide to Herbs & Spices* by Aliza Green (Quirk Books). Used by permission of the author.

LIBRARY OF CONGRESS CATALOGING-IN-PUBLICATION DATA
Flinn, Kathleen.
Burnt toast makes you sing good : recipes of love, loss, and adventure from an American Midwest family / Kathleen Flinn.
pages cm
Includes bibliographical references and index.
ISBN 978-0-670-01544-3
1. Cooking, American—Midwestern style. 2. Flinn, Kathleen—Family. 3. Cooks—Untied States—Biography. I. Title.
TX715.2.M53F56 2014
641.5977—dc23
2014004497

Printed in the United States of America
1 3 5 7 9 10 8 6 4 2

Designed by Nancy Resnick

For my dad, Milton Gale Flinn Sr.,
and to the memory of my cousin
Richard Fridline Jr.

Contents

Part III

"I don't have to tell you I love you. I fed you pancakes."

—My grandmother Inez Monk Henderson

Siblings and offspring of Milton Flinn Sr. and Irene Flinn

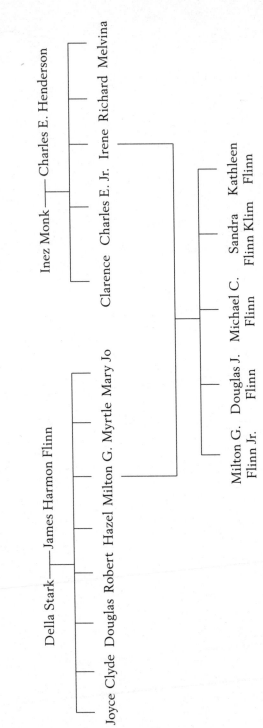

Family Tree of Kathleen Flinn

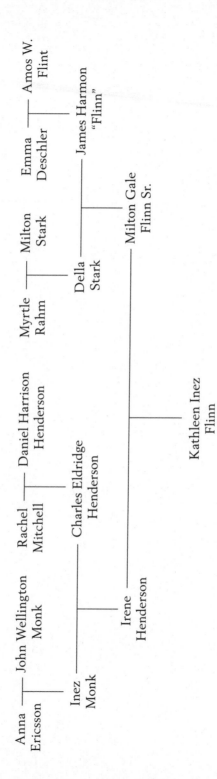

Burnt Toast
Makes You Sing Good

So It Begins . . .

I'm Swedish, which makes me sexy, and I'm Irish, which makes me want to talk about it."

My older sister, Sandy, coined this phrase more than twenty years ago. I use it as if it were mine, just like the forest green sweater that I "borrowed" from her in college, which I wore until it was threadbare and ended up in a box for charity. Isn't heritage community property?

But I didn't stop to think about what it meant until I casually trilled that line for a laugh in a talk during my first book tour. As people descended on the last of the warm white wine and softening inexpensive cheese at a cozy bookstore, an affable blond woman loitered patiently at the end of the line. "I'm Swedish and Irish, too," she said when she appeared at the table where I was signing books. She described a plucky, restless lot who emigrated to America to take on hard lives in their new homeland. "But, then, *my* parents, that's when it got boring," she said with an eye roll. "But yours, they sound so, well, *interesting.*"

Rarely am I struck without a comment. I'm Irish, after all. But my parents . . . *interesting?*

"I mean, you threw a dart at a map and moved to a strange city when you were a teenager and then you followed your dream and went to Paris," the woman continued in my absence of words. "People with normal parents don't do things like that."

I'm a typical American mutt. I didn't know much about my heritage then, not really. The further that I got into it, I discovered that in many ways, my family's story is both unremarkable and utterly fascinating. Poking into the murky edges of my ancestry, I also uncovered that I'm not who I thought I was, that my pithy line wasn't quite accurate. I'm a direct descendant of scrubwomen, a circus worker, a midwife, a bootlegger, a bigamist, an auto worker, and a cop. The most notable thing? That so many of my ancestors cooked, either for a living or as their passion. Until I started this journey, I didn't know just how honestly I'd come to my love of the kitchen.

I consider what follows a multigenerational memoir. I set out to tell my parents' tale and then realized that by extension, the whole thing necessitated sharing the lives of their parents, too.

In early research, I stumbled on a 1951 *Time* magazine article about my parents' age group, the one typically referred to as the silent generation, the children born in the grips of the Great Depression. The so-called greatest generation, which preceded them, inspired tons of ink, as did World War II, the conflict that defined their era. The baby boomers had Vietnam and the resistance and all those cultural counterpoints. By contrast, my parents' generation fought in Korea, sometimes called the forgotten war. *Time* magazine referred to the silent generation as a collective "quiet, still flame."

My parents were rarely still, and never quiet.

I spent a lot of time separating what truly happened from family lore and legend, not always an easy task. It's tricky working off memory, especially when writing from many people's versions of long-ago events. The genesis of this book is a series of stories that my mother put down on paper years ago about my father's childhood, her young family's years in San Francisco, and life on their Michigan farm. I interviewed my mom, recording dozens of hours of conversation as we sat in our Florida cottage. We drank wine and sat in rocking chairs in a gazebo under swaying palm trees as she recalled details of her life going all the way back to the Great Depression. Then I went to work to confirm as much of it as I could. I'm a trained journalist, so along with numerous interviews of relatives, I scoured letters, public documents, military records, and more than twenty years of research conducted by a professional genealogist.

This is a true story. No names have been changed. My cousins are *really* named Larry and Gary.

Part I

"Thanks, God, I can take it from here."
—My mother, Irene Henderson Flinn,
on marrying my father, Milton

CHAPTER 1

That's Amore

Clyde (left) and Milton Flinn at my parents' restaurant, 1960

Hey, Milt!" Uncle Clyde said, calling long distance. "What do you know about pizza?"

With that, my parents sold all their furniture and stuffed the rest of their belongings and three toddlers into the back of their 1954 Chevy Bel Air and headed to my Irish uncle's Italian restaurant in San Francisco.

Dad was Irish American. Mom was Swedish American. Neither of them knew anything about Italian cuisine. They didn't care. "So what if we didn't know anything about the food?" Mom says. "We both believed that life should always be an adventure."

My mother, Irene Henderson Flinn, just twenty-four, was a

pretty, shy brunette with a klutzy streak who favored those bat-wing glasses so popular in the 1950s. She was heavily pregnant, nearly five months along with her fourth child.

My father, Milton, was a twenty-seven-year-old recent college grad and Korean War veteran who had sold life insurance until a major recession swept the country.

Before they met, Mom worked her way through secretarial school and scored a well-paying position with the Michigan Council of Churches. A marine home from Korea, Dad held multiple jobs while juggling a full-time load at Michigan State yet found time to date a half dozen attractive coeds.

At least, until the night he picked Mom up at a roller-skating rink in Lansing.

"Now reverse," the rink's announcer instructed a sea of circling skaters in a bored voice.

Dad turned in unison with the young crowd—and slammed directly into my mom, knocking her to the concrete floor.

As he knelt to help her up, Mom took his hands, struck by his chiseled good looks and solid build. *A bit like Charlton Heston*, she thought.

Then they both noticed they were wearing matching outfits. He wore a butter yellow cotton shirt and gray wool trousers; she was clad in a soft yellow sweater and a similar gray skirt.

"It looks like we came together!" he joked, still holding her hands in his as they stood on the rink. "What are the odds?" Dad skated backward with fluid elegance while she clung to a side wall for support as the hit song "Kisses Sweeter Than Wine" by The Weavers played over the loudspeakers. They chatted without listening to the song's story of a farmer's life filled with children and hardships, but in the end, love made it all worthwhile. After another song, she implored him, "You're such a great skater. You should really go skate without me."

He gently guided her into the brightly lit concession area and bought her a Coke instead. They talked until the staff started mopping up and they realized the place had closed. She was surprised when he offered to take her home, and even more caught off guard when he asked her on a proper date. Mom couldn't believe her luck that such a smart, handsome college guy wanted to date her. As she confided the story to a co-worker her age attending his college, the woman just shook her head and put up a hand to silence her.

"Listen, I wouldn't get my hopes up," she said flatly to my mom as she fixed the circle pin on her shirt. "Don't you know he's dating the Water Carnival Queen? They're the big item around campus. I heard they're getting engaged."

The queen was a leggy, glamorous blonde. Her beauty was legend around Lansing.

Mom decided to check out her competition. She learned the beauty queen frequented a certain hair salon on Saturday mornings. With the deft nonchalance of a detective, she feigned waiting for a bus across the street until the blonde turned up. Mom watched her walk with the practiced poise of someone comfortable with being on display. Her dimpled smile showed off perfect, brilliant white teeth that matched her perfect, delicate gloves.

Mom felt beaten. She got on the next bus that arrived, even though she had no idea where it was going. As she took a seat, she gulped back tears. *How could I be so stupid?* she thought as the bus pulled away, leaving the blonde in the distance. *She's like a movie star. I don't stand a chance.*

After a few dates, Dad pulled into the drive-in movie theater. They'd brought along their own popcorn. He asked Mom to hold the paper bag, and when he took it back he spilled it all over them. "Irene, I've got something to say," he started nervously.

Here it comes, Mom thought. *He's going to dump me.*

"I've been trying to figure out a way to ask you to . . ." He paused and took a deep breath. "Will you marry me?" he blurted.

"But what about the Water Carnival Queen?" Mom asked, incredulous.

"Are you kidding me?" he responded, dumbfounded. He took her hands gently in his. "You're the brightest, most beautiful woman I've ever met. I knew you were the one for me the minute I picked you up off that rink."

Just a few months after getting knocked down, Mom was

happily knocked up after getting married in a town named Hope. First on the scene was Milton Jr., whom they called "Miltie." Douglas, "Dougie," arrived almost to the day the following year, making them what relatives called Irish twins. My sister Sandy came along just two years later.

Sandy's birth coincided with the so-called Eisenhower recession, which began in 1958, a bleak reminder that the postwar boom years couldn't last forever. Michigan always feels economic turndowns harder than other parts of the country. After all, a new car is the last thing someone orders when times get tough. Unemployment hit 25 percent in the state, Great Depression numbers. Every night after they put the kids to bed, my parents stayed up late, figuring out bills, worrying.

On one of these nights, the phone rang.

Uncle Clyde had a successful Italian eatery in San Francisco. Would Milt be interested in coming out to California to learn the restaurant business?

Within two weeks, they were on the road. They sold everything except their clothes, the rocking chair, and a baby carriage. "We really didn't think twice about it," Mom says. "We just decided to go."

In Illinois, when they saw the first sign for the famous highway, Mom and Dad burst out singing "(Get Your Kicks on) Route 66" as the kids cheered. "We felt like those people who went west in covered wagons," she says. Which made sense, since part of Route 66 follows a wagon trail blazed in 1857 by the U.S. Department of War as a way to access the western frontier. By 1926, the government joined other roads to patch together the nation's first cross-country highway.

Mom and Dad drove for seven days. Each morning, they scooped still-sleeping children off the hard beds of cheap roadside motels. They stopped to see a few sites to let the kids run around. They took in a big Paul Bunyan statue in Illinois, the world's largest rocking chair in Missouri, a blue whale in Oklahoma, and a ghost town in California. To save money, they mostly ate sandwiches for lunch and dinner, but they had breakfast out. In Amarillo, Texas, my

Midwest parents discovered people outside the movies actually say "y'all" when a waitress asked, "Y'all happy with your cheese grits?" They had never had them before. They marveled at the flavor of the chorizo that came with their eggs at a diner in Arizona and were enchanted at the sight of tortillas in place of toast in New Mexico.

By the end of the week the novelty of the drive wore off. My parents were exhausted. Dad's left forearm was thoroughly sunburned, the result of hanging it out the window while he smoked his Kent cigarettes. Days of tuneless kids singing "(Get Your Kicks on) Route 66" over and over again grated on their nerves. The restless toddlers argued in the backseat over insignificant infractions ("He looked at me!") as they trudged north in California along small highways. My brothers stopped fighting long enough to take in the sweeping view of San Francisco Bay and the Golden Gate Bridge against the setting sun and commenced swatting each other again.

They found their way to 2335 Mission Street. Uncle Clyde was outside smoking when they pulled up. "Hey, kid brother!" he yelled, waving at Dad, tossing the butt to the ground.

In his younger days, Clyde was devilishly handsome with a solid jawline and piercing blue eyes topped off with a certain "star" quality. Women stopped in the street and stared at him as he greeted the family, slapping my dad on the back and assuring him that "pizza is the future." He led them up to the simple apartment above the restaurant where they would live rent-free until they settled in.

The oldest boy in a family of eight, Clyde took on the sense of quasi-parental responsibility that older children often internalize in a large family. That's why he invited my dad to California. He could have hired someone locally to work in the kitchen and he could have rented the apartment for cash. But that wasn't Clyde. He knew things were bad in Michigan and he'd always been willing to do anything for his youngest brother. When he was twelve, Clyde saved my father's life by pushing him out of the way of an oncoming car. Clyde was hit instead. He spent months in the hospital recuperating. As an adult, his limp was barely noticeable.

While pizzerias existed in Italian-American immigrant

communities on the East Coast, it was still an "ethnic" food in the rest of the country in the 1950s. In Michigan, it wasn't easy to come by. "Pizza was really new then," Mom says. She and Dad had had pizza only once in their lives, at a brand-new place called Shakey's in Lansing* just after they got married. They bit into the crispy crust blanketed with sweet tomato sauce, gooey with cheese, and spiked with the bite of garlic and the unexpected spice of sliced pepperoni. They ate the entire pizza within minutes, stopping only long enough to breathe and exclaim how great it tasted. They had never experienced anything like it.

That was while Dad was still in college and they had their first baby on the way. As much as they loved it, they couldn't afford to go back to Shakey's.

So imagine their delight when they discovered a local grocery carried the new "pizza kit" from Chef Boyardee. The box contained "all the ingredients for a traditional Sicilian-style pizza": a package of add-water-only pizza dough, a small can of tomato sauce, and a packet of dried Parmesan cheese. Following the directions, they spread the dough with oily fingers into an inexpensive pizza pan, spooned the thin sauce over the top, and then sprinkled it with the powdered cheese. Inspired by the pizza they'd had at Shakey's, they added mozzarella and sliced kielbasa sausage on top.

They found it lacking compared to the one they'd had at the pizza parlor. Yet they considered it enough of a success to get two boxes to share with Dad's brother Uncle Bob, who lived in a small, immaculately kept worker's bungalow in Flint. From their meager budget, Mom and Dad bought a second cheap pan for the occasion. They excitedly served the two pizzas to Bob, his wife, Lillian, and their young children, my cousins Larry, Gary, and DeeDee. Lillian took a dubious bite of the tip of one wedge and then dropped it to her plate.

"I don't care for it," she said primly.

Bob had a similar reaction. "I don't know if I'll be able to sleep

---

*Shakey's Pizza, established in 1954, is still in business. My parents ate there the year they opened.

if I eat this. What's this called again? Pizza? I can't see this catching on."

That was my parents' sole experience with Italian cuisine when they arrived in San Francisco. That one of his brothers didn't see pizza catching on and another thought it was the future didn't worry my dad. They'd been raised to be independent thinkers.

Clyde's restaurant had been christened That's Amore after the song made famous by Dean Martin. Outside on Mission Street, it didn't look like much. Once inside, the bony arms of a real oak tree trunk reached up to the ceiling to a hidden grid that held faux leaves and grapes artfully assembled to create the feel of a canopy over the room. Woven through the vines were hundreds of tiny lights. Oil paintings of Tuscan landscapes adorned the walls, while an all-Italian lineup drifted from the jukebox. Chianti bottles fitted with dripping candles adorned the tables, each draped with a red-and-white-checkered cotton tablecloth. With the lights low, the place felt romantic. "It sounds so cliché now, but honestly it was so lovely," Mom says. "It felt as if you had walked into an Italian outdoor café on a cool evening."

Clyde had a knack for the restaurant business. The food was fairly priced and plentiful, the service fast, and the date-night feel ensured they sold a lot of wine. Every night, he positioned a worker flipping dough near the front window to lure in customers, an innovative marketing move at the time. The pizzas were created in twenty-inch-wide new heavy-gauge steel garbage-can lids that Clyde had come across cheap at a surplus sale at The Presidio military base nearby. He removed the handles, turned them over, and voilà! Pizza pans. Back then, you could get one of these huge pizzas—which could feed six to eight—for two bucks.

As soon as patrons sat down, a server brought warm garlic bread. Every dinner came with a salad, so those arrived automatically. The place delivered pizzas using three Volkswagen vans, inexpensive to buy and simple to fix. On Sundays, they offered a special family dinner menu designed for churchgoers and weekend drivers. The Sunday menu included more American-style favorites, such as Clyde's mother's recipe for chicken and biscuits, for those who considered pizza too "exotic." Like his brother Bob. Plus they kicked in a discount for seniors and veterans. The combination proved so appealing that people would stand in line down the block, hoping to get a seat.

That's Amore sold other entrées, but most people came in for the pizza, the spaghetti, and the minestrone soup. The night they arrived, Clyde led the family past patrons chowing on their hot bread and iceberg salads to a giant round table. From the kitchen, he retrieved a pot of the hot soup, stoked with chunks of beef, white beans, and vegetables in a hearty tomato broth. Mom dunked the garlic bread into the minestrone. After a long cross-country drive fueled by cheap sandwiches made on their Bel Air's tailgate out of a secondhand cooler, it struck her as the most delicious thing she'd ever tasted.

Dad began training as a cook the next day. First he learned how to make the "concentrate," by mincing pounds of celery, onion, carrots, dried oregano, and garlic with a heavy grinder. This he cooked at a low, slow simmer in a massive commercial sauté pan with a small amount of ground beef for more than an hour, until it softened and mellowed into its own flavor. Once cooled, this concentrate would be frozen into chunks. When the staff of That's Amore made spaghetti and pizza sauce fresh each day, the cooks simply added the concentrate to cans of diced tomatoes to add in an earthy and "meaty" texture. Even in a sudden rush of business, they could make fresh sauce quickly thanks to the blocks of concentrate.

Then Dad learned to form meatballs, craft ravioli, sear steaks, and dozens of other culinary techniques. Finally, he got a lesson in tossing dough. He was so good that Clyde stationed him in the window. That he looked a bit like Charlton Heston didn't hurt business.

Meanwhile, Mom took care of the kids upstairs. She collected random pieces of furniture from thrift stores: a rose-colored love-seat, a green plaid sofa, and a beat-up laminated dining room table that she covered with a secondhand tablecloth. The apartment opened onto a flat roof lined with a parapet wall. While the roof afforded no view other than industrial rooftops along the street, it gave the kids a safe place to play without disturbing anyone and a nook to hang her clotheslines. The Mission District had some rough spots in the late 1950s. A wave of Central American immigrants was pouring into the largely Hispanic area, prompting a fresh crime wave thanks to a series of violent turf wars. Mom saw none of this, and instead just noticed the area seemed to have a lovely "Latin flavor" to it as she ran errands and walked the short blocks to Mission Dolores Park, where she took the children to play on the swings.

Clyde was great to the family. Almost every night, the staff would bring up big pizzas for Mom and the kids' dinner while Dad worked downstairs. The pies made Mom feel embarrassed about the pizzas she and Dad had made from a box. After dinner, Mom made a huge lemon meringue pie in the pan and sent it back down the next day. Clyde loved it. The arrangement worked well until Mom's doctor told her that even for a pregnant woman, she was gaining too much weight. So Clyde alternated their pizzas with salads and lighter roast chicken dinners.

My folks felt a great deal of gratitude. Before my brother was born in September, they decided to name him "Clyde Michael." Dad's brother was overjoyed. But Mom found herself staring at the newborn. All she could think of was Clyde Barrow, the male half of the famed criminal team Bonnie and Clyde. When the birth certificate arrived to confirm its information, she couldn't hold back. "I just can't look at this baby and call him *Clyde*!" Dad agreed. His name was changed to Michael Clyde and they never told my uncle.

While they had a good thing going at That's Amore, after a year, urban restaurant life started to wear on my parents. The place opened at four in the afternoon and served until well past two in the morning. The din from the dining room made it tough to put the kids to bed. Dad frequently worked twelve- to fourteen-hour shifts and had only Mondays off. It was hard for Mom to get the baby buggy up and down the stairs. The list went on.

Clyde understood.

So they packed up and headed to Marysville, a small town about eighty miles north, not far from Sacramento. The town developed in the mid-1800s as little more than a stop for gold rush era travelers seeking out supplies. Later it became known as one of the towns settled by members of the infamous Donner Party, the tragic wagon train expedition that left its members to resort to cannibalism when they got trapped in the Sierra Nevada Mountains in the winter of 1846. The townspeople named it Marysville after Mary Murphy, one of the expedition's survivors who settled there.

Mom's aunt Peggy had moved to the pleasant town from Michigan years earlier. She found them a house and introduced Dad to someone at a fruit-packing company. He got hired as a manager on the spot. But after a few months, apparently forgetting all the reasons the restaurant business had not been right for them, they decided to use all their savings to start their own.

Uncle Clyde gave them his recipes and plenty of advice. He made frequent trips up to Marysville to help them get started. He even helped Dad pick out a commercial pizza oven. Dad was a history buff, so instead of the charming Chianti bottles and Italian countryside inn look carefully nurtured at That's Amore, Mom and Dad transformed a small storefront into a room vaguely reminiscent of a castle from the latter days of the Roman Empire and dubbed the place The Roman Knight.

Mom found chef uniforms at a local Goodwill. Dad got the tables cheap from a Greek deli that had shut down. They found two pretty waitresses to work the tables and a guy to work in the kitchen. A local printer laminated their menus. They were ready.

Business boomed at first. Mom's older brother, Uncle Clarence, drove out for an extended visit to see if it made sense to move his own family there. Clarence had learned his way around the kitchen from their father, a former army cook. He offered to work in exchange for room and board. They put Clarence in charge of the daily special. One Tuesday, he made a paprika-spiked fried chicken that was so popular, they began to offer it once a week. People began asking for it *every* day. Although the place was a pizzeria, a review in a local paper heralded the chicken. Dad put "Clarence's

Fried Chicken" on the regular menu in his honor, right next to the spaghetti and pizza recipes from Clyde.

Mom worked as a waitress for two weeks. Apparently, she was terrible. She won't even discuss how bad it got before my father gently suggested that perhaps she work in the kitchen. She didn't get on well there, either. Easily flustered when it got busy, she tended to make mistakes. Once, she forgot to add yeast to a batch of pizza dough. Diners promptly sent the pizzas back. When she tried to cut into one to see what was wrong, it nearly broke the knife.

Everyone agreed that it would be best if Mom used her secretarial training to get a job outside the restaurant. She got hired onto an air force project installing air-conditioning into the western missile silos. At that job, she made enough to pay all their bills while she sat in the relative splendor of an air-conditioned government office. After much prodding, Mom convinced her younger sister, my aunt Mel, to move out to California after she finished up business school. Aunt Mel found work nearby with Western Electric as a secretary.

Life seemed good. The restaurant broke even. Thanks to the cold war, Mom had a secure job. The kids had a yard to play in. Mom had both her sister and one of her brothers with her in California. She had a place to hang her clothesline. Dad managed the kids during the day until Mom got home and then headed to the restaurant.

Then came June.

By lunchtime, it grew gruelingly hot in the dining room. The restaurant had no air-conditioning. To cool the place, they brought in fans, but they couldn't compete with the pizza oven. Day in and day out, they watched their savings dwindle as they paid staff to look out over an empty dining room. By August, they decided to just shut the place down. Uncle Clarence headed back to Michigan.

Looking for less stressful work, Dad applied to become a police officer.

More than sixty men applied for two positions in San Bruno, an upscale bedroom community just south of San Francisco. Dad was hired along with an Irishman named Brendan Maguire who was straight off the boat from Dublin, where he'd already worked as a cop. San Bruno required officers to live in the city, so Mom and Dad rented a cute house in a pleasant section of town. By now, they were used to moving.

The drive to her government job proved too much, so Mom quit and stayed home with the kids. They planted a small vegetable garden and lined the fences with roses. From their back patio, Mom could see the lights of San Francisco. Aunt Mel found a secretarial job in nearby San Mateo and lived with them for a couple of months. The children loved Aunt Mel, then single and in her early twenties. Mel enjoyed playing with them, plus she had remarkable patience. She could listen to four kids tell different stories and keep track of every word. One night, Doug even made a special request in his nightly prayers as Aunt Mel waited to tuck him into bed.

"And please, God, let Aunt Mel never get married and just live with us forever. Amen."

Aunt Mel looked up toward the sky. "God, maybe you could just disregard that last part."

All of them spent weekends playing tourist around the city. They visited the waterfront, Chinatown, and picnicked in Golden Gate Park. They went fishing almost every weekend and camped at Half Moon Bay. Mom missed her parents, but Dad's mother, Della, was able to make the trip out. They were young, their kids were healthy, and they loved living in the Bay Area. Everything was wonderful.

Until one day, when the phone rang.

Uncle Clarence's Oven-Fried Chicken

Uncle Clarence deep-fried his popular chicken at my parents' restaurant. Mom adapted it to an "oven-fried" version to capture the same flavors but with an easier and (marginally) healthier variation for home cooks. The key is to lightly glaze the top of the chicken with some kind of fat before it's put into the oven. Mom used margarine; you can use butter or a mixture of equal parts olive oil and melted butter. I'm not talking a token drizzle; every inch of the top of the chicken should be moistened.

Mom says: "Sometimes I add cinnamon to the flour instead of sage or poultry seasoning, just for a little different flavor." This works best with fresh paprika; if yours is vintage, use extra. You can use whatever pieces you want for this if you purchase precut chicken, but if your chicken includes extralarge breasts, cut each one (ribs and all) into two portions. This will make them appropriate serving sizes and assure they'll cook more evenly.

Note: If you don't have buttermilk, you can make your own by adding 1 tablespoon (15 ml) white vinegar or lemon juice to 1 cup (240 ml) milk and let it sit for about 5 minutes. No poultry seasoning? Check out the recipe for a salt-free homemade version on page 252.

Makes 4 to 6 servings

6 tablespoons (90 g) margarine or butter, melted
About 1½ cups (375 ml) buttermilk
1½ cups (200 g) all-purpose flour
2 teaspoons (10 g) coarse salt
1 teaspoon (5 g) ground black pepper
1 cup (125 g) crushed cornflakes
½ teaspoon (2.5 ml) poultry seasoning, or dried thyme and/or sage
One 3½-pound chicken, cut into 8 to 10 pieces (about 1.5 kg)
1 tablespoon (8 g) paprika, for dusting

Preheat the oven to 375°F (190°C). Using about 2 tablespoons (30 ml) of the margarine, coat the bottom of a roasting pan or a baking dish large enough to hold the chicken pieces in one layer without touching.

Place the buttermilk in a shallow bowl or dish. In another bowl, mix the flour, salt, pepper, cornflakes, and poultry seasoning. Dip each chicken piece into the buttermilk. Shake off the excess and roll in the flour mixture to coat. Place the chicken pieces in the prepared roasting pan, skin side up.

Drizzle the rest of the margarine evenly over the chicken. Dust the chicken liberally with paprika. Put the roasting pan on the middle rack of the oven, uncovered.

Bake for about 1 hour, until the chicken is golden and cooked through. (Small pieces may be done at 45 minutes, so check.) To confirm, push an instant-read thermometer into a meaty section; it should register at least 165°F (74°C). Serve warm. Leftovers reheat nicely in a toaster oven.

CHAPTER 2

The Farm on Coldwater Road

Family portrait, San Francisco, 1961

Milt," my uncle Bob began. "It's Hazel."

In 1964, a five-minute long-distance phone call from Michigan to California cost the equivalent of twenty-five dollars. People didn't call for a casual chat. Hazel was my dad's older sister and they were close. Hazel had taken care of Dad as a kid when he was diagnosed with rickets, a painful bone disorder. It was Hazel who shimmied up an apple tree to get them something to eat one afternoon when they were hungry kids fishing together. They lost their hard-found worms and, too poor to buy any more, she put the apple cores on their hooks. In her nine-year-old logic, she argued, "We like apples, maybe the fish will, too."

Some people find the silver linings in the darkest of clouds. Hazel was one of those. When she was diagnosed with lung cancer, everyone was sure she would beat it.

"She's dying," my uncle said. "It could be a day, a week, or a month. She's in bad shape. She keeps talking about you . . . and . . ." He couldn't go on.

Hazel was just thirty-six years old.

Dad turned ashen. "No one told me it was that bad," he said, stunned. He stared blankly at my mother across the room. Without a word, he handed her the phone. He sat on the couch, his head in his hands, still in his police uniform.

Bob pulled himself together to talk to Mom. "It's just a matter of time now. She's been talking about Milt and she wants to see him. It's"—his voice broke—"her dying wish."

Mom's heart dropped. "We'll get him there one way or another just as soon as we can." Then she quickly hung up to avoid costing Bob any more money on the call.

Practical people, they talked about the options. Bob had mentioned flying back to Michigan. A flight would cost about $600, equal to $4,670 today, or about ten times the monthly rent on their house. Plus, they agreed, if he went back for a week, would that be enough?

"Maybe we should consider moving back to Michigan," she said gently. "It won't cost any more for all of us to move than it would for you to fly back one time." Dad kept a hard gaze on the floor. "We've got enough money for the trip and some to hold us over until you find work. It's been a great adventure but maybe it's time we went home."

With that, my parents left California just as quickly as they got there. Dad gave notice the next day. His Irish co-worker Brendan Maguire bought some of their furniture and agreed to sell off the rest and send them the proceeds. Two weeks later, they were on the road.

The morning they left, my mother walked through their empty

house and into the sunny backyard bedecked in all shades of pink and yellow roses. She went to a climbing bush with fuchsia blooms, took a deep inhale, and stared up at the clear, cloudless March sky. Then she fished into her pocket for a small pair of scissors and snipped off one of the larger roses.

After they hooked up with Route 66, this time heading east, they stopped less often now that the kids were older. To avoid their experience with the "Route 66" song on their way out, Mom brought a stack of songbooks with her in the front seat. When the kids got tired and started to fight, she taught them another song. "Kids can't fight when they're singing," she says. One from *The Boy Scout Songbook* became a family favorite:

> *Oh, Mr. Johnny Verbeck, how could you be so mean*
> *We told you you'd be sorry for inventin' that machine*
> *Now all the neighbors' cats and dogs will nevermore be seen*
> *For they'll all be ground to sausages in Johnny Verbeck's*
> *machine.*

Days later, they hit a blizzard in Ohio. Mom reached into the glove compartment, where she'd stashed the fuchsia rose. She cradled the limp flower in her hand for a last smell of California. As they crossed into Michigan, the petals fell apart, scattering in her lap.

It's hard to visualize a person you've never met but everyone loved. When I hear stories of Aunt Hazel, I think of the character Elizabeth Montgomery played in the television show *Bewitched*. People describe her as a lovely blonde with deep green eyes and a mischievous yet sweet presence. Just before her cancer diagnosis, she wore a fetching green satin dress with a stylish hat to a family wedding. Men clamored to dance with her. For fun, my aunt Mary Jo, her youngest sister, asked one of the men how old he thought she was. "Gosh, I didn't think of that," said a handsome soldier. "I hope she's at least eighteen."

Hazel started smoking at age thirteen. She got a job at fourteen, and then married at sixteen. She didn't marry well. Her husband turned to booze, and by her twenty-fourth birthday, she was a divorced woman with three kids, a minor scandal in the early 1950s. But Hazel was as tough as she was kind, and, like her seven siblings, she'd been brought up to work hard. She hadn't told anyone when she was first diagnosed with lung cancer. Hazel believed she could fight anything.

Back in Michigan, my parents were unprepared for the sight of her. Hazel's thick blond hair had turned to wisps, her skin stretched taut across her cheekbones to expose the outline of her skull. Her green eyes had dulled with pain to a tired gray. At just seventy-five pounds, the skin on her arms barely seemed to cover her bones.

After a teary reunion, the pragmatic Hazel asked weakly where they were looking to move. "There's a farm for rent, not far away from our family's old little house over in Davison. It's on Coldwater Road. You should go look." Dad nodded that they would.

After their first visit, my parents went to the car, hugged each other, and cried.

🍓

"We can't possibly live here—this place is a wreck," my mother declared. "The pipes are all frozen up. There's not even any heat."

Although March, it was a classically unpleasant late winter day, frigid, damp, and gray. Mom stamped her feet on the floor of the living room to keep them from freezing.

The front door to the small farmhouse had been left open by the previous tenants. Who knew how long it'd been open? Snow banked into a pile in the front of the entry hallway. Beat-up carpet lined the floors and the wallpaper was peeling off in the living room.

Dad listened as he looked around. When they saw the FOR RENT sign out front, he'd had a good feeling about the place. Settled on ten acres with an orchard backing up to an expansive wood, it would be big enough for energetic kids. Plus it was cheap, just forty-two dollars a month. "It's in a great school district," Dad said, trying to sell her on it. "The little schoolhouse where I went as a kid is just down the street."

Mom said nothing and pulled her coat around her to step outside to call the children in from the car. The kids rushed in with gusto. "Which room will be mine?" my brother Milt asked, bouncing around the living room.

Mom remained neutral. "Let's look around a bit."

My sister, Sandy, then one month shy of five years old, clapped her hands together in new pink mittens and twirled around the room. "I like it. It made the sun shine."

Mom peered out the bay window. The weak winter sun had indeed come out and the house seemed transformed by it. The rooms suddenly felt a bit bigger and less forlorn.

Dad guessed the farmhouse had been built around 1895. They headed to the cellar, where squared-off hardwood logs made up the floor joists in the basement. The walls were made from piled granite rocks. "Looks really well built, solid," my dad said cheerfully, banging against one of the logs.

"Feels kind of creepy," replied my mom, still hugging her wool coat to her.

Nestled into a deep set of shelves in the basement sat seemingly hundreds of dusty canning jars. Under a muslin drop cloth, they found an incubator for baby chickens. A pair of slanting double doors and stairs led to the outside. "Good for tornadoes," my dad said. "If you can't get up the stairs, you can still get out."

Didn't help Dorothy in The Wizard of Oz, my mom thought, but said nothing.

They went back upstairs to inspect the bedrooms, two on the first floor and one big room up on the upper floor. The ceiling of the upstairs room had the lines of the pitched roof and took up the width of the house with a window on each side, the top of a large tree visible from each one. At seven and eight years old, my oldest brothers weren't worldly kids. This was the first time they'd been in a two-story house. To them, it felt as if they'd stumbled into a mansion and now had the chance to live among the trees.

Just then, they heard a voice downstairs. The owner's wife,

Molly, had shown up. She was a sturdy woman in a musty men's winter coat and heavy farm boots and wearing a touch of frosted lipstick. She told them not to worry about the toilets—frozen solid with the water still in them—or the furnace, which appeared not to be working. Her husband was coming to sort it out.

"We had some people here and they got behind in the rent," she explained in a husky voice. "We didn't really get after them about it. They just left one night and didn't tell us. Can't figure someone doin' somethin' like that." She shook her head. She handed my mom a basket piled with eggs. "We got us more eggs than we need. Just got these this mornin'."

Farm fresh eggs! This was something they didn't get in California. Mom was touched by the thoughtful gift. Maybe she could keep an open mind.

In the kitchen, a large window over the sink afforded a view of the massive backyard, layered with a thick coat of pristine snow. Mom noticed a massive bare oak. *Good for a tire swing, probably has a lot of shade in summer,* she mused.

Molly took them outside and pointed out the naked limbs of dozens of fruit trees, seven varieties of apples, yellow cherries, plums, pears, and a massive mulberry tree. She led them past a whitewashed chicken coop beyond the ample barn to show off an aging tractor under a haphazard tarp. "You can use it all you want. Come in handy if you plow a garden." She nodded to the woods. "In summer, you can find all kinds of mushrooms and lotsa wild-flowers."

Dad looked at Mom. The kids were running around happily in the snow, throwing themselves down to make snow angels, some-thing they had learned just a day earlier. My sister flapped her arms, beaming as she singsonged, "We're going to live here!"

Mom bit her lip. Born in the Great Depression, she had been raised on a series of farms. So what if the wallpaper was peeling? Or the living room seemed to have a bit of a slope? She had four small children, her husband was unemployed, and they spent half their savings moving from California. Who knew what the future held? But if they had fruit trees and a garden, at least they wouldn't starve, not once summer came along.

"Okay. Let's do it," my mom said. "Until we find something else, anyway."

The next day they left my uncle Bob's house and moved in. Molly's husband fired up the furnace. The pipes thawed admirably. My folks bought beds at a secondhand shop and wrestled them into the back of my uncle's truck during a break in the snowfall. Mom made each bed with linens brought from California.

The rest of the house remained empty as they settled in the first night. Mom sorted through boxes of kitchenware to unearth a heavy-bottomed stockpot. Her parents had come to greet them within hours of their arrival back in Michigan. "You're back!" her mother, Inez, had said, throwing her arms around her in a suffocating bear hug. Her father, Charles, a hulk of man standing at six feet four inches, threw his arms around them both. On the long drive, Mom had had second thoughts about moving back to Michigan. In the long double embrace of her parents, she wished she'd moved back earlier.

Then Grandpa Charles stood back and took a look at her. "Look at you, such a skinny thing," he said, shaking his head.

Grandma Inez nodded, wiping tears from her eyes. "You ain't been eatin' enough," she agreed before blowing her nose loudly into a Kleenex.

Charles reached to the ground and picked up a hefty burlap bag and set it on the table. Inside the bag were smaller bags holding twenty pounds of mixed beans that he grew and dried on his farm in central Michigan. Along with the beans, he'd packed onions and carrots from his cold house and a thick slab of cured pork belly from his most recent hog. "Welcome home, sweetie."

So Mom dug into the bag and pulled out a pound of dried beans to make a pot of soup for their first meal in the old farmhouse. As it began to gurgle, the warmth from the stove crept through the lower rooms. Her fourth move in five years, she began to systematically empty each of the worn boxes marked "KITCHEN" and figure out where to put things away—no easy task, given that the small room had only one drawer and few cabinets.

As she started on the third box, the walls creaked slightly at a strong gust of wind. She stopped to look out the steamy windows at the long, barren stretch of land outside her new home. Hard to imagine that only three weeks earlier, they'd been happily living in the warmth of California. What would the place look like when it thawed, she wondered.

I can always plant some roses, she thought.

All-Afternoon Bean Soup

Midwest budget cooking at its finest, this basic recipe offers potentially endless options. Just swap out the type of beans you're using, the flavoring meat, and the seasonings as noted in the variations. True to its name, it will take at least 2 and up to 4 hours to simmer its way into velvety, hearty goodness.

One key is to start with dried beans, not canned. You can utilize virtually any variety, such as navy, pinto, great northern, red, lima, and so on; refer to the packaging for guidance on cooking times. Mixing beans yields more complex flavor; bags of various beans ready for soup are available at most supermarkets. Old beans take significantly longer to cook to make tender, something to be aware of if you're using beans of unknown provenance or those that have been languishing like a stubborn stain in the pantry.

As for a meat to flavor the dish, options include a ham bone, a ham hock, chopped ham, diced thick-sliced bacon, diced pork, or even a lamb shank. All may be bypassed to create a vegetarian version. For a flavorful meatless soup, increase the amount of seasonings and puree 2 cups of the beans to return to the final soup to offer extra body.

How much salt you'll need depends on your flavoring meat. To avoid over-salting, use a minimal amount at the start of cooking and taste toward the end to see if it needs any more. Mom says, "Dad 'finished' a pot of beans by adding hot sauce to give it some kick." This is slow cooker–friendly, but if you've got a small one, you may need to halve the recipe the first time you try it to assure it doesn't cook over the sides.

Makes 8 to 10 one-cup servings

One 16-ounce (450-g) package dried beans
2½ to 3 quarts (2.5 to 2.85 L) liquid, any combination of water, chicken
    stock, or vegetable stock
1 chicken or vegetable bouillon cube (optional)
1 large onion (340 g), chopped (about 2½ cups)
5 stalks celery (285 g), chopped (about 2 cups)
3 large carrots (285 g), peeled and chopped (about 2 cups)
3 garlic cloves, chopped
About 6 ounces (170 g) flavoring meat (optional)
2 tablespoons (30 ml) Worcestershire sauce
1 tablespoon (15 ml) dried thyme
2 teaspoons (10 ml) celery seed
2 teaspoons (10 ml) garlic powder
1 bay leaf
One 14.5-ounce (400-g) can diced tomatoes
2 teaspoons (10 ml) salt, or to taste
½ teaspoon (2.5 ml) ground black pepper or cayenne pepper, or to taste
Hot sauce (optional)

Put the dried beans in a pot with enough water to allow 3 inches (8 cm) of water above them. You can either leave the beans to soak overnight or do a "quick soak": Boil for 2 minutes, remove from the heat, cover, and let stand for an hour. Either way, drain the beans and rinse with cold water before proceeding.

Combine the beans with 2 quarts (2 L) of the liquid, the bouillon cube (if using), onion, celery, carrots, garlic, meat (if using), Worcestershire, thyme, celery seed, garlic powder, and bay leaf in a large pot. Bring to a gentle boil. Lower the heat, partially cover, and simmer for about 2 hours, occasionally skimming off foam or excess fat as it collects on the surface.

At this point, the soup should be quite thick. Add the tomatoes with the liquid and another 2 to 3 cups (500 to 750 ml) of water or stock. Taste and add salt and pepper as needed; if you've used ham hocks or bacon, it might not need salt. Simmer for an additional hour, or until the beans are tender. Check every so often to assure there's enough liquid to cover the beans by at least an inch.

Before serving, discard the bay leaf. If using a ham bone or hock or a lamb shank, pull it from the soup. Chop any meat clinging to the bone into bite-sized pieces and return the diced meat to the soup. Check the seasonings again and finish with a few shakes of hot sauce, if desired. Once chilled, left-overs should be stored in an airtight container for 5 days in the fridge or for up to 2 months in the freezer. When reheating, you may need to add some extra liquid, as the soup will thicken while it is stored.

A Few Flavor Variations

Cajun: red kidney beans + hot sausage + lots of cayenne pepper

Italian: white cannellini beans + rosemary + Parmesan cheese

Cuban: black beans + smoked pork hunks + cumin

Greek-esque: garbanzo beans + lamb shank + oregano

Hearty vegan: porcini mushroom bouillon cube + Bragg's liquid aminos in place of the Worcestershire sauce

CHAPTER 3

Morels in May

Aunt Hazel with my cousins Andy and Ruth Brimmer, 1957

Within two weeks, spring transformed the resting farm. The dense snow retreated. Small tendrils of leaves peeked tentatively from barren tree branches. By the end of April, the place exploded in color. In the orchard, fragrant white blossoms blanketed the apple and pear trees, while deep pink blooms covered the plum and cherry trees. Mom said it seemed as if each tree were trying to outdo the other. The grass, once tough and grayish patches that showed through swatches of ragged snow, shifted into one lush carpet of green. Bulbs planted by long-forgotten tenants sprang up everywhere: blood red tulips, brilliant yellow daffodils, and wine-colored crocus. Volunteer tomatoes struggled up in a crazy patchwork near the barn.

Whatever reservations my mother had about the farm drifted away with each passing day. Mom and Dad bought seeds and hoes from a local store and borrowed a rototiller from my uncle Bob to wrangle the neglected garden soil ready for planting. Dad got the old tractor working, and its hacking and coughing engine could be heard for miles. The kids did their part, raking dirt and pulling weeds. They helped to set up strings along the freshly tilled beds to assure everything was planted in straight lines. Mom and Dad taught them to carefully count off two of their little steps and then stop to plant seeds. Two more little steps, a couple more seeds.

The interior of the house, too, was coming along. Mom dipped rags into paste and then smeared and smoothed it on the ailing wallpaper. It left a hardened surface that could be concealed with— what else?—more wallpaper. Mom covered the hideous carpet with a fleet of cheap floor rugs. Dad poked strips of old rags into the cracks around the windows to seal them up tight.

Dad hunted for work, but didn't turn up much. Police officers in Flint earned half as much as his salary in California. Dad thought he could do better. The men in his family had a strong entrepreneurial streak. After all, one of my great-uncles had started a lucrative business making clocks out of grindstone into the shape of Michigan. During the years Dad had been in California, his brothers had started a window and aluminum-siding business called Century Products Inc. They invited my dad to work on commission as a salesman. It turned out he was good at it, and he soon earned as much as he had made in uniform in San Bruno.

Just as the farm seemed to explode with sheer delight that winter was finally over, life seemed to be settling in.

May first was a day meant for picking wildflowers, Mom says. After spending the morning working in the garden and planting roses, she asked the kids what they wanted to do. Invariably, they always answered, "A picnic!" Of course, they'd say they wanted a picnic in the dead of winter, but on that day, it seemed like a good idea. Mom instructed Miltie, then eight, to make peanut butter and jelly sandwiches. Five-year-old Sandy was charged with wrapping two oatmeal cookies per child in plastic wrap; she weighed the cookies carefully in her hand to assure no one got more cookie than anyone else. Doug made strawberry Kool-Aid in the big canteen that they had used on their cross-country trips. Mike, just four, insisted on carrying the blanket, but in truth, he mostly just dragged it on the ground.

As they walked through the apple orchard, it felt like a carefully directed scene from a movie. Tiny petals cascaded from every tree, showering them as they walked through the sweet, fragrant air. They laid out the blanket and nibbled on their lunches under the falling petals. Mom could have stayed there all afternoon. After an hour, however, the kids decided they needed more adventure.

Miltie jumped to his feet. "Let's go to the woods," he suggested.

"Okay," Mom agreed, propping herself up on one arm. "We can pick some flowers."

Miltie led the pack as usual, looking back as the rest sauntered along. At the wood's edge, he began jumping up and down, waving his arms wildly. "Come on! See what I found!" he yelled. "Hurry!"

They ran. Mom assumed it was a rabbit or some other small woodland creature that he could taunt and prod before pretending to track through the woods.

But what he'd found was no rabbit. She couldn't believe it.

"Wow!" she cried. "Oh, no, we don't have anything to gather them in!"

A thick layer of hundreds of morel mushrooms spread out from under the canopy of a black walnut tree. Mom had never seen that many in one place. She'd started hunting them as a young girl with her dad. Morels, also known as species *Morchella*, are a gray-brown mushroom with a distinct pointed spongy honeycomb. Normally, hunters consider finding a dozen or so a bonanza.

"I'll run back to the house, Mom," Miltie volunteered.

"Me, too," Dougie said, and the two boys sprinted to the house.

"The big round laundry basket," Mom called after them. "Bring a couple of sheets, too!"

Sandy stood in the woods in her standard attire. No matter the planned activity, she demanded to wear a frilly party dress and formal black patent leather Mary Janes, what she called dancing shoes. That morning before the picnic, Mom had insisted that in order to go into the woods, she had to wear last season's dancing shoes. While they waited for the boys to return, Sandy decided to pick some wildflowers for Hazel. "I'll pick these for her and you can take them to the hospital, okay?"

"Hey, the boys," Mike shouted, pointing, and he ran on his little legs to meet them.

Mom lined the laundry basket with the sheets and showed the children how to pick the morel mushrooms the way her own father had taught her when she was around five or six. She carefully twisted each so it broke off at the base, leaving a root of sorts, so more mushrooms could come back the following year.

Within forty minutes, they'd accumulated a heaping bushel* of morels. Sandy kept picking flowers, amassing an armload of white, pale lavender, and yellow blooms. Mom and the kids carefully carried the treasures back to the house.

When he returned home from selling siding that day, Dad was shocked at the sight of that many morels. He'd never found more than a few at one time. That night, Mom prepared the morels the way she always did, with a simple toss in flour stoked with salt and pepper and maybe a bit of paprika, then fried quickly in butter. The result was a crisp, hot burst of savory mushroom with an almost nutty flavor.

Mom prepared a plate of fried mushrooms to take to Hazel in the hospital. "I know she doesn't really eat much anymore," Mom said, sighing, as she carefully covered them with foil. "But maybe she'll have a few."

Since their return, Hazel's health had plummeted as the cancer seeped into her bones. She was in pain most of the time. In the 1960s, federal law restricted the use of morphine even for terminally ill patients. Every four hours, she could have a shot of

---

*A bushel is a volume measurement roughly equivalent to eight gallons.

painkiller. The problem was that after two hours, it began to wear off. The last hour she spent in agony. Hazel had zero chance of recovery, yet she spent six hours or more every day in agony. She never felt sorry for herself. Hazel bit her lip and didn't talk about the pain.

When they arrived with the flowers and mushrooms, she shrieked in delight. Dad asked how she was doing. "Well, I just got a shot so I'm okay," she said brightly. "I don't know what they're worried about. That I'll get addicted to it? Not like it's going to kill me."

Although she normally had to be prodded to take a few bites of the soft food they fed her in the hospital, Hazel set a land speed record for consumption of fried morels. Within minutes, they were gone. "I haven't had anything so good in years!" she exclaimed, smacking her lips as she sat back against her pillows. She had my mother arrange the flowers on her tray so she could smell them. "This is almost as good as being back in the woods." With that, she went to sleep.

Although dying of lung cancer, Aunt Hazel still smoked, even in the hospital.

Ironically, the source of all her pain was one of the few things that gave her pleasure. Even in her declining state, she still managed to smoke half a pack a day.

The hospital insisted that someone be with her when she smoked. So Dad's oldest sister, Joyce, worked out a schedule. Dad took the early shift, waking at four A.M. so he could spend time with Hazel before he started his day's work. Mom took turns on the day shift while the two boys were in school and a relative watched Mike and Sandy.

Two weeks after their morel bounty, Mom woke up to the smell of apple blossoms drifting gently on a soft breeze coming through her open bedroom window. That morning, she cut off an armload of branches loaded with the fragrant flowers.

"Hey, beautiful," Hazel said to Mom when she entered the

hospital room, her once light, musical voice now hoarse and brittle. She swooned at the sight of the blossoms. "Come hold them close so I can smell them." Mom took them over to her bedside and Hazel buried her head in the flowers and breathed away.

"Can we have a little prayer together?" Hazel asked. "And today, don't pray for me to get better, please pray for me to have a safe trip home." When she grabbed Mom's hands in hers to pray, they felt as fragile and light as a piece of spun glass.

Hazel was in a strangely alert and talkative mood. "You know, I've been lucky. I've got good kids and a great family," Hazel began. Mom thought, *That's just like Hazel. She's dying, yet she feels she's lucky.* "Hey, open the window. I want to smell the spring air." Mom opened the window the small wedge that its industrial design would allow. "Have you ever seen the sky so blue? It's lovely." Hazel looked at the sky for a long time, as if seeing it for the first time and trying to comprehend it.

That was how the day went: lots of chatter, a cigarette, sips of water, talking, pain shot, blanket on, blanket off, rub lotion on her feet, another cigarette. She refused her lunch of soft food. It was then that Mom noticed Hazel's hands looked oddly dark. Hazel kept up her singsongy chatter. Dad's youngest sister, Mary Jo, had lived with Hazel for a few years. The two were close. "Mary Jo will be here soon, right?" Hazel asked.

As if on cue, Mary Jo and her husband arrived and sent Mom home.

On her drive to the farm, Mom felt unsettled. Dad was home from work and starting dinner for the children. Mom told him about Hazel's peaceful day, the chatter, and her dark hands. Dad had felt the same way that morning when he'd been there to see her. When he thought back to their conversation, he realized his sister was saying good-bye to him.

They read each other's thoughts. "We should go back to the hospital," they said in unison. They rushed to collect coats and get boots on the children.

Then the phone rang. Hazel had just died.

In the weeks that followed, Mom and Dad worked diligently on the garden. Mom planted more than a hundred rose bushes. It was as if they'd transferred the emotion and energy they'd spent on Hazel to the earth that surrounded the old farmhouse. They felt so strongly about the place, that summer, my parents arranged to buy it from the owners.

"I always felt that we were meant to move back to Michigan, and that Hazel led us to the farm on Coldwater Road," Mom says. After all, it was Hazel who had told them about the house. Although she'd been in the hospital for months, no one could ever figure out how she knew about the place.

Mom and Dad found more morels in the woods, but nothing ever equaled the bounty of that first spring.

Morels Sauteéd in Butter

This recipe is well suited to other delicate wild mushrooms, such as chanterelles, and also works nicely with soft vegetables such as diced eggplant and zucchini. Don't be tempted by dried mushrooms that have been reconstituted; they won't work. One key is to avoid getting too heavy a coating of flour on the mushrooms. It should be even and light. I serve these straight from the pan to people standing around my kitchen to assure they're good and hot. You can also sprinkle them with fresh chives before serving.

Makes 4 appetizer servings

 ½ pound (225 g) morel mushrooms
 ½ cup (65 g) all-purpose flour
 1 teaspoon (5 ml) coarse salt, plus more to finish
 ½ teaspoon (2.5 ml) ground black pepper
 ¼ teaspoon (1.25 ml) paprika
 About 5 tablespoons (80 g) unsalted butter, plus more if needed

Soak the morels in cold water for a few minutes to rinse off any impurities or critters. Drain them well and lightly dry with paper towels. If they're large, slice them in half lengthwise.

In a large bowl, stir together the flour, salt, pepper, and paprika. Add the mushrooms and toss carefully to coat them lightly in the flour. Shake off any excess flour and set the mushrooms aside.

Melt the butter in a large skillet over medium-high heat. When hot, add the mushrooms. Shake the pan to prevent them from sticking to the bottom. Panfry until they are golden and slightly crispy, turning them once. Add more butter if necessary, especially if the butter becomes dark and grainy. Sprinkle a bit more salt on the cooked mushrooms. Serve warm.

CHAPTER 4

The Queen of Mancelona

My grandparents Charles and Inez Henderson
at the Sanford Farm, 1959

My maternal grandmother, Inez Monk Henderson, was a hand-some, soft-figured woman, with a light fringe of mustache, who favored cotton housedresses from Sears and polyester pant-suits from Kmart. She rarely left the house without a well-worn knee-length baby blue down coat. At least, that was by the time I knew her. No matter. My grandfather would stare at her wistfully across the sheet-protected furniture. She'd be in the dining room, sweaty and swarthy-skinned, bluntly butchering a chicken into pieces to ready it for frying. He'd just sigh. "She's the most beautiful woman I ever saw," he would say, ignoring *Hee Haw* on the television.

To understand my grandmother, you'd have to meet my great-grandmother, Anna Erickson Monk, even though I never did.

Anna Erickson was the third of six children born to working-class parents in Utterbyn, Sweden. In 1896, her parents sent her to America with a single piece of luggage. The seventeen-year-old couldn't speak English, so she spent the voyage studying a phrase book meant for tourists. From New York, she made her way to friends of the family in the Swedish immigrant community of Newberry in the Upper Peninsula of Michigan.

By the time she arrived, more than a million Swedes had emigrated to the United States. In their home country, laborers paid high taxes to the monarchy, yet lived in something of a caste system. Education, voting, and property ownership were reserved for the upper class, making social mobility impossible. So lower-class Swedes flocked to America, lured by the prospect of cheap farmland in the Midwest, good-paying jobs in urban factories, and an education for their children.

At first, Anna worked as a household servant. When she discovered cooks got paid a little more, she shifted her sales tactics. "Yaah, I'm a cook," she told everyone, although she knew little beyond the basics she'd picked up while helping her mother in Sweden. Thanks to Anna, more than one household was introduced to Swedish pancakes, pickled herring, gravlax, spritz cookies, and *äppelformar*, her mother's apple and almond muffins.

Although she moved to the country very young, for the rest of her life she had a strong Swedish accent. Still, she boasted that she didn't have one.

"Yaah, ven ah left Sveeden vor Amee-ricka, ah speak Amee-rickaan, so ah no och-cent, yaah," she'd say. "Ah leav-in mah och-cent een Sveeden."

Two of Anna's brothers joined her in Michigan. After years of working and scrimping, the three sent enough money to Sweden to bring over the rest of the family. By then, she was set to marry a lumberman thirteen years her senior, John Wellington Monk. He'd been born and raised in Maine, but moved to Michigan to work in busy upstate lumber camps. John operated boilers that powered saw mills and the steam log loaders that picked up the freshly cut timber and moved them to waiting railroad cars.

Anna continued to work hard after her marriage, taking in laundry and filling in as a cook for various families. She studied midwifery and delivered dozens of children. She had a flair for making medicinal balms and soups to cure the ill. The pair seemed happy enough. Then, one day in 1927, John went to work and didn't come back.

One of the camp's boilers built up too much pressure. When a valve designed to alleviate the pressure failed to work, my great-grandfather held it together with all his might, yelling to warn the twenty-two men to leave before it exploded.

He saved all their lives, but didn't make it out himself.

Anna was left with five kids, no husband, and, despite John being killed on the job and saving the other workers, no compensation from his company. My grandmother Inez, not quite sixteen, left school to take care of her younger brother and sister so her mother could work full time.

When Charles Henderson met Inez at a church picnic, it was love at first sight. Her older brother had just started at the iron company where Charles worked. Charles told him he was going to marry her.

"Are you kidding? You're an old man," her brother said, laughing. "Why would my sister even go out with you, much less marry you?"

At twenty-nine, Charles was twelve years older than the teenage Inez. Yet he was a solid man with dark features, a gentle laugh, and a decent job. He was as good a prospect as Inez might find in northern Michigan. Plus he had one quality that clinched it for her.

Charles could cook.

He courted Inez not with flowers but with food. Charles brought around vats of hot chili and sweet cornbread, savory stewed chicken, and biscuits scented with rosemary.

Charles was born and raised in the impoverished hill country of Carter County, Kentucky. Some men worked in mining, a few got jobs in lumber, but a lot of them made and sold moonshine and homemade whiskey, a tradition in the region. Men handed down methods for the hard liquor the same as women did with recipes. For most, the moonshine sales yielded slight incomes. Even before national prohibition took hold in 1920, the federal government sent "revenuers" out to the area to catch scofflaws. When he was seventeen, Grandpa Charles and a couple of friends tried to sell some homemade whiskey to a man who turned out to be an undercover sheriff. He spent six months in the county jail.

When Charles received his army draft notice in 1918, he wanted to fight, but his earlier run-in with the law complicated things. So Charles was shipped off to Fort Sam Houston in San Antonio, Texas—then the largest army base in the continental United States—to train as a base cook.

The army put my grandfather through an intense on-the-job culinary school, one that taught him culinary fundamentals along with the complexities of ordering supplies and managing inventory for a high-volume kitchen that fed more than ten thousand soldiers and base workers daily. He was exposed to chili peppers, hot sauces, and cayenne powder for the first time. The base kept extensive gardens that he helped tend in his off-hours. He took pride in his ability to nourish the troops training for the war, and was known as one of the best cooks at the base. "The men, they would weep at my beef stew," he boasted years later.

Charles was a born chef. He was a gifted cook, but also excelled at managing a kitchen and training staff. After the war, the army wanted Charles to move up the culinary ranks. But he missed his family, most of whom had moved to northern Michigan to work in the booming lumber camps. So he headed to Mancelona. His first week there, Charles landed a plum job at the Antrim Iron Company.

Founded in 1882, Antrim Iron demolished more than fifty thousand acres of virgin timber during its years of operation. The company converted the wood into charcoal to fuel a sixty-foot furnace and dozens of kilns in the process of smelting iron ore into pig iron bars, which could later be transformed into steel. The bars were shipped by rail to mills in Chicago, Pittsburgh, and Buffalo.

Antrim was a classic company town. The founder, John Otis,

personally platted the settlement just outside Mancelona, and then built houses that the company rented or sold to its workers. The company pumped all the waste and by-products from iron production into a nearby clear pond that became known as Tar Lake. The company shut down operations after exhausting the timber supply in northern Michigan in 1945, just after it shipped its last lucrative war contract.

Grandpa Charles's job was to load the finished bars onto waiting railroad cars. Standing six feet four inches and a sturdy 220 pounds, Charles had remarkable strength; he could carry pig iron bars alone that normally took two men.

For doing the work of two men, he earned a man and a half's wages.

The company didn't pay its employees in U.S. currency. Instead, Antrim Iron issued its own form of tender known as scrip. Essentially a form of credit, scrip could be used for 100 percent of its face value at only one place: the company store.

Each family had a ledger in which they would track their purchases, whether it was coffee or fabric or even the mortgage due on a house. The amount was subtracted from the wages due, and whatever was left over was given in coin form by the company. Local retailers sometimes took the company scrip, but never at face value. If a worker wanted to use scrip for cash required to buy postage stamps, train tickets, or an order from the Sears Roebuck catalog, Antrim charged a 10 percent "exchange" fee.

Company scrip, also known as a truck system (from the French word *troquer*, which means "to exchange" or "to barter") wasn't unusual in logging and coal-mining towns in the 1800s through the early 1950s. In some cases, the camps were so remote that physical cash wasn't that easy to come by. But more often, companies leveraged scrip as a lucrative—and potentially exploitive—way to manage labor and induce "loyalty" among its workers. Many workers "outspent" their earned scrip, accruing so much debt with the company store or their mortgage or rent on company housing that they could never leave. Hence the phrase that refers to owing one's soul to a company store made famous in the song "Sixteen Tons."

Although the lyrics describe the life of a coal miner, the arrangement was exactly the same at Antrim.

Inez didn't worry about the scrip, though. She agreed to marry with one stipulation. "On Saturdays, if we have the money, I want to get my hair done."

"Honey doll, I'm going to treat you like a queen," Charles replied, relieved that she had such a simple request. After they married in June 1928, he would affectionately refer to her as "Queenie" or "the Queen of Mancelona." They bought a modest house in "the horseshoe," a workers' neighborhood that resembled a massive cul-de-sac. In the center of the horseshoe was a big field where both the workers and their kids would play endless games of baseball.

They moved a couple of times during the Antrim years. Frustrated by the lack of space for a garden at their first house, Charles convinced Inez to rent a rambling farm on twenty-five acres outside of town. They called it the "Old 25." The farmhouse didn't have any electricity or running water. Mom and her younger sister were too small to use the wide hole in the ancient outdoor privy at the Old 25, so Inez found herself cleaning out "thunder jars," portable pots small children used as toilets in those days.

The thunder jars weren't nearly as bad as the laundry situation. The house they left in the Antrim horseshoe had the latest domestic luxury: an electric wringer-style clothes washer. Since there would be no electricity at the Old 25, Grandpa Charles sold it along with the house.

To wash clothes at the Old 25, Inez had to send her three sons to shuttle water from the windmill-driven pump well. They brought the water in with buckets to a massive charcoal-fueled copper boiler. Queenie poured the hot water into a steel container with soap flakes, and scrubbed the clothes against a ribbed board, rinsed them in fresh water, and fed them through a hand-cranked wringer. Then she and the boys lugged them out to the line to dry. Charles got filthy loading pig iron six days a week, so she spent what she later described as "all damn day" doing the wash.

Charles suggested they buy the place after their year-long lease was up. "What do you think, Queenie?" Grandpa Charles asked her.

She got up from her stool in the kitchen, slammed the door, and planted herself on the ground with her arms folded across her chest.

They moved to a house on the end of the horseshoe on a plot with several acres so Charles could have his garden. Queenie got a new electric washer.

Years of loading pig iron wreaked havoc on Charles's legs, engraving them with deep varicose veins that caused him pain for the rest of his life. When Dow Chemical recruiters arrived in town at the start of World War II, he jumped at an offer to train as a boilermaker. The money was better, the work week was five days, not six, and it was less taxing on his body. The company paid legal tender and offered a pension plan. At first, the family lived in the military-style barracks the government set up for workers flooding into Midland to work on war-related Dow projects. In 1943, Charles found their final home in a tiny hamlet near Sanford Lake.

That Sanford Farm was set on ten acres at the edge of a generous wood, not unlike the house on Coldwater Road. Charles planted a mammoth vegetable garden that included every kind of bean he could get seed for. Somehow, he even coaxed chili peppers to ripen during the Midwest summers. They kept a small flock of chickens, and for a few years they raised turkeys. In the woods he shot squirrels and rabbits that Inez roasted or braised for dinner. He grew hogs that he'd butcher and turn into hams and sausage.

The house came with electricity and a pump house that provided running cold water. The day they moved in, Charles conducted the traditional "christening" of the outdoor privy by installing a small shelf for a Sears Roebuck catalog. It wasn't for reading. Let's just say the tissuelike index pages went first.

Inez had use of her prized washing machine. She would collect eggs, can vegetables, and even kill chickens, but that's where Queenie drew the line. She refused to step foot in the garden. "Never learn to milk a cow or clean a fish," she counseled my mother as a young girl. "Otherwise, you'll do it for the rest of your life." My grandmother never learned to drive a car or write a check, presumably for the same reason.

Charles and Inez held hands everywhere. Mom would catch

them smooching in the kitchen from time to time. "Oh, we were just talking," one of them would say as the pair would pull away from each other, embarrassed. Then, out of habit, Inez would give my mother a chore. "Well, don't just stand there. Here's a broom. Go sweep the porch."

On Sunday afternoons following church and a big dinner, Charles and Inez would take their usual nap. They'd head into their bedroom around two P.M. with strict orders to the kids not to knock. "Even if the house is burning down," Inez told them. They could play outside and visit with friends as long as they were home by six P.M. Sometimes Charles would emerge after an hour half dressed to use the bathroom, and then fetch a beer and a bottle of sweet wine from the fridge and return to the bedroom. Occasionally, the kids heard laughter behind their door.

Mom thought this was normal, and that all parents napped for up to four hours most Sunday afternoons. One day, when she was thirteen, a friend stopped by. Mom was reading. She shushed her friend. Her parents were napping, she explained.

"They ain't nappin' in there," the girl scoffed. "I know what parents do. They're doin' sumpin' naughty."

Mom had only a vague working knowledge of such things. The thought horrified her. "No, they're not!" she shouted in protest. "They're too old for that kind of stuff!"

In Sanford, with his regular work hours and higher pay, Charles finally made good on his original marital promise. On Saturday mornings, Inez would change out of her usual housedress and put on lipstick. A friend or relative would pick her up to take her into town "to get her hair done." In truth, Inez had naturally curly hair, so she rarely went to the salon. Instead, she used it as a chance to do some of her "sunshine work." She'd visit elderly relatives who might be lonely, write letters to send to distant friends, or run errands for a sick neighbor. To Grandma, sunshine work meant thoughtful deeds done for others with nothing expected in return.

On the weekend, Charles took over all the care and feeding of the children. He figured Inez did enough of it during the week. On Saturday mornings, he'd make scrambled eggs with his homemade sausage or stacks of pancakes that everyone would soak in "sugar syrup," a thin syrup made from white sugar boiled in water. While the kids cleaned up the breakfast dishes, he commenced with his Saturday ritual: making chili.

"It's hard to explain how exotic chili was back in the 1940s where we lived in Michigan," Mom says. "I grew up eating it and thought it was normal. But sometimes the kids would not know how to react the first time they tasted it. For a lot of them, it was the first time they ever tried anything spicy."

Charles started by browning beef and onions in the bottom of a huge twenty-quart kettle. Then he added home-canned tomatoes, dried beans, and dried chili peppers from his garden. He mixed the powdered chilies with paprika, oregano, and other spices to make his own "secret weapon" chili powder. Back then, the J.R. Watkins company sold its herbs and spices via door-to-door salesmen. Thanks to all the chili he made, Grandpa Charles was their rep's best customer.

Around one P.M., kids began to drift over to their house. Every kid within miles knew they were invited for chili on Saturdays. Each one got a dish of steaming hot chili and a fistful of oyster crackers that Charles bought in big bags from the A&P. Sometimes Charles would slip a few pounds of dried beans and some extra vegetables to the poorer kids or those from families without gardens.

Like all their dishes, the bowls they used for chili had come from inside boxes; back then, oatmeal and cereal boxes often included inexpensive bowls as a sales incentive. Laundry detergent brands offered glasses, while gas stations would often add in a plate with a fill-up. Movie theaters even had a "dish night" to attract theatergoers. All the dishes had simple designs, such as stamped-on wheat or strawberry patterns. The idea was that you'd keep buying the oatmeal or detergent until you had a complete set. But invariably, the manufacturers changed the designs too frequently, so it was nearly impossible to get more than three or four items. Every household Mom frequented growing up had the same random assortment of mismatched dishes. Mom promised herself that one day she'd have a matching set.

After Hazel died in May 1964, Mom packed up the kids and

drove the two hours north to Sanford. Grandma Inez came home early from "the salon" and changed into her usual Sears housedress. Grandpa Charles greeted the kids with chili and oyster crackers. Although Mom had made meek versions of his infamous chili, none of the kids had ever tasted anything quite like it. My brother Mike's eyes grew wide at the first bite.

"Is it too spicy for you, young man?" Charles asked. After all, Mike was just four.

"I like it," he said, beaming. "It tastes like firecrackers!"

The kids learned quickly that Grandma Inez was herself something of a firecracker.

She settled arguments between her hordes of grandchildren swiftly and effectively, by sending each kid in a different direction with a chore. "You got time to argue? Then you've got time to sweep the kitchen. Here's a broom." Then she'd turn to the other child. "And you, here's a rag. Go dust the living room."

In her presence, a kid never tattled—snitches got punished worse than the kid who was ratted on. You didn't even *think* about whining.

Toast was a great example of how Grandma Inez approached life.

While she embraced some emerging technologies such as an electric tea kettle, others she dismissed as fads. A toaster was among those items. Who needed a toaster when you had a perfectly good oven? she'd argue. She made her own bread twice a week; she could certainly do something as simple as *toast* it. She lined the hand-sliced bread on racks in the oven. Invariably, she'd get distracted and burn at least half of it. Sometimes she made the effort to scrape off the blackened portions with a knife. Other times she didn't. The most blackened pieces went to the youngest kids. When they protested, she had a simple retort.

"Eat it. Burnt toast makes you sing good," she'd tell them. "Everyone knows that." When the queen of Mancelona told you to do something, you didn't argue.

Grandpa Charles's "Mich-Mex" Chili

Debate rages about what "belongs" in chili. Purists say no beans, and others debate the use of tomatoes. As a laborer with a family to feed, Grandpa tended to use less meat and more beans. Most often he used beef, but he'd sometimes use venison. The vegetables shifted with the seasons. In summer he used fresh tomatoes and heaped the pot with bell peppers and shucked corn.

Since Grandpa Charles grew an abundance of beans and dried them himself, his chili might use any combination of kidney, pinto, cannellini, black, navy, and great northern beans, or even black-eyed peas. Feel free to experiment.

Strong seasoning is chili's hallmark. Try to use fresh spices and a quality hot chili powder. (See page 252 for a homemade version.) Grandpa employed whole chili pods in his pot. At the end of cooking he opened one pod and dumped the contents in the chili if making it for kids, two if making it for a mostly adult crowd. Finally, he served each hot bowl with a fistful of oyster crackers.

Makes about ten 1-cup (240-ml) servings, but can easily be doubled or halved

> 1 pound (450 g) dried beans, such as kidney, pinto, or black beans, or
>   four 15- to 16-ounce (425- to 450-g) cans, drained
> 1½ tablespoons (22.5 ml) ground cumin
> 2 to 3 tablespoons (30 to 45 ml) hot chili powder
> 2 tablespoons (30 ml) vegetable oil
> 1 large onion (340 g), chopped (about 2 cups)
> 2 green bell peppers (400 g), chopped (about 2 cups)
> 1 pound (450 g) lean ground beef
> 6 garlic cloves, chopped
> 2 tablespoons (30 ml) dried oregano
> 2 tablespoons (30 ml) all-purpose flour
> 2 teaspoons (10 ml) coarse salt
> 1 teaspoon (5 ml) ground black pepper
> One 6-ounce (170-g) can tomato paste
> 6 cups (1.5 L) water
> 1 bay leaf

6 whole dried red chili pods, such as chile de arbol
One 28-ounce (794-g) can whole tomatoes
1 tablespoon (15 ml) molasses
1 tablespoon (15 ml) red wine vinegar

If using dried beans, put them in a 4-quart (4-L) or larger pot with enough water to cover by 3 inches (8 cm) and soak overnight. Alternatively, boil for 2 minutes, cover, and let stand for at least an hour. Either way, drain the beans and rinse with cold water before proceeding. If using canned beans, drain and discard the liquid.

In a small dry skillet over medium heat, toast the cumin and chili powder for about 2 minutes to bring out the flavors. Put in a bowl and set aside.

Add the oil to a 5-quart (4.5-L) or larger pot or Dutch oven over medium-high heat. Cook the onion and green peppers until softened, about 3 minutes. Add the ground beef, stirring to break it up into small chunks, and cook until the exterior starts to brown, about 4 minutes. Turn down the heat to medium, add half of the garlic, and cook, stirring occasionally, until the meat is thoroughly browned, about 8 minutes.

Add the oregano, flour, salt, black pepper, cumin and chili powder, and tomato paste, and stir thoroughly into the mixture. Simmer for about 2 minutes.

Add the drained beans, water, bay leaf, chili pods, and tomatoes, crushing the whole tomatoes roughly with your fingers or a spoon as you add them to the chili. Bring to a boil, then turn down the heat and simmer for an hour.

Stir in the molasses, vinegar, and the rest of the garlic. Taste and add more salt if needed. Simmer for another hour or until the beans soften, or about 20 minutes more if using canned beans.

Remove the chili pods and bay leaf. Depending on how hot you want the final result, cut off the ends of 1 or 2 of the chili pods and stir the seeds into the chili. This can be refrigerated for up to 5 days or frozen in an airtight container for up to 2 months.

CHAPTER 5

Playing Chicken

Grandma Inez with cousins Julie and Pam
in front of the Fridline chicken coop

My parents decided that since they had a ready-made chicken
coop with a fenced yard out back, they ought to get some
chickens.

In the basement, they had found a chicken incubator—a contraption resembling a gigantic heated gerbil or hamster maze. It
wasn't exactly state of the art, but it had a built-in system of troughs
for chicken feed and water.

One dark afternoon, they dropped the kids with relatives and
headed to a nearby feed and farm supply. In the cold lofty room, a
vast horde of peeping chicks kept piling over one another in a

waist-high enclosure built of (what else?) chicken wire. Each cost mere pennies.

They were *so cute* and *so cheap.*

"Let's buy fifty," Mom said impulsively.

Dad countered as if at an auction. "How about a hundred?"

About then, the owner came strolling over. A hard-bitten farming type with a deeply weathered face, he said little as he rolled a piece of straw around his mouth. He looked at my parents, their faces shiny with enthusiasm at the prospect of raising their own chickens. He offered them a deal. If they bought 125, he'd give them another 125 *for free.*

Mom and Dad headed home with a crate filled with 250 white leghorn chicks, gallons of the specially treated water they had to drink until a certain age, and a few bags of feed. They felt like they'd hit the jackpot.

At first, the kids loved the chicks, a welcome break from winter boredom. They developed a game they called football. One kid would give a tiny speck of bread to a chick and watch the others chase it. Trying to save its treat, the chick scurried as if its life depended on it. Invariably, the peeping mob brutally tackled the treat-holding chick to the ground and pecked one another savagely in a furious rage to snatch the fumbled bread. For a few days, the kids gleefully clapped at the chicks' misfortune and the ensuing battle until they tired of the chicks in general.

Baby chicks need round-the-clock attention. The family could rarely leave the house together. If one escaped the incubator, it would cry in a shrill staccato series of panicked chirps, "*CHEEP! CHEEP! CHEEP! CHEEP! CHEEP! CHEEP!*" Oddly, despite the chicks' small size, the terrified cheeps were loud enough to be heard throughout the house. The whole flock freaked out, suddenly mimicking the escaped chick. It was a terrified cheeping multiplied by 250. Others would attempt to escape to save the lone chick. In minutes, dozens would spill out and spread onto the floor—and quickly die if not returned to the life-giving heat of the incubator. Virtually every night, the entire household was awakened by the cheeping. Worse, the smell of chicken poop permeated every inch of the farmhouse. The kids started to sleep with washcloths over their faces. After a couple of weeks, the kids found the once adorable chickens annoying.

"When are the chicks going out to the coop?" young Miltie asked Mom one morning around three A.M. after plodding from the upstairs room down to the basement to help her pick up an armload of chirping chicks and stuff them back into the incubator. The chicks fit comfortably in the first three weeks, but by April, they grew so much they barely fit.

Mom saw the opportunity to turn the kids' irritation into motivation. "Pretty soon," she replied. "You know, we'll need to clean out that old coop to get it ready for the chickens. The sooner it gets cleaned out, the sooner the chicks will be out of the house."

The next morning, Miltie rallied the troops. The obedient children worked like slaves, clearing out stale hay to make way for new, washing down the repugnant walls and nests. It was nasty, dirty work. They would do anything to get the damn chicks out of the house.

Days later, they installed the now adolescent chicks into the coop. By that time, they were growing fast and consuming an alarming amount of feed. As soon as they could add other food to their diet, Dad bought a bushel of dried corn from a neighbor. They dug out an old coffee grinder from the basement and took it to the drafty barn. The boys sat for hours, taking turns churning to grind the corn.

The birds always seemed starved. Mom began to toss all the peelings and leftover food from the house into the chicken yard. She'd drop the food and then leap back to avoid being injured as they attacked it, wildly chirping, wings flapping, beaks poking. In seconds, it would be gone.

By mid-June, they were spending more to feed the chickens than to feed the rest of the family. They were now about two to three pounds, fryer size. The decision was made to start collecting on their investment. Dad bought a huge secondhand deep freezer. With the help of his brothers Doug and Bob, they dragged it through the storm doors and set it up in the basement.

Mom was no stranger to what happened next. She had helped her mother kill and clean chickens. Mom didn't enjoy the process, but she liked fried chicken.

One warm June morning after school let out, she casually explained to the kids that the time had come to prep some chickens to put into the freezer. Only my oldest brother had a sense of what might happen next.

"You mean kill them?" Miltie asked, alarmed. "Who is going to do that?"

"I am, son," my mother explained matter-of-factly. "I'm a farm girl, and I have killed and cleaned plenty of chickens in my day. It's no big deal."

The kids took this news in stride. None of them liked the chickens. Churning corn proved an unpleasant chore. The once tidy coop smelled horrifically of drying poop. The hens pecked at the kids if they got too close to the yard. All were scared of the mean rooster. They were more curious about the process than upset by it.

Mom filled a sixteen-gallon pot she used for canning with water and put it over a fire pit outside to boil. She explained to the wide-eyed kids that this would be used to scald the dead chickens to remove the feathers.

She took the boys out to an area behind the coop where she set up a block of wood. Placing a flapping chicken's neck on the block, she took a sharp ax and lopped off its head with one quick *thwack!* It flapped around for a bit. When the bird quieted, she dipped it in the scalding water and sat down on a bench to demonstrate how to pluck off the feathers.

The boys didn't seem fazed by any of it. Mom set up an assembly line. Mom killed the birds, dipped them in hot water, and handed them to the boys to pluck. She never let them use the ax or kill them, since they were too young. But they took to the plucking quickly. They enjoyed sitting next to her, chatting.

"When you have tasted a chicken you have raised yourself and cleaned, it's just so much better than what you buy in the store," she said, ripping the feathers off a dead bird. "Our chickens ate a lot of grass and fruit and vegetable peels along with their feed, so they're going to be very tasty."

After they had killed and plucked six chickens, she headed inside to clean them. First, she singed off the tiny pin feathers over a gas burner. Then she gently bathed and washed the skin with a bit of mild soap and rinsed them several times until the water ran clear.

The kids asked a lot of questions. Among them, why did she give the chicken a bath?

"Just think about how dirty you would be if you ran around in the yard and didn't get a bath for two months," Mom replied.

Finally, she wrapped each chicken tightly in butcher paper and then tucked it into a freezer bag. She slapped a piece of white tape on each one and wrote the date on it with a marker. After cooling in the fridge for twenty-four hours, she packed them into the freezer downstairs.

Six chickens down, she started the whole process again. The first day, she dispatched eighteen chickens to the fridge. It took a good eight hours.

That night, she made beef burgers for dinner. As a treat for all their hard work and cooperation, Mom let each kid have a glass of strawberry Kool-Aid. They all toasted to a great achievement.

The kids thought the whole thing was a one-time event. Little did they know.

The next day, an older neighbor kid, Alfred, came over to help out. They killed and cleaned about 20 chickens a day for a solid week. She was finished when she'd sent 150 chickens to the freezer.

Each day, Mom rewarded the kids for their hard work. She also wanted to associate something fun with the brutality of the effort. She got store-bought ice cream to make banana splits one night, strawberry shortcake another. The final night, she supplied a box of Oreo cookies. The kids looked at the package with solemn reverence. Oreos were a *big* deal—everyone knew that they were for rich people. She rationed the package over two days. The kids ate them slowly and in silence, recognizing their value.

Cutting the flock down to a hundred birds significantly helped reduce the feed bill. By August, the remaining chickens began to lay eggs. Soon they were flooded with them. Mom began to hunt for recipes to employ them all. She made angel food cakes, lemon meringue pies, and French toast. She would add four or five eggs to a loaf of bread or a cake, anything to use the eggs.

She put a sign out in front of the farmhouse: Eggs for $ale. All proceeds went back to the feed bill, but the income from the eggs didn't make a dent in what it cost to keep them.

They had to face the truth—that they still had too many chickens. They tried to give some away to relatives. While everyone graciously took a cleaned dead one, no one wanted the live ones.

By fall, they put an ad in a small weekly paper and got a fair price for half of what remained. A month later, they decided that fifty chickens were still too many. They sold off another two dozen, until they were left with about twenty, a perfect number. They yielded a lot of eggs, but not enough to sell. The feed bill felt worth the fresh eggs they retrieved daily.

All seemed well in chicken land as winter descended again on the farm. Dad convinced Mom to set aside ten fertilized eggs to hatch into chicks to refresh the pack. After months of chicken drama, things seemed right.

Then one morning, it happened.

Mom had just finished making Dad breakfast before he left for work early on a wintry Saturday morning. He'd done so well as a salesman with his brothers' company, Dad decided to buy into it as a partner.

As light crept across the dark sky, Mom heard the rooster crow. She might as well get the first feed over with, she thought. Wearily, she threw on heavy winter boots and a thick wool coat. Mom grabbed the five-gallon bucket off the back porch and filled it halfway with warm water. Stopping by the barn to collect some meal and ground corn, she headed to the coop.

Mom set the water bucket and food inside. She closed the door, propping it open slightly with a long two-by-four piece of lumber to let in some fresh air but not let the heat escape. The coop was well lit even at this hour with five large incandescent lights. The lights gave off heat and prompted the hens to lay more eggs.

Some of the hens jumped down from their roosts when she entered and rushed at her. Inside the coop, Mom kept a long stick to poke at the rooster in case he got too protective and tried to attack. She loosened the frozen chunk of ice from the container with the warm water and refilled it. Next, she heaped the feed into the troughs. The hens clucked loudly, ate greedily, and slopped up the water. Mom sighed relief. At least this chore was done. In winter, the coop didn't smell too bad since everything was frozen. She picked up her empty buckets and turned to leave. Somehow, the mean rooster had gotten between her and the door.

He cackled at her. She got her stick and shooed him away nervously. Anxious to get out, she pushed on the door. It wouldn't budge.

The two-by-four she had propped open the door with had fallen and wedged the door shut from the outside.

She was trapped in the coop.

Mom began to yell at the top of her lungs. "HELP! ANYONE! I'M STUCK IN THE COOP!!"

After a few minutes, she realized screaming was futile. The rooster began to cluck and cackle loudly, puffing up its feathers. At his cue, the hens began to get hysterical.

Mom realized the severity of the situation. The coop sat well behind the barn, the distance of at least a football field from the house. The closest neighbor was acres away. It was below freezing and not quite seven A.M. on Saturday morning in an unheated coop with a rooster that might attack at any minute. She tried not to panic. With the chickens swirling and pecking around her, she considered her options.

She could break one of the small windows. But how would she get through broken glass? The sound could also spur on the already agitated rooster to attack.

The only other way was out the dreaded small hole the chickens used to get into their yard. She shivered at the thought. The rooster eyed her and scratched his left foot into the ground as if prepping for a fight.

She looked at the hole again. Resigned, she took off her jacket and stuffed it through the hole as the rooster clucked at her wildly.

Mom removed the poop-splattered plank the chickens used to walk down to the yard. She got down on her hands and knees and tried the hole. It was smaller than she realized. No way, she thought. She took off her sweater and jeans and threw them through the hole. Her boots, too, had to go. That left her in only a bra, under-wear, and thin socks. Mom reached out of the hole with one arm and then pulled her head through and then the other arm . . .

And then she was stuck.

She kept trying to squeeze out through the hole but it was too tight. She could imagine the headlines if she died this way, a half-naked woman attempting to escape a chicken coop. Mom screamed for help again only to feel her voice carried away by the freezing north wind.

After struggling for a few minutes more, she relaxed. Any minute, the rooster was going to start scratching or pecking at her legs. Tak-ing a deep breath, she located the edge of a sturdy post inside. Using all her strength, Mom made one huge push with her feet, wriggling her hips through, scraping off a layer of skin on each side. She dropped the two feet into the snow-covered chicken yard. The rooster appeared, crouching its head out the small hole.

Mom grabbed her clothes—now wet with snow—and clung them to her chest as she ran toward the chicken-yard fence. She climbed and jumped, half falling over the other side.

Freezing now and clad only in panties, bra, and socks, she ran as fast as she could the 125 yards to the house and jerked open the door leading to the kitchen.

Standing in front of her were four sleepy children in their pa-jamas.

"Mom, what's happening?" my brother Milt asked in a small bewildered voice.

Still in her underwear, clutching her clothes, Mom stood shiver-ing, her voice shaky. "I'll explain later. Miltie, please make the kids some toast with peanut butter and jelly. Dougie, please pour them some milk."

They stood motionless, staring at her.

"It's okay. Mom will be in a bath for a while. Milt, why don't you turn on the TV after breakfast so you can watch cartoons?"

With that, she turned toward the bathroom and immediately started to fill the bathtub. Over the water, she heard Miltie say, "Okay, sit down, kids." He corralled them to the table. The first touch of hot water against her skin felt like glass breaking through her veins. As she settled in, she could feel herself unthaw. How lucky, she thought, that she was slender enough to get through the small hole. How fortunate the rooster had not genuinely attacked her. How lovely that secondhand Zenith television could reliably tune in only one channel at the moment so the kids couldn't argue about what to watch.

After he came home from work that day, Dad went out to the coop to install an adjustable air vent into the door of the coop plus a new latch that could be opened from both sides. As he banged the nails in place, the rooster protested loudly. Dad poked him with the stick, but the rooster kept up his offensive, fluffing his feathers and scratching threateningly on the floor. The bird looked at him with a fixed stare and lunged straight at him.

Dad returned to the house awhile later. He kicked off his heavy boots and came into the warm kitchen, rubbing his hands to warm them.

"Did you fix the coop?" Mom asked, stirring a pot of soup on the stove.

"Yep, and I fixed the rooster, too." The next day, dinner was chicken and biscuits.

....

Chicken and Biscuits

This dish was the fate of a mean rooster who chased my mother. Mom would cut up a chicken into eight pieces, keeping the back intact. This way, she could pull the chicken pieces out once they had cooked through but not yet toughened. Leave in the back to flavor the stock for the gravy. Another option is to utilize the legs and thighs, then add chicken necks, a few wings, or the saved carcass from a roasted chicken to keep flavoring the stock after the other pieces have cooked.

This takes about 2½ hours from start to finish, but the stewed chicken portion can be made a day ahead, reheated, and served with freshly made biscuits. Dad liked crispy biscuits, so Mom cooked them separately rather than on top, but that's up to you. To make this a bit lighter, remove the skin from the chicken before start-ing. If you don't have poultry seasoning, you can make your own (page 252).

Makes 6 to 8 generous servings; the accompanying biscuit recipe makes 6 biscuits. I usually double the biscuit recipe and bake some or all of the bis-cuits separately.

> 2 tablespoons (30 ml) vegetable oil or butter
> 5 large carrots (285 g), diced (2 cups)
> 6 stalks celery (250 g), diced (2 cups)
> 2 large yellow onions (680 g), diced (4 to 5 cups)
> 3 garlic cloves, minced
> ¼ cup (35 g) all-purpose flour
> One 3½- to 5-pound (about 2-kg) chicken, cut up into 8 pieces
> 2 teaspoons (10 ml) coarse salt
> ½ teaspoon (2.5 ml) ground black pepper
> 1 tablespoon (15 ml) poultry seasoning
> 2 quarts (2 L) water or chicken stock, enough to cover the chicken
> 1 bay leaf
> 1 large potato (12 ounces/340 g), peeled and diced
> One 10-ounce (283-g) package frozen peas (2 cups/500 ml)
> 1 cup (250 ml) half-and-half or whole milk
> ½ teaspoon (2.5 ml) paprika
> ¼ to ½ teaspoon (1.25 to 2.5 ml) cayenne pepper, red chili flakes, or chili
>   powder (optional)
> Biscuit dough (recipe follows)

Add the oil to a 6-quart (5.5-L) or larger pot and cook the carrots, celery, and onions over medium-high heat until softened, about 8 minutes. Add the garlic and stir through. Sprinkle with the flour and stir to lightly cook, about 2 minutes, until the flour absorbs into the vegetables and thickens slightly.

Season the chicken pieces with 1 teaspoon (5 ml) of the salt, the pepper, and half the poultry seasoning. Add the seasoned chicken, water, the remaining salt, and the bay leaf to the vegetables and stir. Bring just to a boil, then reduce the heat to simmer gently, partially covered. Skim regularly to remove any foam or fat from the surface.

Remove the breast and wing pieces after 30 minutes. Remove the dark meat after 50 minutes, but leave in the chicken back. Simmer uncovered for an hour to reduce and thicken the sauce.

Once the chicken has cooled, discard the skin from the cooked chicken pieces, remove the meat from the bones with your fingers, and shred the meat.

When the sauce has thickened to your liking, remove the chicken back from the gravy. Then stir the shredded meat into the stock along with the diced potatoes, peas, half-and-half or milk, paprika, the remaining poultry seasoning, and the cayenne, if using. Taste and add salt and pepper as needed. Discard the bay leaf. Let it simmer while you make the biscuits. This is a good time to heat the oven to 450°F (180°C).

If you want to bake the biscuits on top of the stew, you can put them atop the gravy and then bake for 13 to 17 minutes until they are slightly browned. (If desired, you can pour the simmering mixture into a casserole dish for baking and serving.) If you choose to bake them separately, just continue to simmer the chicken mixture on top of the stove until the biscuits are done and the potatoes have softened.

Easy Herb-Scented Biscuits

These biscuits use only three ingredients, four if you add dried herbs. Self-rising flour has baking powder and salt already incorporated into it. You can make your own self-rising flour if you don't have it on hand. For each cup of all-purpose flour, simply add 1¼ teaspoons of baking powder and ¼ teaspoon of salt and mix to combine. Grating the butter is a key to making the biscuits rise; it will take a few minutes but is worth the effort. Don't overknead or handle too much while rolling out the dough. Make sure the oven is hot before you put the biscuits in to bake.

¾ stick (6 tablespoons; 85 g) cold salted butter
2 cups (256 g) self-rising all-purpose flour
½ teaspoon dried herbs such as thyme or rosemary (optional)
1 cup (237 ml) whole milk, cold
All-purpose flour for dusting

Put the oven rack in the middle position and preheat the oven to 450°F (180°C). Partially freeze the butter for about 10 minutes. Using a cheese grater, grate the hardened butter into a bowl. Cover. Put the butter back into the freezer to chill again, about 5 minutes.

Combine the flour and butter in a mixing bowl. Blend together with a pastry blender or your fingertips until the mixture resembles coarse meal with some small (roughly pea-sized) butter lumps. Stir the herbs into the milk (if adding herbs). Then add the milk to the flour and butter and mix with a fork just until a sticky dough forms.

Turn the dough out onto a floured surface and gently knead 6 or 7 times. Do not overwork, or the biscuits will be tough. Pat the dough out to about ⅓-inch thickness. Cut out 5 circles using a biscuit cutter or the floured rim of a drinking glass. Bundle up the extra dough and pat into a sixth biscuit. Alternatively, you can roll it out into a square or triangle and cut it into individual biscuits. Place on an ungreased baking sheet or, if making chicken and biscuits, directly on the stew. Bake until golden brown, 13 to 17 minutes. Cool slightly, serve warm.

Part II

"God doesn't subtract from your time on earth the hours you
spend fishing."
—Dad's variation on a Babylonian proverb

CHAPTER 6

Birthday Dinner

Cousin Diane (left) with the Flinn family, 1967

When I started dating, Mom said, "If a boy says, 'Trust me, you won't get pregnant,' then you tell him, '*I* was a trust me.'"

In the sticky heat of August 1966, my parents got ready for a wedding an hour away in Detroit. Dad looked snazzy in his best jacket. Mom appeared from their bedroom and posed for a moment in a body-hugging jade green dress. She'd found it new with tags still attached at the thrift store. Dad let out a wolf whistle.

"Wow, isn't your mother a knockout?" Dad said to the kids gathered around the living room to witness the excitement of the evening. My parents were going out! On a date! "Wow, that dress looks like it was made for her!"

Mom and Dad kissed the kids good-bye and left final instructions for our cousin Diane, then fourteen. She'd recently moved in with our family after her father had died. She was a quiet girl, mature for her age.

"Okay, kids, all of you are going to mind Diane and Miltie, right?" Dad said. The others nodded. "Good. We'll be home late, so go to bed when they tell you to."

At the reception, after the roast beef buffet, the lights dimmed as the band started to play. Couples drifted to the dance floor. Candles flickered on the tables. Mom and Dad swayed with her head on his shoulder as the band played covers of Frank Sinatra's "Strangers in the Night" and "Pretty Woman" by Roy Orbison. Over the evening, Dad had a couple of beers, Mom drank sparkling wine. It was the first night they'd gone out by themselves in years.

"You look just the same as the day I married you," Dad told her as he twirled her around at the start of "My Girl" by The Temptations and softly sang along into her ear for a moment. Then he said, "Hey, I've got an idea."

When the song ended, Mom giddily fished a dime from her purse as they stood at the pay phone in the hallway.

"We're going to spend the night in Detroit," Dad told Diane. "Are you okay with keeping an eye on the kids?" She said no problem. Sandy and Mike were already in bed.

When they reached a roadside motel, Mom warned that she wasn't prepared for, well, what was going to happen. "Trust me," he said. At age thirty-two, he suggested that Mom was probably too old to get pregnant anyway. They rose early the following morning and were home in time to make the kids breakfast.

A month later, my mother called Dad at his office.

"TRUST YOU!" she yelled into the phone. "You said I wouldn't get pregnant!"

The news was greeted by Diane and my siblings as if they were all getting new bikes and kittens. They cheered, hollered, and danced around the room.

My sister, then nine, had started Sunday school at the First Baptist Church in Davison. She took church seriously. Sandy would pray several times a day. Even though we were Baptist, she somehow got her hands on a rosary and would work it fervently between her small fingers. One night, Mom overheard Sandy as she kneeled for her bedtime prayer: ". . . and God, please tell my baby sister that I love her and that I'm here waiting for her. Amen."

Mom helped little Sandy into her covers. In the late 1960s, there remained some mystery to childbirth. Ultrasound machines existed but weren't yet sophisticated enough to detect the gender of a fetus. Mom said tactfully, "You know, God might not give you a baby sister. He might give you another brother."

Sandy shook her head, appalled. "Oh, no, God would NEVER give me another brother." Whenever Mom would try to introduce the subject of a possible brother, Sandy wouldn't hear of it. She insisted that she'd worked it out with God. She was getting a sister.

Mom worried less about the gender and more about how they would manage with a new baby. After all, they were completely broke.

Century Products started as a producer of faux bricks made of concrete with a weatherproof brick exterior. Around the time Dad came back from California in 1964, the company had just added an aluminum siding option using subcontractors to tap into the booming 1960s siding craze. They also built custom windows, aluminum screen enclosures, and window awnings of all sizes and shapes.

Not long after they returned to Michigan, Dad's brothers offered him a partnership. He had to come up with $25,000 to own a third of the company, about $180,000 in today's currency, equivalent to about five years of his San Bruno police salary. They organized bank loans and approached relatives and friends to raise the rest of the money. My parents had never been in debt before. They knew it was a risky move. But Century Products was growing so fast that they felt certain it was a good investment, the kind of business that could develop into something substantial, a share in a solid company that Dad might be able to leave to his kids someday.

Besides, Dad's hero was William C. Durant. Better known as Billy Durant, he founded the Coldwater Road Cart Company in 1885. The business morphed into the Durant-Dort Carriage Company, and by the turn of the 1900s it was the largest manufacturer of horse-drawn carriages *in the world*. In 1904, Durant took a risky move and shifted all of his focus into the infant automobile industry by joining a small horseless-carriage company called Buick. Within a few years, Durant would pull several companies together and rechristen the endeavor General Motors. All of that started just a few miles down the very road from us.

If Billy Durant could find success starting an endeavor on Coldwater Road, Dad figured he could, too. He didn't expect Century Products to grow into the equivalent of GM, but he felt he was on the ground floor of something big.

The partners drew small salaries so they could pump the rest of the profits back into the company. They had thirty-five employees, a dozen vehicles, plus a number of subcontractors, and developed a great reputation for solid work and expanded their service area. They started to routinely beat competitors out of sought-after contracts.

In the midst of this growth, the partners were approached by a local investor. He outlined a strategy that involved an infusion of his capital and a small business loan so they could expand even more quickly and then go after major commercial accounts. They agreed to make him a nonworking capital partner.

Counting on the coming infusion of cash, the company ordered new equipment after it was approved for a $100,000 loan, equivalent to $750,000 today. All that was needed was to finalize the documents.

But the investor didn't return his paperwork for weeks. Then he returned the documents unsigned. The guy never explained why. The new equipment arrived the day they learned he backed out.

The dominoes fell. The partners scrambled to save the company. They sold off the newly ordered equipment at a loss to a competitor. They laid off workers. Their two largest clients decided it would take too long to get their orders and took their business to another company—the same one that bought the equipment they couldn't afford to keep. Then came the day they didn't have enough cash to pay the subcontractors or the payroll. They were forced to liquidate the assets, selling even the desks in the office. Within a few weeks, the once thriving Century Products folded.

Mom and Dad were stunned.

Rumor had it that the investor was a silent partner in the competitor that bought their equipment and took over the contracts. It might have been a shrewd but cut-throat move to run them out of business. Or he might simply have changed his mind with unfortunate timing.

People told Dad that he should declare bankruptcy. But Dad knew the individuals who had lent him money on little more than his word would not be repaid. If they defaulted on their bank loans, they would lose the farm and their credit rating would be shattered.

Dad, a U.S. Marine, was not about to lose the most valuable thing of all: his honor.

They developed a repayment plan with the banks and each of the individuals who had lent them money. It would take at least six years to pay it all back, with interest, as promised.

Dad's hero Billy Durant had his own setbacks. In 1910, Durant became overextended and lost control of GM to banking interests. His response was to start a new motor company with Louis Chevrolet, an American racing champion of French descent. The company was so successful that Durant was able to buy enough General Motors stock to own a controlling interest. He took his young wife, Catherine, out for hamburgers one evening and casually told her, "I took back GM today."

Her response: "Well, then, you could have taken me to dinner at the Plaza."

If Durant could stage a comeback, Dad could, too.

Given Dad's fascination with its founder, perhaps fate led both my parents to work for GM. Mom got a job as a secretary in the personnel department at the AC Spark Plug plant in Flint. Dad knew someone at Chevrolet and got hired on the assembly line.

Mom's position in personnel turned out to be a blessing for the extended family. General Motors received thousands of applications every week. Since most of the jobs were blue-collar positions that didn't require much experience, a résumé meant little in terms of getting hired for jobs on the line, or even in middle management. In "the shop," as it was called, getting hired often depended on who you knew.

When Mom started to work, GM was testing a program at AC Spark Plug to train foremen who oversaw workers on the line. Foremen had historically been hired from the ranks, but this didn't always work out. Someone might be good at assembly, but it didn't necessarily translate into being an effective manager. The head of the training program was impressed by Dad's entrepreneurial spirit and his background in the marines. Plus he had a college degree in business. They had never hired a foreman from "the outside" before. Dad was the first.

Thanks to Mom, other relatives got into the shop, too. Aunt Mary Jo was hired into a coveted position as a stock chaser, a kind of higher-level go-fer who would watch the line and warn when supplies got low. Aunt Mel's new husband, Rich Fridline, joined as a plant security guard. Potential line workers had to pass a dexterity test. Aunt Lillian got one of the highest scores in the history of the testing. Her manual prowess earned her a place as a winder, rapidly wrapping wire around spark plugs, a job she held for thirty-three years.

At first, both my parents worked days. All the children were in school. Diane monitored the kids for a couple of hours after the bus dropped them off.

Every cent of Mom's paychecks went toward their debts. As they were children of the Depression who believed firmly that the economy could always go wrong, a portion of my dad's income went into savings. This left them little cash after they paid the sixty-three-dollars-a-month mortgage on the farm. But they had the garden and orchard, chickens producing eggs, and a basement filled with canned goods. The most important thing was that they wouldn't go hungry.

When Mom went on maternity leave in late April 1967, Dad was unexpectedly laid off. Although the rest of the U.S. economy remained steady, auto sales plummeted in February and March. Some economists blamed the year-long news reports swarming around GM in relation to political activist Ralph Nader and his ongoing crusade for improved safety measures such as mandatory seat belts in American cars and design issues with specific models, notably the Chevrolet Corvair. Others pointed to an increased appetite by urban dwellers for smaller vehicles from foreign manufacturers such as Volkswagen. Whatever the reasons, GM scrambled to lay off workers throughout the ranks.

Still heavily in debt with a baby on the way, Mom and Dad made the best of it. They took the kids on all-day fishing adventures at nearby Holloway Reservoir and for picnics in the woods. They would make a big bonfire behind the farmhouse and cook dinner over the fire. It was like camping without having to pack up the car.

Mom's original due date was May 16—the same day Dad's sister Hazel died four years earlier. Nothing happened. After a week passed, the kids got impatient.

"Come out, baby!" eight-year-old Mike would implore loudly at my mom's stomach. "We're all waiting! Are you always going to be late?"

With time on his hands in good weather, Dad decided to cover up the old farmhouse with some of the white siding he'd bought wholesale from Century Products. "Might as well do it now," he told Mom. "We're just waiting on this baby."

Installing siding is hard work; it normally takes at least a couple of strong, skilled men. The boys liked it. They spent days fetching siding as Dad perched perilously atop ladders. Dad had enough left over that he even put siding on part of the barn, which didn't really match its rustic wood exterior.

He finished around midnight the last day of May aided by work lights. At one A.M., he fell into bed exhausted. As soon as he drifted off, Mom poked him awake. "I think this is it," she said. Dad wearily got up and rushed her to St. Joseph's Hospital.

They weren't too surprised by the onset of labor. She'd felt a lot of movement on the days Dad had been installing the siding. When the nurse went to listen for the heartbeat, she couldn't find it right away. After checking Mom over, she stood back. "This baby is breech," she said grimly. "We'll have to get it turned around."

Apparently, I was a tiny baby luxuriating in a relative lap pool of amniotic fluid. The attending nurse was a hulk of a woman. She massaged the exterior of Mom's belly, pushing and kneading until she thought the baby's head was down, not a particularly comfortable experience for my mother. "All right," she declared. "I think we're set."

Within minutes, I flopped back into breech position, as if pushing off a wall at a swim meet. The nurse tried her maneuver again, this time trying to tie off a possible retreat route by securing towels around Mom's stomach. At seven A.M., I flipped back into breech again. The nurse put her hands on her hips, exasperated.

"I feel like I have to push," Mom said. She'd been trying to fight her involuntary contractions. "But I know that I shouldn't." After all, her baby was in a potentially dangerous position and the doctor wasn't yet in the room.

The nurse, a veteran of hundreds of deliveries, told her to go ahead. "If I can't deliver this baby, I shouldn't be here," she assured Mom. After a single mighty push, she heard the nurse say quickly, "It's a girl." With a second push two minutes later, she heard a timid cry. I had come out feet first, one arm casually flung over my head, the other arm down at my side. My shoulders never squared, so I slid right out. Minutes later, the doctor arrived, a mask held in place over his mouth. "Well, well! What have we here?" he exclaimed. He picked me up from the weighing table, to assure he got his fee.

At 6.2 pounds, I was the smallest of my parents' offspring and, after the initial scare, by far the easiest birth. Dad called the house with the news. The kids had been up since nearly three A.M., and screamed in celebration. Then Miltie, ever practical, asked when Mom was coming home to make them breakfast.

"Your mother is very tired," Dad explained. "She and your sister won't be home for a few days." In the late 1960s, women remained in the hospital for up to a week following delivery. Mom basked in the quiet luxury of the hospital. She slept late every morning. Someone brought her bland meals on a tray and changed her baby. A few days without five kids and laundry felt like a trip to a spa.

On the sixth of June, she took me home in a tiny newborn outfit sprinkled with roses, a gift from my aunt Mary Jo. The novelty of a new baby gripped the household. My brothers and sister fought to hold me and to give me a bottle. The older kids couldn't wait to change my diaper. Mom had spent years washing cloth diapers, a complicated and messy process. I was the first child born after the common availability of disposable ones. To her, tossing a diaper in the trash was nothing short of a miracle.

Sandy, proven correct in her divination that she'd get a sister, took on secondary-mother status. At nine, she became a sudden expert in all things infant. "Don't hold her like that, it will make her throw up," she'd scold one of the boys. Or, overseeing a diaper change: "No, that's not how you do it. Give her to me." If a brother or cousin Diane heated up a bottle, she'd check it against her wrist and nod her approval.

A week later, Mom got a call from AC Spark Plug. She thought it might be someone confirming she'd be back after her maternity leave in September. Instead, the caller informed her that she was being laid off, too.

Despite their debts, my parents were thrilled. On maternity leave, she had no pay. With a layoff, she would be eligible for a small unemployment check *and* be able to stay home with the baby and the kids while they were on summer break. "Rocking chair money," she called it. Mom couldn't believe her good luck.

The next day, her boss at AC called personally. "Great news!" he started. "We've created a job just for you! It's a new classification so that we could bring you back from the layoff. But this means you'll have to come back on Monday, not after your maternity leave."

So Mom went back to work. In mid-August, when Dad got "called back in," the nomenclature used by auto workers to signal the end of a layoff, he asked to be moved to second shift. For the first months of my life, my parents rarely saw each other so that one of them could always be home with me.

The next June, Dad got transferred to days. Their differing-shift child-care strategy wouldn't work anymore. Cousin Diane had moved in with her older sister in Saginaw, so they'd have to hire someone to watch me. Even though Mom's salary was helping them pay off their debts, they decided it didn't make financial sense to spend so much on child care. She quit working at AC.

People were shocked. No one "quit" working at GM. If you got lucky enough to get in—especially at a desk job like Mom's—you stayed until you got your pension. But her four kids were ready to break for summer. She had already missed so much of her baby's first moments. She wasn't home for my first steps, nor did she hear my first word. In the two years she worked at AC, they'd paid off a big chunk of their debt. Quitting meant they would have to live off a small portion of my dad's paychecks.

"Some things are worth more than money," Mom says.

As young parents, they were always financially strapped. They couldn't afford to get each kid an expensive toy for his or her birthday. Instead, we would get a small token gift. The *real* present was we could "order" whatever we wanted for breakfast, dinner, and dessert.

This evolved into an annual event of immense proportions. Extraordinary amounts of time went into discussing and developing birthday menus. Mom served the whole family whatever the child ordered, so deals were made to assure that the selected menu didn't contain any yucky items, such as peas.

Despite the hours of consideration, in the end, we tended to order the same thing each year. Sandy always wanted spaghetti and meatballs, corn on the cob, and "sweet salad," a simple cabbage slaw made with bananas and apples in a mayonnaise and sugar dressing. Her dessert was always angel food cake; she considered it the most extravagant food in the world since it required twelve to fourteen egg whites. Mom would collect the eggs for days to get enough and then carefully save the yolks for French toast or homemade noodles. Sandy would watch as Mom whipped the egg whites into stiff peaks and folded them into a frothy batter. Angel food cake was so special it even had its own pan.

Miltie preferred bone-in chicken to the stewed variety Mom served routinely with biscuits. For his birthday dinner, he ordered fried chicken with blanched green beans and cornbread, and a chocolate cake for dessert. Doug wanted hamburgers with real buns, not slices of bread, and chocolate chip cookies for dessert. (Otherwise, Mom never made chocolate chip cookies; the morsels were too expensive.) Mike usually wanted steak, a delicacy rare on the farm, with off-the-ear corn and mashed potatoes, and a banana cream pie for dessert. Diane stayed with us until I was about a year old, but when she lived on the farm, she ordered fried chicken, mashed potatoes, biscuits, and strawberry shortcake. When I got old enough, I ordered roast chicken with mashed potatoes, herb dressing with thick sage gravy, and lemon meringue pie.

But all of us ordered the same thing for breakfast: cinnamon rolls.

Mom regularly made pancakes and French toast. They both allowed her to use up her many eggs. Cinnamon rolls were reserved for special occasions. My grandmother's recipe required two stages of letting the dough rise, so they took a couple of hours to make from start to finish. They couldn't be prepped the night before, either. In order to have them in time for the kids' breakfast before school, Mom had to get them started by 5:30 A.M.

Mom didn't mind. She and Dad rose early anyway. She'd pad to the kitchen on each of our birthdays and start to mix the dough before she had her coffee. During the years they paid off their debts, the kids never had new clothes, fancy bikes, or enough money for hot lunch at school. My mother's heart sank as the children would spend dinnertime telling stories of their friends' trips to Disneyland or summer camp. Once, Sandy needed shorts for gym class. In a thrifty move, Mom made her a pair from Mike's old Cub Scout trousers, which were threadbare hand-me-downs worn first by Milt and then by Doug. Mom cut off the legs and hemmed them to fit Sandy's tiny frame. The girls in school noticed the trademark dark blue color with the bright yellow piping. A group cornered her at gym and taunted her.

"Are those Boy Scout pants?" a tall girl asked, mocking her.

Another piped in, "You can't afford real shorts, can you?" Sandy gritted her teeth and endured the shame, her face hot and ready for tears, but she held them back. The taunting continued on the bus ride home. She jumped off the bus at the farm, ran into the house, buried her head in a pillow, and cried for hours.

The next morning, Mom got up and made Sandy cinnamon rolls even though it wasn't her birthday. She knew that her children were paying the price of a risk that didn't pan out and the cost of keeping promises. As she left the dough to start its first rising in her quiet predawn kitchen, my mother figured it was the least she could do.

Cinnamon Rolls

The key to these cinnamon rolls is to make sure they get adequate rising time. This whole process takes about 2½ to 3 hours from start to finish. These are great to make on the weekend when you know you'll be off somewhere for an hour for the first and/or second rise, whether it's church, soccer practice, or a long walk with the dog. Alternately, it's a great recipe to work on in between batches of laundry.

A stand mixer simplifies things, but if you don't have one, simply use a large spoon and some muscle. A handheld mixer just isn't strong enough, but you are! If desired, frost with Cream Cheese Frosting while the rolls are still warm, but it's not necessary.

Fresh cinnamon makes a huge difference in the flavor intensity. If your cinnamon harks back to ancient times and has little smell, double the quantity and buy some fresh before you make your next batch.

Makes 16 to 20 rolls, depending on how you roll them out and how thick you cut them

> Two ¼-ounce (7-g) packages active dry yeast (4½ teaspoons/22.5 ml)
> ½ cup (120 ml) warm water (90° to 110°F/32° to 43°C)
> 1½ cups (360 ml) milk
> 2 teaspoons (10 ml) coarse salt
> ½ cup (100 g) granulated sugar

8 tablespoons (120 g) unsalted butter or margarine, softened, plus more
    for the pan (if not using nonstick spray)
3 large eggs, beaten
6 cups (780 g) all-purpose flour, plus more for rolling out the dough
2 tablespoons (14 g) ground cinnamon
½ cup (110 g) dark brown sugar
1 large egg white
Nonstick cooking spray (optional)
Cream Cheese Frosting (recipe follows; optional)

In a large bowl or the bowl of a stand mixer, combine the yeast and water.
Let stand for at least 5 minutes.

Meanwhile, scald the milk in a small saucepan by heating it until it
gets frothy and barely bubbles, just at the edge of boiling. Remove from the
heat and let it cool to room temperature. (If the milk is too hot, it will kill the
yeast.)

Add the milk, salt, granulated sugar, and 4 tablespoons (60 g) of the butter
to the dissolved yeast and mix until incorporated. Add the eggs and 3 cups
(390 g) of the flour and beat thoroughly, until the eggs and flour are incorporated. Add the remaining flour and mix thoroughly again. Remove the dough
to a lightly floured surface and knead lightly for about 3 minutes, until soft
but starting to stiffen. Shape the dough into a ball and put it back in the
bowl. Cover loosely with plastic wrap or a clean kitchen towel and let it rise
in a warm place for about an hour, or until it has doubled in bulk. The dough
should feel soft, light, and a bit airy.

Return the dough to the floured surface and roll it out to a square about 16
x 16 inches (41 x 41 cm). Melt the remaining 4 tablespoons (60 g) of butter.
With a pastry brush or the back of a spoon, apply a light layer of the butter
across the dough. Combine the cinnamon, brown sugar, and egg white in a
small bowl. Sprinkle this damp mixture across the entire surface of the
dough. Carefully roll up the dough.

Coat two 9 x 13-inch baking pans with nonstick cooking spray or lightly butter
them. Slice the roll of dough into pieces ¾ to 1 inch (2 to 2.5 cm) wide. Lay the
slices flat in the pans, leaving at least ½ inch (1.5 cm) on each side of each slice.

Cover the pans lightly with plastic wrap. Let the dough rise again in a warm place until the slices have doubled in bulk, about an hour. They should have expanded to the point where they touch and start to crowd one another.

When the rolls are ready to bake, preheat the oven to 350°F (175°C). Bake for about 20 minutes. The rolls should be light brown and still a bit soft and doughy when they emerge from the oven. If frosting, do so while hot and serve while warm. Store leftovers in airtight containers in the fridge and reheat briefly in the microwave.

Cream Cheese Frosting

Soften the butter by either leaving it out at room temperature for 20 minutes or microwaving it on medium power for about 10 seconds; do not melt it. Soften the cream cheese by either leaving it out at room temperature for the same amount of time or, after removing it from its packaging, microwaving it, covered, on medium power for about 20 to 30 seconds. If you don't have a mixer, a rubber spatula will work better than a whisk, and the resulting frosting will be a little thinner than if mixed by machine.

Makes about 1 cup, enough to generously frost about 20 rolls

> 4 tablespoons (60 g) unsalted butter, softened
> ½ cup (60 g) confectioners' sugar
> 4 tablespoons (60 g) cream cheese, softened
> ½ teaspoon (2.5 ml) vanilla extract
> ¼ teaspoon (1.25 ml) orange extract (optional)
> ¼ cup (60 ml) water
> 2 pinches salt

Beat the butter and sugar together until creamy. Add the cream cheese, vanilla, orange extract (if using), water, and salt and beat until smooth. Using a spoon, coat the top of each cinnamon roll with 1 teaspoon (5 ml) to 1 tablespoon (15 ml) of frosting, depending on taste.

CHAPTER 7

Pie for Radio

Sandy teaching me to read while listening to the radio, 1969

It's the strangest thing," Dad said one day around the time I was four. "Every day this week, I've heard that John Denver song. You know, that one I like about driving home."

Mom was pulling fresh bread from the oven in the farmhouse kitchen. She dumped it onto clean dish towels. With a distracted note, she responded, "Oh, really? Huh. Which one?"

Dad needed little excuse to sing. He rattled off a couple of lines of "Take Me Home, Country Roads" by John Denver in his steady tenor voice.

"You know, it just really makes my day to hear a great song when I'm on my way home," Dad said brightly as he wrapped his arms impulsively around her waist. He gave her a quick peck on the cheek. "I'm going to go change out of my work clothes and head out to the barn."

As Dad left the kitchen, Mom turned to where I sat at the table. She put a finger to her lips. "Shhh," she said. "It's our little secret."

What Dad didn't know was that my mother routinely called the DJ at the station he listened to during his drive home in his Chevy pickup.

To assure her requests got played she employed her own brand of payola. For years she'd been plying a local DJ with pies. At first, she requested "Kisses Sweeter Than Wine" by The Weavers, later "My Way" by Frank Sinatra, and then shifted to the likes of "Take Me Home, Country Roads."

A month earlier, we pulled into the small white concrete bunker of a building nestled at the foot of a huge antenna somewhere in Flint. She looked so pretty with a light rain jacket over her teal wool sweater, black flats, and tight black trousers à la Mary Tyler Moore in *The Dick Van Dyke Show*.

"Don't move, I'll be right back," she told me as she smoothed the foil over the top of a still-warm apple crisp and walked over to the gray door. Minutes later, she plopped back into the front bench seat with a satisfied smile as she pulled down on the three-on-the-tree shifter to lurch our 1964 white Biscayne station wagon into reverse. She turned on the radio.

"And I'd like to thank a special lady who just dropped off a warm pie here to the studio," the deep-voiced DJ announced. "Ladies, you know, all donations are welcome to your bachelor announcer here . . ."

Although the 1960s and early 1970s generally evoke mostly television memories from those who grew up in that era, radio played a big part in our lives on the farm.

While there are many reasons we didn't watch a lot of TV, you had to start by blaming the encyclopedias.

Mom came home one day after they married to find that Dad had purchased a full set of the *World Book* encyclopedia from a door-to-door salesman.

Encyclopedia salesmen were a fixture of suburban America in the 1950s and 1960s, widely mocked by comedians. Regardless of the brand, the hard sell invariably included an expression of grave concern that a potential client's children would suffer without having a "library in the living room." Most offered a payment plan to help ease the impact of the investment, which could be the equivalent of half a year's rent.

They lived in Lansing, the home of Michigan State University. In those days, college towns offered a buyer's market when it came to encyclopedias. Lured in by the promise of easy money, college students flocked to work on a commission-only basis for one of the big three encyclopedia companies. This pitched them against one another in heated competition for a relatively small geographic area. Dad listened to several of the salesmen's pitches. He got to know their strategy, and figured out what kind of discounts they were authorized to make. One day, a brand-new *World Book* salesman came knocking. By then, Dad knew more about encyclopedia sales than the guy at the door. He ended up getting a complete nineteen-volume set with the matching world atlas and the small bookcase that came with it for nearly wholesale.

Internal research at *World Book* showed that the average owner of their product opened an encyclopedia twice a year. Not my dad. Still in college, he referred to them for virtually every paper and started a lifelong habit of reading the encyclopedia for entertainment. The set was one of the few possessions they moved to California and back again.

At the farmhouse, he'd disappear for hours into the only bathroom. Kids would get restless and start jigging up and down outside the door. Finally, after insistent knocks, he'd exit, a heavy, oversized volume in his hand and a newly acquired fact at his dispatch.

"Did you know that in ancient Rome, most of the homes didn't have kitchens?" Dad would say to the kid rushing into the vacated bathroom. Talking through the door, he might continue: "And the Circus Maximus could hold 150,000 spectators. Isn't that amazing?"

Or, after another session: "I was just reading about the state of Connecticut. Their state motto is 'He who is transplanted still sustains.' So interesting."

Later: "You know, the term *Patagonia* comes from the name of the giants Europeans thought lived in the area when Magellan ended up there in 1520." He'd point to an in-line photo. "See, they expected them to be fifteen feet tall!"

Dad loved the encyclopedias so much that he would bring along a volume or two on camping and fishing adventures to read aloud. "Okay, who wants to know about the history of the gold rush?" Or, "Who wants to hear about bats?" He selected topics that weren't too long, and he was a good reader, so it didn't seem that strange.

When he tucked me in at night, he'd sometimes bring along a random volume and read a passage in lieu of a children's book. From those nocturnal readings I learned about the Greek goddess Athena; the migratory habits of northern songbirds; the life of the first female American lawyer, Arabella Mansfield; and that the rings of Saturn are made up mainly of ice particles, dust, and debris.

When Dad finally read through the entire set of encyclopedias, he started to pick up used history or science textbooks at garage sales. He'd take one with him into the bathroom early on Sunday mornings, settle into an hours-long bath, and read the entire thing cover to cover.

To free up the bathroom and to encourage reading as a sought-after form of leisure time, for a few years Mom tried to get the whole family involved in reading on weekend nights. This proved complicated by the time I entered the scene. Miltie liked to read, but Mike liked to draw and Doug was more interested in doing anything outdoors. For years, she'd dragged my brothers and sister to the library on Saturdays. As children, each would routinely take out the maximum number of books allowed—six. By the time I was reading at age four, only Sandy and sometimes Mike would come along. Sandy would check out a couple of novels and Mike would investigate some records or books on art. Just as the kids had once done, I'd take home all six allowed books.

At home, if my parents didn't have plans to visit relatives and play cards, Mom would make popcorn and turn on the radio in an attempt to revive her family's Saturday night ritual during her childhood in Antrim and later the Sanford Farm.

From the time Mom was eight her family would head to the drugstore on Saturday evenings, where each of them would pick up a pulp magazine. The term referred to the cheap wood pulp paper on which the magazines were printed and became synonymous with the sensational writing in genres that ranged from comics to mysteries to westerns. The pulps pumped out a plethora of cheap entertainment each week; for a cover price between a dime and a quarter, you could get 100 to 250 pages' worth of short stories. Dozens of prominent authors got their start writing for pulps, from Isaac Asimov and Agatha Christie to F. Scott Fitzgerald and Tennessee Williams. In the 1930s, when Mom was a kid, a pulp could sell a million copies of an issue.

Inez preferred mysteries and romances, while Grandpa Charles favored detective tales. Mom's brothers usually bought comic books, known then as hero pulps. Mom leaned toward confessional-style tales such as *True Story*. Despite its famous subtitle, *Truth Is Stranger Than Fiction*, even then she realized that most of the confessional-style works in *True Story* were made up. Typically, the stories involved good girls gone bad, ones who suffered dire consequences after making poor life choices. Grandma Inez knew it was kind of racy, but she let it slide. She had to let her daughter rebel in some way, and if it involved reading, then fine.

They'd get home giddy with anticipation. Grandma would make a big kettle of popcorn and each of the family members would find a comfy location throughout the house. They'd munch popcorn, read, and listen to the *Grand Ole Opry* on the radio.

My brothers and sister weren't interested in the radio on Saturday night. That was for *old people*. They would eat the popcorn, but they wanted to watch television. That's what all their friends did.

They talked about it at school. Television made up a significant part of the social language, and if you didn't speak it, you were uncool.

Sure, my parents worried that too much TV would somehow suck out our brains. But the main reason they curtailed our viewing time was simple. Like a lot of people in the 1960s, we had terrible TV reception on the farm. It just seemed like a lot of work to my parents, and with the exception of Julia Child and Dad's favorite show, *Star Trek*, most of the viewing options weren't worth it.

Watching television required tuning in one of the five channels then available in the greater Flint area. Dad bolted a massive steel antenna to the back of the house. It must have been four stories tall. It required grasping the raw steel between both palms and trying to twist it with sheer strength to maneuver it in a circular pattern one way or the other. The antenna was finicky and highly directional; a tiny fraction of a turn could mean the difference between watching a show or snow, which is what people called the visual static displayed when a channel wasn't properly tuned in.

The Detroit PBS affiliate, WTVS, was on UHF and came in easily in the afternoons when the station ran back-to-back reruns of *The French Chef* with Julia Child. We barely had to deal with the antenna to get it tuned in. My sister and I would park ourselves in front of the black-and-white set on an oval braided rug, heads on hands as we watched the show, each of us transfixed. She whipped eggs into omelets and fixed broken Hollandaise sauces. Julia explained what made a rooster a capon (castration, something I didn't quite get then). We couldn't get enough of her.

Prompted by Julia's influence, Sandy plastered our shared small bedroom with posters of France. One day, as she spread a print of the Eiffel Tower on one wall, she explained that as an adult, she was going to go live in Paris. I sat on our bed, clutching a naked doll.

"Where's Paris?" I asked her.

Sandy stretched to place a tack into the top edge of the poster. "France," she said over her shoulder. "It's in Europe, very far away."

I lifted up my baby, pretending to burp her, to mask my alarm. "When are you going there?" I worried she'd leave me alone with my brothers.

She reached down to tack the bottom edge in place and then stood back, admiring her handiwork. "There's a famous university there, the Sorbonne. I looked it up in the encyclopedia. I'm going to study there, I've decided."

Sandy was nine years older than me, almost fourteen. She seemed like a grown-up, always certain of everything.

"When are you going?" I asked meekly.

"When I graduate from high school," she said, collapsing on the bed. She picked at a pillow on top of our comforter, one of several my mother had just purchased from the thrift store and re-covered in a soft floral fabric. "It's college, really, so don't worry. That's a while away."

When I was little, nothing mattered more to me than being like my sister. So I nodded. "Okay, and then I'm going to go live in Paris, too."

Dad always wanted to watch *60 Minutes*, but the CBS station from Detroit proved nearly impossible to get in the evening, heavily dependent on luck and the weather. Flint had its own NBC and ABC stations, of which the NBC station was the more reliable. Sometimes the boys would have to run outside and move the antenna. In the winter, it could be punishing to stand with a gloved hand on an ice-cold metal rod.

"Right there, that's perfect," my dad would yell out to them.

"There?!" one of my brothers would respond, letting go of the pole.

"Wait, that's no good. Put it back," my dad would yell.

"Now is it good?" yelled back a brother, clutching the pole. "It gets bad when I let go."

"Perfect! Just stand there and hold it," my dad would reply.

When the boys shifted, we'd lose whatever we were watching.

As a result, television was less enthusiastically embraced in bad weather. Sometimes the family would decide it wasn't worth it and would break out a board game such as Monopoly.

Despite the antenna hassle, on Sundays, we invariably watched

Mutual of Omaha's Wild Kingdom. One episode, in which they catch leopards in a net, we watched so frequently that my brothers and sister knew exactly when each crow sitting on the trap mechanism would caw. As the host, Marlin Perkins, introduced the segment, they'd all groan.

"Dad, we've seen this one!" one of the kids would say.

"I haven't seen it," Dad would reply.

"Yes, you have. It's the leopards with the net."

He'd light another cigarette. "Well, I don't know how it ends."

You didn't argue with Dad. He'd just as soon turn the TV off if the kids argued. The best part of the show for us was near the end when Marlin Perkins would launch into a sales pitch for life insurance with a line such as "While Jim seems to have his hands full with that leopard, I'd like to tell you how Mutual of Omaha could help your family . . ." as a frenetic battle of man and beast ensued on a screen behind his large desk.

If the kids were too restless to watch TV, Dad would make them go out and "touch the post."

Touching the post was a sort of game/punishment that my parents invented not long after they moved into the farmhouse.

To burn off some of their endless energy, my parents first taught the kids a game called go run around the house. They'd run in a circle until they got tired. As they got older, they could run around the house in just a couple of minutes, not long enough. One day walking out to the woods, Dad passed the post, a stubby white-washed wood pole that marked the border between the farm's private property and the public lands of the woods behind it. It was roughly a quarter mile away from the house. The goal was to run to the post, touch it, and then run back as fast as possible, a full-speed eight-hundred-yard sprint, enough to wear out anyone, especially when running in snow.

If the kids started fighting or being rambunctious, he'd enthusiastically cry out: "Hey, which one of you can touch the post first?"

The kids would stop in their tracks. Naturally competitive, they'd all jump up and down and wave their hands.

"Me!"

"No, I can!"

"No, you can't, I'm way faster than you are!"

Then Dad would lead them to the back door. The kids would put on their sneakers or, if it was winter, their snow boots. Then he'd vaguely assure that each kid had an equal start. With great fanfare, he'd yell, "GO!"

The kids would haul off at top speed. As they ran back to the post, Dad would stand on the porch and tap out a fresh Kent cigarette. Even a fast kid took at least ten minutes to run a half mile. By the time the kids arrived back at the porch, ragged and tired, breathing hard, Dad would have finished his cigarette and be back inside drinking a beer. Once in a while, one trip to the post wasn't enough. Dad would see a too energetic kid arriving back at the house.

"Hey, you didn't touch it," he'd say to the kid.

"Yes, I did, Dad. I swear."

He'd shake his head. "No, I was watching. You've got to go back and touch it again."

Without fail, the kid would grudgingly turn and jog back to the post.

Every morning when my mother wasn't working, she parked in front of our radio to listen to *Party Line*, broadcast by WFDF-AM in Flint. The host was a folksy, pragmatic woman from Flint's sister city, Hamilton, Ontario. Born Betty Monas, she was rechristened Betty Clarke by the show's producers, who wanted a catchier name.

The show focused on household hints and recipes, the usual fodder of "women show" material back in the day. At least once during her program, Betty would offer recipes by reading through the ingredients list, pausing to allow enough time for the listener to write each one down before moving onto the next item. Literally, it was

"One cup of sugar" (pause) "One teaspoon baking powder" (pause) "One teaspoon salt."

My mother would sit at our kitchen table, pen in hand. She'd write down Betty's tips for removing stains, gardening, or saving money on groceries. But mainly, she waited for the recipes. They weren't fancy. Dump-and-stir cakes, casseroles, variations on meat loaf, that sort of thing. But every so often, Betty would introduce listeners to some culinary novelty, such as fondue or stir-fry. She would go to the Flint library to research items such as soy sauce, which Midwest home cooks were unfamiliar with in the 1960s and early 1970s. Mom's culinary landscape changed thanks to Betty on the radio and Julia on television.

Our local supermarket was Hamady Brothers, the Flint-based chain founded in 1911 by Michael and Kamol Hamady. They were immigrant cousins from Lebanon but referred to themselves as brothers for the sake of the business. At a time when most shoppers requested items at a counter rather than selecting them off store shelves, the Hamady brothers pioneered self-service shopping for a simple reason: They spoke little English. By the late 1960s, it was the largest chain of grocery stores in the area.

Reflecting the shifting tides of the food world, Mom increasingly came across unusual items at Hamady's: fresh pineapple in the produce section, curry powder in the spice aisle, Italian-style sausage in the meat department. Food started featuring ingredients on the labels. Strange new products hit the shelves: Hamburger Helper, SpaghettiOs, and Cool Whip topping. Mom puzzled over such developments. To her mind, why would anyone need a box to make a hamburger skillet? Who would eat canned spaghetti? What was wrong with plain whipped cream?

Mom remembers the first time she ever came across a kiwifruit. She didn't buy any—they were too expensive—but she immediately went to the encyclopedia to look it up when she got home.

"I heard that song again today!" Dad said, walking through the door. He hummed the chorus of the John Denver song as he wrapped Mom up in a hug. Then she told him all about the origins of kiwifruit. He wanted to know more about New Zealand, so he got out the *N* volume of the *World Book*. They sat at the kitchen table, reading aloud to each other.

Even without tasting the fruit, my parents fed each other as they always did, in every way possible.

Apple Crisp

My mother made this dish every other day during the autumn and well into the winter. She stored apples in our unheated Michigan basement in bushel baskets, protected by layers of newspaper. They would last through early March, when the trees began to bloom again. A fast, easy, and flexible dessert, this works with most kinds of apples, from good eating apples such as Gala, Golden Delicious, and Honeycrisp to tarter baking varieties such as Granny Smith. An apple cutter—one that cores and cuts the apple into eighths—will cut the prep time down to less than 10 minutes. This works well with Anjou or Bartlett pears, peaches, cherries, berries, and most noncitrus fruits.

Note: The top may not brown, but should be a bit dry and crunchy.

Makes about six ½-cup (120-ml) servings

½ to 1 tablespoon (15 to 30 ml) unsalted butter, softened
3 apples (1½ pounds/680 g)
2 teaspoons (10 ml) fresh lemon juice
¼ teaspoon (1.25 ml) ground nutmeg
½ cup plus 1 teaspoon (110 g) dark brown sugar
1¼ teaspoons (6.25 ml) ground cinnamon
½ cup (65 g) all-purpose flour
1 cup (85 g) quick-cooking oats
½ teaspoon (2.5 ml) coarse salt
5⅓ tablespoons (80 g) unsalted butter, melted
Vanilla ice cream or frozen yogurt, for serving

Preheat the oven to 375°F (190°C). Coat a shallow pie pan or 9-inch (23-cm) square baker with the softened butter.

Peel the apples. Core them and cut into wedges, aiming for 8 slices per apple. Place the apple slices in the buttered pan, sprinkle with the lemon juice, nutmeg, 1 teaspoon (5 ml) of the brown sugar, and ¼ teaspoon (1.25 ml) of the cinnamon, and toss to coat.

In a small bowl, combine the remaining brown sugar and cinnamon, the flour, oats, and salt. Add the melted butter and stir until crumbly. Spread the crumb mixture evenly over the apples.

Bake for 45 minutes, until the apples are tender and cooked through. Let cool slightly before serving. Serve with a simple vanilla ice cream or frozen yogurt.

CHAPTER 8

Fish Stories

Sandy (in a tiara) and Mike showing off the family's catch, 1970

Our family had a rule when it came to fishing: You got your own pole with a hook when you turned seven or were as tall as my dad's belly button, whichever came first. Until then, you got a beer can tab at the end of your line.

My parents never explained the shadowy origins of this rule, and we kids never questioned it. Instead, we celebrated the day when we finally swapped our beer can tab for a hook on which to snare an actual worm. That was the other rule. My dad, the marine, had an iron-clad "no wimps" policy. You baited your own hook or you didn't fish.

It's a testament to my parents that we kids would spend years staring at a bobber, waiting for a bite, when we were fishing not only without bait but without a hook, either.

Since I was so much smaller than the other kids, I was the one with the beer can tab through our family fishing vacations, which meant *every* vacation, as we didn't take any that didn't involve fishing.

My father loved to fish, an endeavor he considered both pastime and a second religion. He had a saying, "God doesn't subtract time from your hours on earth that you spend fishing."

As a kid, Dad started out with a switch made from a slender hickory stick. His brothers showed him how to find a sturdy limb that had just enough give at the end. They'd hew off the tiniest limbs with a sharp rock, scraping them into submission. Then they'd sit and rub them until smooth. If they couldn't get standard fishing line they'd use cotton kitchen string or twine. Their grandfather, a quiet gentleman named Milton Stark, brought packets of shiny hooks with him on his occasional visits, along with pieces of candy. The candy was nice, a rare treat, but the kids treasured the hooks. You could manage a pole from a limb, you could find worms on your own, and string could be had almost for free. A discarded bottle cap could be used as a weight. But you couldn't fish without a hook, so *those* were valuable.

When Dad turned ten, Milton Stark gifted his namesake grandson with a cane pole made from a thick, rigid piece of bamboo, and then-new nylon fishing line. It was the cheapest kind of pole, but a big step up from a stick. For years, it was Dad's most valuable possession.

During summer, Dad, his friends, and his siblings arose at dawn to prowl mowed fields for earthworms that made their way to the surface in the cool night dew. They'd pluck them before they retreated back to the dirt at the first warmth of sun and drop them into a coffee can filled with dirt. Kids didn't catch much in the area's small lazy rivers with a stick pole. For them, it was a reason to be lost in the woods on a sunny afternoon in the rare hours when they had no chores.

Dad was different, though. He had a gift when it came to fishing. With a graceful arc, he'd cast into the water and give his line the tiniest tug. Another pull, another tug, and then—a bite! It had something to do with the intuitive way he teased his line, mimicking something a fish might find delicious. Other kids tried to copy him, but they couldn't get it quite right. It was just a strange knack that came naturally.

So while the others headed home empty-handed, Dad lugged several fish crammed into a metal water pail. Another kid would invariably ask: "What'd you use for bait?"

Dad would shrug. "Worms. Nothing special." And it was true.

Combining the two loves of his life, Dad took Mom fishing for their honeymoon.

He planned a weeklong trip at Hulbert Lake not far from the home of my mother's Swedish grandmother, Anna, outside Newberry in the Upper Peninsula. They stayed in a cute, rustic cabin and rented a small wooden fishing boat with a tiny, sputtering motor. They got up at dawn to strategize where to fish as Mom made coffee, toast, and eggs.

Mom was a sport. She embraced the whole thing on the condition that she never had to clean any fish and she could bring along a book in case she got bored. They'd pack a picnic lunch and head out for their planned location. They'd spend the morning quietly chatting, making plans for their new life together, my dad gently sharing his stories with her as naturally as he teased the fish below. As the sun gathered strength, Mom put on a wide-brimmed hat and poured the last of the coffee from the cup of their thermos. At lunchtime, if the fishing was going well, they would munch on their sandwiches right in the boat. If the action was slow, they would find a shady spot to spread out a thin blanket and listen to the gentle sounds of nature along the lake. After lunch, they returned to fishing for a couple of hours. Dad would sip on a Coke or a beer. By then, Mom was usually into a book.

After a day of fishing, they hopped into Dad's Chevy Bel Air and drove the twenty or so miles to Anna's small farm, a bucket of fish wedged on the bench seat between them. The lakes of Michigan can yield more than a hundred varieties of fish. Most often, they snared yellow perch, but they scored the occasional smallmouth bass or other fish lured by worms.

A true Swede, Anna adored any kind of fish. She believed that meat was toxic but consuming fish offered a life-giving, age-preserving elixir. Given that she lived to be ninety-six with no major illnesses in her life, she might have been onto something. Dad would present the fish to Anna, who would declare them beautiful. He would grin at the acknowledgment of a good day's fishing and duck outside to clean them, spreading the discards in her garden as fertilizer. Meanwhile Anna heated up a cast-iron frying pan. The aroma of fresh baked bread filled the room as Dad poured Mom a cold glass of sweet local wine and settled down at the table with a beer.

"Vee veady, yah?" she'd ask in her heavy Swedish accent, looking them in their eyes. They'd eagerly nod yes. She believed the secret to frying fish was all in the timing. "Fish vait vor no von," Anna would say. "*You* vait vor da fish."

My grandmother Inez later interpreted this to mean: "Never cook a fish for someone until you can see the whites of their eyes."

As a mix of bacon fat and shortening melted into the fire-hot pan, Anna dragged the fish through cornmeal and flour seasoned with salt and pepper. The fish hit the hot pan with a loud *szzzzzzzzz*. As soon as the edges turned an opaque white, she flipped the fish with an oversized spatula. A minute later, it landed on a plate. Anna, Mom, and Dad sat around her sturdy wood table and feasted on fried fish and warm bread slathered with salty butter until they couldn't eat another bite.

Dad would pull Mom across the bench seat and wrap his arm around her as they drove back to the cabin in the cool night air. They sat outside and watched the stars and the reflection of the night sky in the clear water, wrapped in the thick homemade quilt that Anna insisted on lending them their first day, worried they might catch cold. The quilt contained pieces of clothes Mom recognized from her childhood.

At the end of their honeymoon, Dad and Mom delivered a final mess of fish and the quilt to Anna. In return, she handed them a basket of crispy fried chicken, dill-studded potato salad, and a fresh loaf of bread as a picnic lunch for their five-hour drive home. She'd killed one of her chickens—a real statement since she herself never ate meat and a certain sacrifice since she kept them for the eggs. Anna wouldn't dream of sending the newlyweds away hungry.

"A lot of people would say that spending your first week together fishing and hanging out with your grandmother isn't much of a honeymoon," Mom says. "To me, it was perfect."

Once they had children, my parents found fishing had yet another upside. It was a cheap way to keep kids occupied and quiet for hours. "Shhh, you'll scare the fish," Dad would say, and the kids would immediately pipe down and stare into the water at their lines, whether they were fishing with actual hooks or just beer tabs. Early on, rules had been laid out: If you couldn't be quiet, you couldn't go fishing. No one wanted to miss out.

We fished all year even though the average temperature peaks above seventy degrees only three months of the year in Michigan and it's been known to snow in May.

In spring and summer, we spent a lot of hours at the two-thousand-acre Holloway Reservoir. Mom would haul a cast-iron skillet to cook the fish over an open fire built by my brothers. She updated Anna's recipe by coating the fish in almonds. The nuts crisped up the fish enough to allow them to be used as leftovers for breakfast the next day. Amazingly, the kids would fight for it, something you wouldn't expect of day-old fish. It was that good.

In winter, we embarked on the curious sport of ice fishing.

Usually, we'd head over to Lake Nepessing outside Flint, a popular spot since it was a shallow lake that reliably froze early in the season. For years, Dad shared an ice shanty there with his best friend Bill Wilson, an affable co-worker who claimed to be part Chippewa.

Once they reached the edge of the frozen lake, Dad would bring out his ice spud, a tool on a long handle that looked like a chubby trident. No matter how many people were on the ice, Mom and the kids weren't allowed until he had a chance to "spud it out." Using the spud like a walking stick, he'd smack the ice in front of him soundly, searching for thin spots, until he decided it was safe.

Ice fishing is a fairly simple concept. You make a hole in the ice and fish through it. Bill owned a fancy holer, a manual drilling contraption. The boys would spin the handle around and around until the cutter broke through the ice like a corkscrew. Then the men would drag the ice shanty from the lake's edge and position it over the hole.

An ice shanty is exactly what it sounds like. Theirs was a handbuilt shed made from lumber seconds and scraps of wood. In the darkened shanty, they could see the fish against the opaque cover of the frozen water, illuminated by the sun shining through the ice.

Fishing under such conditions seems crazy. "But you have to know how good the fish tastes when they're cold like that," Mom says. The fishermen would take their catch off the hook and toss it out onto the ice, a reckless yet effective method of preservation.

Of the kids, only Milt, Doug, and Mary Jo's oldest son, Steve, had the perseverance for ice fishing. Sandy preferred to skate. Other cousins amused themselves with sleds or a particularly slippery brand of kickball. I chose to cling to my mother as she made beef stew right on the lake.

Building a fire on ice doesn't seem like a good idea. My dad explained that the ash acts as a layer of protection from the heat. That, plus a lack of air under the wood, keeps the ice from melting. Once the boys got the fire going, Mom would sear meat in her six-quart cast-iron kettle, the kind with three legs. She'd pile in onions, carrots, celery, and potatoes that she'd cut up at home, add some water, and let it simmer for hours while the men fished and the kids played. Gusts of chilly wind carried wafts of the smell of stew haphazardly around the lake.

Done fishing, the men would leave the "comfort" of their shanties to retrieve all the fish. Peeking inside our cooler, we'd see that the fast freezing left all the fish with the same startled look of surprise.

Everyone dipped a ladle into the hot stew, the beef now fork-tender and the vegetables softened and mellowed from the long, slow cooking. They'd stand, eating their stew, gathered near the fire. As the sun set and the wind kicked in, we'd sit with burning faces and frozen backs as we crouched on the cold ice, toasting marshmallows.

As the lakes began to thaw, the spring ritual of smelt dipping began.

Smelt are small fish that resemble salmon but mature to an average size of about eight inches long. Like salmon, smelt run at different times of the year as they return to their spawning streams, often running in large shoals along the coastline to get to their destinations. Smelting requires little skill. Essentially, you stand in water with a mesh net and scoop them out. You just need luck to be in the right place at the right time.

For the extended family, smelting was essentially an excuse to hold a tailgate party in the middle of nowhere late at night. According to Dad, the best smelting happened around midnight. My aunts, uncles, and cousins would meet with potluck dishes and coolers filled with beer. The older boys would construct a bonfire. The men would stand around in their waders chatting and eating, or even play cards at portable tables by the light of camping lanterns. We kids would play kick the can or hang out by the fire. A couple of people were put on "water watch." They'd stand in gentle currents of shallow water just above freezing and keep a steady gaze toward the bottom with a flashlight in hand or a headlamp attached to their forehead. Once they saw smelt, they'd yell.

"The smelt are running! The smelt are running!"

Everyone would drop their beers, grab their nets, and go into the water. They'd scoop and scoop hoping to swallow up the darting, silvery pools of fish.

Smelting was then, and remains now, a feast-or-famine sport.

Once, after six hours of waiting, Dad scored only eight of the small fish, barely a handful. But when they hit, Dad and the boys dipped and scooped as fast as they could. Once the fury was over, they'd pack a thirty-gallon garbage can full of the glittering, fidgeting little fish.

Everyone would then sit around with scissors to cut open their bellies to scrape out the tiny bit of entrails. Mom would pack the smelt with their heads intact into plastic bags with water so they would freeze solid without any freezer burn. When thawed, she drained, dried, and rolled them in flour seasoned with paprika, salt, and pepper, not unlike her method for morels. Then she'd panfry them until they were crisp and golden.

Fried smelt are meant to be eaten whole; part of the appeal is the satisfying crunch of their tiny bones. "Everyone loved smelt," Mom says. "We ate them like French fries."*

Smelting signaled something important: Summer was on its way. The height of the fishing season was about to begin.

Not long after they arrived at the farm on Coldwater Road, Dad purchased a twelve-foot aluminum skiff from a client of the siding company. The guy needed the money to finish paying for the windows Dad was helping to install on his house.

It was a push to get all the kids plus two adults into the boat. Not the ideal, but it was a *boat*, something Dad had lusted for his entire life. We dragged it thousands of miles behind our station wagon.

As we spent more time on the water, the cuisine shifted to sandwiches made with homemade bread and store-bought olive loaf lunch meat. Unlike bologna, which is pumped into a casing like sausage, olive loaf is made more like meat loaf. Once beef and pork are minced and mixed to a batterlike consistency, whole olives are

---

*Smelt should not be confused with whitebait, a delicacy common in many countries, notably the United Kingdom, New Zealand, Australia, and Japan, where it's known as *shirasu*. Smelt are harvested as adults. Whitebait involves the immature fry that would grow into larger fish such as herring, salmon, sardines, mackerel, bass, and others—not exactly an ecologically viable foodstuff. Several countries have banned it or are working toward banning it, concerned that removing fish at such a juvenile stage before they've reproduced might severely reduce future fish stocks.

gently stirred in before it's put into molds and baked. Mom said we ate a lot of it because it was cheaper than bologna and Dad liked it better. Mom would add a thick slice of tomato, which paired strikingly well with the olives.

When I was a toddler, our neighbor, a kindly bachelor known as Uncle Bert to us kids, saw my dad hitching the boat up to "Bisquick," the name I use in hindsight for our Chevrolet Biscayne station wagon. We thought then that Uncle Bert was incredibly old, but he was just in his forties.

"You know, I've got a sixteen-foot boat," he started. "You got another little kid there and those boys are so big now, maybe that would work better for you? I'm not using it much these days."

"Well, you know how we're doing, Bert," Dad replied, putting down the hitch and wiping his hands. "We don't have any extra money for anything given what happened to the business. We couldn't afford it."

Uncle Bert raised his eyebrows. "Oh, no!" He shook his head. "I wasn't suggesting that. No, no. You've all been so kind to me, and your wife's always sending over biscuits and pies. I figure you can just borrow it whenever you want. Kind of my way of paying you back for all your generosity."

Four feet doesn't sound like a lot until you're talking boats. The sixteen-footer was not only longer but also much deeper. It swallowed up the supplies that had filled the other boat, with plenty of room left for more.

The extra space accommodated the now-teenage boys and offered me a place to sit—something the other boat didn't provide.

For the next three years, Bert let us take his boat whenever we wanted. Mom made sure he got plenty of pies and Dad always reserved some of the fish we caught for him.

We spent most weekends and some weeknights fishing in the summer. Mom and Dad found a small cabin at a rustic resort on St. Joseph Island in Canada, just over the border from Sault Ste. Marie in the Upper Peninsula, at the northern tip of Lake Huron. This one-week fishing trip was the only summer vacation my family took for years.

Dad's ice-fishing partner, Bill Wilson, also rented a cabin on the lake for his wife, Beverly, and daughters, Cindy and Kelly. During these weeks, we'd see how people with money lived.

The Wilsons owned a zippy new motor boat that they'd bring up to the lake so everyone could water-ski, although the water was so cold that anyone who attempted it left with a bluish cast to their skin. Their two cute daughters always had brand-new shorts and bathing suits. They had all manner of big boxes of "sugar cereal" to choose from at breakfast. At least twice during the week, they *ate out* at a local restaurant. Their mother read *hardcover* books that she *bought* at a store, not used paperbacks or library books. Plus, the Wilson girls brought along their Barbie dolls, something Sandy and I coveted but never owned.

Every year, it went the same. We'd load up Uncle Bert's aluminum skiff tied behind Bisquick with poles, tackle, cans of night crawlers, coolers loaded with food, bags of flour, cans of shortening, waders, nets, a secondhand blow-up canoe for the kids, a couple of lanterns, insect repellant, a few board games, a pile of books, and a couple of encyclopedia volumes. It took hours to pack the boat and then deft organization to make it all fit. Even though the limit was one duffel bag of clothes per person, it still meant seven or eight heavy bags, each stuffed to test the seams.

We'd drive north, up "past the straights," as Grandpa Charles called them, through the Upper Peninsula to the border crossing at Sault Ste. Marie, about a five-hour drive from Davison. Once through the border crossing, it was about forty miles to the cabins on the island, and until the early seventies, the only way to get there was via a car ferry. Boarding the ferry officially marked the start of vacation.

Once at the cabin, Mom assigned each kid a sleeping spot. The cabin had a huge table, a decent-sized living room, three small bedrooms and a sleeping porch, electric lights, a cold water sink, and a gas stove that also burned wood. There was no toilet or shower in the cabin; those were both located in a central bathhouse a short walk away, unless one was brave enough to use the outdoor privy.

The island epitomized the natural grandeur of the region. Thick, old-growth pine trees reached well into the sky around the edges of the deep, clear lake. Cleaners that boast of pine scent had nothing on this place; one inhale and you felt as if your lungs had taken a breath mint.

Each day afterward, the family would be up and out fishing before dawn. We'd break for olive loaf sandwiches at lunch, then fish some more. By about three, we'd head back to the cabin to clean our catch, take a swim, lie out in the sun, or read a book before heading over to take a shower before dinner.

Every night was a fish fry. Since the place had electricity, Mom left her cast iron at home and instead brought along her favorite appliance: a large rectangular electric frying pan. Beige with brown piping, the thing was big; it could hold a chicken and a half or several fish at once.

The Wilsons would come over most nights for dinner. Afterward, Dad made a huge bonfire by the water and everyone shared the story of their day.

Bill always trolled in his boat for the elusive walleye. He never caught one.

Dad went mostly after perch and lake trout. One year, Dad bought some walleye off another fisherman. When the Wilsons came over for dinner, Dad announced that he'd caught them himself. Bill was shocked.

"You're kidding! How did you do it?"

Dad shrugged. "They seem to like worms."

Bill was dumbfounded. Everyone knew that walleye couldn't be caught with worms. He swore under his breath. What could he possibly be doing wrong? Then Dad burst out laughing.

"Oh, Milt," Bill said. "You almost had me."

When the fire died down and the kids couldn't eat any more marshmallows, the adults headed inside to play cards for hours.

The days went on with little variation. Sometimes Sandy and

Mike would stay behind and play with the Wilson girls. Everyone would meet up in the afternoon. Dad would grab one of the encyclopedia volumes to carry over to the shared bathrooms. The boys would explore the woods. Everyone loved that week.

One year, after packing up the boat as usual, then hauling it nearly five hours to the border, came "the incident."

The border agent asked the usual questions. "Any firearms or alcohol?"

My parents shook their heads. "What about potatoes?" In the late 1960s, Canada was at the start of what would be a decades-long fight against what's known as late blight of their potato crops.

Dad was quiet. Mom piped up. "Yes, yes, we do, officer," Mom said in a loud voice, leaning over Dad from the passenger seat. "We have ten pounds of potatoes packed in the boat." Dad looked at her with a mix of shock and dismay, and then rolled his eyes.

For the next two hours, the whole family unpacked the boat as customs agents looked through every item. Finally, they found the sack of potatoes languishing at the very bottom. No one spoke to Mom as they all wearily packed it back up, a process that took yet another hour.

Settling back in the car, Dad turned to Mom. "Next time, let me do the talking."

Mom remained indignant. "So you would *lie* in front of your children to an official of the government?" Dad decided it was best not to argue the point. Silently, he started the drive toward the island. "See? I didn't think so."

That was the year Grandma Inez came along. I'd just had my first birthday, and even in my family, I was still a little young for fishing. She agreed to watch me for the week. She cooked and cleaned all day long. While everyone else was out on the boat, she laundered every blanket, cleaned the cupboards, scrubbed the walls and floors, swept the flagstone path all the way down to the lake, and even scoured the floor behind the stove.

But mostly, she loved cooking on the wood-burning stove. It

reminded her a bit of the early days in Antrim. She woke every day at 5:30 A.M. and made berry pancakes, eggs, and sausage for breakfast along with authentic maple syrup produced right on the island. She brought along some of Grandpa Charles's famous jam, which she served each afternoon with hot freshly made bread or biscuits. She cranked out coleslaw and vats of ham and beans. She shucked dozens of ears of sweet corn that she boiled in a big pot on the stove. For dessert, she made a fresh lemon meringue or berry pie. We got cinnamon rolls almost every day.

Mom worried she was working too hard the whole week. "Put your feet up, Mom. Here, I'll get you a glass of wine."

Inez would take the wine, but kept working on whatever she was doing in the kitchen. She cooked as if her life depended on it.

When they dropped her off at the farm in Sanford, Mom thanked her for the hard work.

"Work?" Grandma Inez protested. "This was the best vacation of my life! I got to eat fish, drink wine, and then cook whatever I wanted and everyone loved it. Who can ask for a better vacation than that?"

"Dad, we found this island and we wondered if we might be able to go and camp on it for a few days," Miltie said with authority. "We're old enough and we're Scouts. We know how to live off the land. What do you think?"

The family was spending the day at the Holloway Dam reservoir. Now that they were both thirteen years old, Dad let Miltie and Mary Jo's son Steve take turns driving the small skiff out alone around the two-thousand-acre lake to conduct reconnaissance on potentially good fishing spots. Doug, then twelve, went along. They came back excited.

"No way," Mom said to my dad. "Leave three boys alone to camp at their age?"

My brother Mike and Mary Jo's son Danny, both nine, clamored to go too. Mary Jo's other son, Bryon, had just turned eleven. He didn't want to be left out, either.

Dad knew how to get to Mom. "C'mon, it will be a great adventure for them," he said. He argued that it wasn't exactly *Lord of the Flies* territory. They were all related and had known one another all their lives. The island was in a public park with security thanks to the nearby dam that then supplied Flint's drinking water. They would have a boat to get on and off the island, plus plenty of food. As Miltie noted, they were all Boy Scouts.

Mom relented. She convinced a reluctant Mary Jo.

They went home, loaded up tents, sleeping bags, her big cast-iron skillet, fishing poles, loads of worms, a cooler filled with food, a big vat of water, and everything else the boys might need for a few days' camping. The only way to the island was by boat. It took three trips to move the supplies and the six boys out to the small island, which was more of a bump of land in the reservoir, laden with some trees and a ring of hardscrabble beach.

Dad got the boys settled. "Okay, we'll be back tomorrow at five," he said. "We'll honk three times to get your attention." Then Milt and Steve drove Mom, Dad, and Aunt Mary Jo back to the shore in the skiff and circled back to their island.

The boys loved it. They set up camp, striking up tents. They made a huge bonfire on the beach. They made gooey grilled cheese sandwiches in the cast-iron skillet. They sat around the fire until late, roasting marshmallows and scheming plans for the next few days. When Mike went into the cover of trees to relieve himself, mosquitoes the size of Buicks attacked him en masse. He barely slept and woke covered in puffy blisters.

The next morning, the boys awoke to find Miltie reviving the slumbering fire. With Steve's help, the pair made a breakfast of eggs and sausage. Then they set out in the skiff. That first morning, they caught a whole string of fish. They fried up the fish for lunch. That afternoon, one of them caught a catfish. It wriggled about wildly in the small boat, one of its stingers hitting Danny's foot.

When Dad honked his horn three times at five o'clock, Milt and Steve hopped in the boat to pick him up. They handed over a pail of the extra fish they didn't think they could eat. Mike and Danny went back with Dad. Between the mosquitoes and the catfish, they'd had enough adventure. The next day, Bryon came home. He preferred TV to the island.

Milt, Steve, and Doug stayed out for three more nights. They fished and made bonfires, and explored the entire reservoir in the small skiff. On the last evening, Mom went for the daily liaison and took them a basket heaped with fried chicken and a quart of potato salad. They greedily ate it. They didn't want to admit it, but they were getting a little tired of fried fish.

On the sixth morning, the boys reluctantly agreed to leave the island behind. To this day they say that week was one of the best times of their lives.

"Your dad was right," Mom says. "If you say you believe that life should be full of adventures, then you have to be willing to let your kids have them, too."

Panfried Fish with Almonds

Don't burn the almonds and you won't overcook the fish. That's the idea behind my mother's take on the classic trout amandine. Mom most often made this with the fresh perch that we caught, but all manner of whitefish lends itself to this treatment, including halibut, tilapia, rockfish, cod, and haddock. Just look for fillets ⅓ inch (8 mm) thick or less; any thicker and the almonds will burn before the fish cooks.

Mom says, "The most important thing is that your eggs are very well beaten. Put the lemon juice and mashed garlic right in the eggs. Always salt and pepper the fish itself before starting." Also critical is my grandmother's advice: "Don't cook a fish until you can see the whites of your diners' eyes."

Avoid olive oil for frying; its smoking point is too low and it will yield a bitter flavor. Go with peanut, grapeseed, canola, or coconut oil if you've got it.

For quick cleanup, put the flour and almonds on sheets of parchment or wax paper instead of in bowls, then toss when you're done. Wrap up leftovers tightly and the crispy cold fish will make good next-day leftovers.

Makes 3 to 4 servings, but is easily expanded to feed more

2 garlic cloves, peeled

2 large eggs

2 teaspoons (10 ml) lemon juice

½ cup (70 g) all-purpose flour

1 teaspoon (5 ml) coarse salt, plus more for seasoning the fish

½ teaspoon (2.5 ml) ground black pepper, plus more for seasoning
    the fish

½ teaspoon (2.5 ml) paprika

Up to 1 cup (90 g) sliced almonds

3 tablespoons (45 ml) peanut, grapeseed, or coconut oil

1 pound (450 g) skinless fresh fish fillets

Lemon wedges, for serving

Mash the garlic with the edge of a fork. Add it to the eggs and lemon juice and beat together well in a shallow bowl so the garlic flavors the egg mixture. Mix the flour with the salt, pepper, and paprika on a sheet of parchment or wax paper. Put the almonds on a second sheet of paper.

Add the oil to a large heavy skillet over medium-high heat. Season each piece of fish with salt and pepper. Coat with the flour, then the egg mixture, and finally roll in the almonds, pressing them into the fish. Carefully place the fish in the hot oil in batches to fit the size of your skillet. Vigilantly monitor the fish as it cooks, adjusting the heat so that it cooks quickly but the almonds don't burn. After 2 to 3 minutes, the almonds on the bottom should be brown. Carefully turn over the fillets. Cook for another 1 to 3 minutes, depending on the thickness of your fish. Add additional oil to the pan if needed before each batch. Serve the fish hot, with lemon wedges for squeezing on the fish.

CHAPTER 9

Top Picker

Canned jars in the basement, date unknown

B y the end of each summer, my mother would turn into "The Claw." Today domestic DIYers look on canning as a rewarding and tranquil endeavor. At the farm, it was a full-scale military production.

When they moved in, Mom found more than two hundred jars in the cellar. The cache felt like a good omen. As a girl growing up on the Sanford Farm, she always seemed to be washing jars and canning with her mother. Her brothers would work alongside Grandpa Charles in the field, weeding, hoeing, planting, and picking. Mom had small hands, so the task of washing the jars inside and out invariably fell to her.

Most often, Grandma Inez cold-packed, a process in which food is put into jars and then processed in a hot water bath. For example, she'd peel and quarter tomatoes, then pack them into jars with a bit of kosher salt and top them with a lid. That was it. Soil, sun-shine, and a little bit of salt, that's what a quart of tomatoes cost.

These jars would then go into Grandma Inez's blue speckled twenty-one-quart enameled steel pot equipped with a metal rack for jars. Once in place, the pot was covered until the water came to a boil. While the cans "cooked" for their allotted time, Mom and Grandma Inez would spread heavy towels on the kitchen table. They'd remove the hot jars with specially made tongs and put them, lid down, on the towels to cool overnight. As the vacuum created by the process took effect, they could hear the lids emit a solid *dink* as the metal went concave, finalizing the seal.

Open-kettle cooking was a little different. If Grandma was go-ing to make a dish to be preserved, such as chili sauce, a kind of unsweetened ketchup they made with ground onions, green pep-pers, and stewed tomatoes, the jars had to be sterilized. Mom put freshly washed jars upside down in Grandma's big roasting pan, then poured more hot water over them. As they put the boiling food into the still-hot jars, Grandma would always say, "Check the windows, Irene." Mom would dart around the house to make sure none was open. Even a slight breeze could cool the jars too quickly, shattering the glass.

Grandma Inez did all the canning except the jams and jellies. Those were left to Grandpa Charles. Canning relies on science, but Grandpa's jam was nothing short of an art. Mom and her brothers would collect pails of blueberries and raspberries in the woods be-hind the farm. They were free and there were tons of them.

"We're gonna have fun like Saturday night in San Antonio!" Grandpa Charles would declare when Mom joined him in the kitchen for jam making. He'd turn up the radio and sing along. One of his favorites was "Shortnin' Bread," thought to have derived from an old Southern plantation slave song. It was reworked by blues singers and eventually made famous by the Andrews Sisters:

> *Put on the skillet, slip on the lid,*
> *Mama's gonna make a little shortnin' bread.*

Mama's little baby loves shortnin', shortnin',
Mama's little baby loves shortnin' bread.

He'd talk her through recipes. They'd laugh and sing songs together. He'd share his tips. "Now, don't add too much sugar, or you'll overwhelm the berries."

When people visited, he'd give them at least one jar of jam so they could sample his artistry. If they protested, he'd wave them off. "I'm making a ton for this year."

Grandpa Charles also showed Mom how to make wine, including his famed dandelion variety. He'd take one of Grandma's big five-gallon crocks and combine dandelion petals, yeast, sugar, and water.

"Just the petals," he instructed Mom as he secured the cover. "You use the whole blossoms, you'll get bitter wine." They'd walk back to a spot near the barn where he'd dug a deep hole. Grandpa Charles would tie a wire onto the crock and lower it in. The ground would keep it cold while it fermented for three months.

They also made wild blackberry, plum, and blueberry wine. They'd start by smashing the berries together in a bucket by hand, a process that resulted in red-stained skin. Then he'd make simple syrup with water and sugar on the stove. He'd let it cool and add it to the berries. While it was warm but not too hot, he'd add in yeast. They'd stir it up, cover it with cheesecloth, and put it in a corner of the kitchen for a week. Then they'd strain out the berries and put it into big gallon glass jugs with a bit more sugar syrup and siphon out the extra air. When it was ready, he served it straight from the siphoning tube. Someone asked him why he didn't bottle it.

"You kidding?" he'd scoff. "My wine's so good it's never 'round long enough."

They always had a full house of friends and relatives at the Sanford Farm. Visitors in the summer left not only with jams and wine but often with boxes of food: dozens of ears of corn, baskets of tomatoes, a half bushel of vegetables. In winter, he gave away bags of dried beans. Grandpa Charles made a point to give food away to people who lived in more populated areas where they didn't have a garden or to neighbors who didn't have much. He had a saying that he'd learned as a young boy in church:

> When you leave this world for a better land someday,
> The only thing you get to keep is what you gave away.

His generosity rarely went unrewarded. People would routinely stop by with all kinds of bounty: freshly shot squirrels and rabbits, bottles of home-brewed beer, sweet homemade blackberry wine, books, bundles of pulp magazines, jars of preserves, paper-wrapped packages of venison, homegrown popcorn, even the occasional game bird. One guy even left them a dog.

Grandpa Charles inevitably responded, "See, you can't give anything away; it always comes back to you."

Grandpa set up melons for local kids to steal. He included his kids on the scheme. He planted an extra row of watermelons well away from their fields toward the closest neighbor. In the summer, Mom and her siblings would tell their friends they were going to steal a watermelon from their neighbor. They'd hide salt shakers in their clothes and furtively sit in the melon patch as they cracked open a melon. "Grandpa figured a stolen melon made it that much sweeter," Mom says.

On the Coldwater Road farm, Mom followed Inez's methods. Dad bought her a twenty-one-quart cold packer, just like the one her parents used. Often in summer, Dad would hit the fields just past dawn and pick what looked ready. It cleared his mind to be in the cool morning air alone with just the sound of nature, a stark contrast to the loud, hot atmosphere of the AC plant. Often, my mother would open the door to find a bushel of green beans or rhubarb or corn, patiently waiting. Most days, she'd have it canned by the time he got back home.

The quantity she produced each year was nothing short of dazzling:

> 80 quarts of applesauce
> 120 quarts of tomatoes

80 quarts of peaches
40 quarts of pears
40 quarts of jam
40 quarts of green beans
60 quarts of bread and butter pickles
24 pints of corn relish
24 pints of berry syrups
24 pints of chili sauce

Halfway through this list, her hands would ache and almost deform from the constant cutting of produce and twisting of the rings around the lids of the jars; hence, the term The Claw.

Every year, they ran out of the bread and butter pickles first. Mom made grilled cheese sandwiches with Velveeta and sliced homemade bread slathered with butter. She says she bought Velveeta, a "cheese-food product," not only because it was cheaper than real cheese but because in the 1960s, the ads heralded Velveeta as nothing short of a nutrition "superfood." It was even endorsed by the American Medical Association. It melted particularly well, making it perfect for grilled cheese sandwiches. Something about the cool, sweet pickles hit just the right note when paired with the hot Velveeta sandwiches. The family could go through a whole quart in one lunch.

She quickly filled up the jars in the basement and scoured estate sales for boxes of used ones. Mom never had a problem finding used jars then. By the late 1960s, many suburban types all but gave up canning and instead relied upon buying fruits and vegetables at grocery stores. The prices had come down within reach of average shoppers as the food industry increasingly streamlined transportation that included refrigeration trucks.

In autumn, Mom sent my brothers and male cousins into the orchard with bushel baskets to pick apples. The boys would head out to the orchard with good intentions, but eventually, one would be unable to resist the urge to fling a rotten apple at another boy, leading to the invariable retaliation. We'd hear yelling from the trees as the game ascended into an all-out battle. Eventually they'd return, their bushel baskets full, smelling like apple vinegar, their clothes splattered with nasty, gooey round blotches. A solid hit with a bad apple could produce an angry welt or a bruise. By October, my brothers' and my cousins' arms were covered in them.

Mom and Dad didn't use any pesticides in the garden or in the orchard. Neighbors called this foolish. They'd get higher yields if they'd just give in and spray, the neighbors argued. But Mom's grandmother Anna insisted that pesticides weren't good for the kids.

"Yah, so you get da vorms," Anna told her. "But yah, vith so many trees, vie not share vith da vorms?"

Anna coached them on how to use natural means to repel bugs. In the orchard, Dad would fill a traditional bug sprayer with soapy water; worms, like people, didn't like the taste of it. But worms still found their way inside a few apples. Mom agreed with Anna; they had enough apples and didn't mind losing some to the worms.

Mom would wash the apples and then cook them until soft. The boys got the task of feeding them through a big steel food mill, stirring and churning, stopping sometimes to bang it against a garbage pan to dislodge peels and seeds, which would then be fed to the chickens. The resulting sauce was put back into the kettle and cooked again to boiling to make applesauce.

Mom and Sandy got so adept at canning together that they could put up cold-packed jars in record time. One Saturday, the family was headed north to the Sanford Farm for the weekend when a neighbor stopped by with a bushel basket of concord grapes in her hands.

"I told the kids to pick some grapes," the woman started, a tone of frustration in her voice. "I meant a few but they got carried away and picked a whole bushel. We can't use all these, do you want them?"

We didn't grow grapes. They were expensive to buy. It was a windfall.

Mom and Sandy rushed to transform the bushel of grapes into sixteen quarts of jelly. Mom had never made that large a batch; she wasn't even sure it was going to turn out. Sandy got out the clean pillowcase they kept just for canning. She squeezed the cooked grapes through the pillowcase until all that was left inside were the skins. They made the jelly, set the hot sterilized jars upside down on a towel, and left to head north.

When they came home the next evening, Mom tried a jar, expecting the worst.

It turned out to be the best jelly she'd ever made.

Every summer for years, Milt, Doug, and Sandy would work mornings at Smith's Strawberry Farm down the road from our house. Mom would drop them off around 5:30 A.M. They had to start early to pick as much as they could before the heat of the day set in, as there were no trees in the fields.

All three worked hard. They were paid seven cents a quart unless named "top picker." The top picker received a premium—ten cents a quart. Hypercompetitive, Miltie routinely earned the title by picking ninety to ninety-five quarts, even beating out the adult field hands who went from farm to farm.

Each picker was assigned a row in the field and given a small basket that held six to eight quarts. The goal was to pick as many strawberries as possible before being driven out by the heat. "The farm insisted that the top green stem had to be left intact, or they'd be considered seconds and wouldn't count toward your haul," Sandy explains.

Each quickly developed an individual rhythm to pick efficiently, clipping the stems off the berries as they went. When they filled their basket, they took it quickly to a pickup truck near the field, where they'd carefully put their berries into quart containers and wait while the overseer tallied their count.

The key to winning the coveted top picker status was not only quickness but a willingness to stay out in the heat. Milt, Doug, and Sandy—entrenched in their own personal competition—were often the last ones in the field, outlasting the adult workers. Most weren't true migrants, but just people down on their luck, trying to earn whatever money they could. Sandy got to know some of the women who worked year to year, feeding their families with their picking money.

By ten A.M., they'd be done. That's when the field opened for the u-pick crowd, who were given the rows already scoured by the paid pickers.

One day, Sandy picked a hundred quarts, earning ten dollars. She was rich! To celebrate, Mom agreed to drive them to McDonald's in Flint, where they each got a burger, fries, and a milk shake for fifty cents. It was the most wonderful day possible. She'd bested her older brothers *and* she got fast food.

Sandy quit picking the summer she turned thirteen. One day, she was out in the fields working, sweating and dirty. She looked up and saw the owner's son, the object of her most recent crush. He was standing near the pickup truck where they deposited their baskets, flanked by a pretty girl and another boy she knew from school. They stood there, just hanging out. Sandy tried to hide her face, but before she could, her eyes connected with the owner's son. She nearly died of embarrassment.

Sandy held back, waiting to take her basket to the truck. But finally she had to; it was getting late and she was the last one in the field. As she walked past them, the three were laughing, just being kids, with their clean hands, clean faces, and nice clothes. The owner's son gave her a little nod.

Sandy got her wages and then bolted to the car, where Mom and the boys were waiting. How could that boy ever like her now that he viewed her as a lowly farmhand, the hired help?

She never worked in the fields again.

Strawberry picking had an unexpected, yet somehow not that surprising, effect. Milt, Doug, and Sandy came to loathe strawberries. When Mom picked the kids up, sometimes the owner's wife would offer her an incredible deal on seconds turned in that morning. Mom would take them home and freeze them whole or make jelly.

In the winter, Mom would bust out the frozen fruit to make strawberry shortcake. Dad, Mike, and I loved it. Back then, out-of-season fruit wasn't common in grocery stores. When you did find strawberries in January, the price was exorbitant. Guests would be amazed, often remarking, "Wow, we're having strawberry short-cake in the winter!"

But Milton, Doug, and Sandy would look at the heaping mounds of strawberries on top of their fluffy biscuits topped with freshly whipped cream and heave a deep sigh of disappointment.

Milton would ask: "Mom, why can't we just have chocolate cake?"

Bread and Butter Pickles

Mom served these pickles with grilled cheese sandwiches. Dad loved them so much that even though Mom put up dozens of jars every summer, they still ran out. Before starting, be aware that the cucumbers will need to soak overnight with the onions.

Makes about ten 1-pint (500-ml) jars

Overnight Soak

8 pounds (3.6 kg) medium cucumbers
4 pounds (1.8 kg) small onions
1½ cups (300 g) coarse or pickling salt
4½ quarts (4.5 L) water

Cooking and Pickling

7 cups (1.75 L) white vinegar
9 cups (2.25 L) water
6 cups (1.2 kg) sugar
½ teaspoon (2.5 ml) ground ginger
1 tablespoon (15 ml) mustard seeds
1 tablespoon (15 ml) ground turmeric

For the overnight soak: Wash the cucumbers well. Trim off the hardened end and slice into ¼-inch (6-mm) rounds. Peel and slice the onions and rinse in cold water. In a large stainless-steel or enameled preserving kettle, combine the vegetables with a brine made by combining the salt and water. Cover the kettle. Let it stand overnight.

To cook and pickle: Drain the vegetables and rinse with cold water. Return to the kettle. Cover with a solution made with 3 cups (750 ml) of the vinegar and the water. Place on high heat. Bring just to the verge of boiling, then immediately drop the heat to low. Do not boil. Keep hot until the cucumbers are translucent and tender, about 30 minutes, stirring frequently with a wooden or silicon spoon.

While the cucumbers and onions are cooking, sterilize ten 1-pint (500-ml) canning jars and lids according to the manufacturer's instructions. Keep hot.

Remove the pickles from the heat and drain. Pack the pickles in the hot sterilized jars to within 1 inch of the tops.

In a large saucepan, combine the remaining 4 cups (1 L) of vinegar, the sugar, ginger, mustard seeds, and turmeric to make a pickling syrup. Blend thoroughly. Place on high heat and bring to a boil. Pour the boiling syrup over the pickles to within ¼ inch (6 mm) of the tops of the jars. Run the blade of a silver knife or the flat handle of a wooden spoon down the inside of each jar to release the air bubble. Seal at once. Once opened, refrigerate the contents.

CHAPTER 10

Deer Hunting Season

Dad, Milt, and Doug deer hunting at the Sanford Farm, 1972

True fact: Hunting is so ingrained in Michigan culture that even the blind can take part.*

Every November, my father, grandfather, brothers, male cousins, and uncles converged on the Sanford Farm for the two-week masculine bond-fest known as deer hunting season. No one discussed

---

*In his story "Six to Eight Black Men," humorist David Sedaris says that the blind can go hunting by themselves; that is not true. The state's Department of Natural Resources requires that a twenty-one-year-old or older sighted person accompany a blind hunter.

the ethics, or debated gun ownership. Sitting in the woods quietly freezing with a rifle in your hand was simply a rite of passage.

As each reached age fourteen, my brothers enrolled in a gun safety and basics of hunting program with the Davison Gun Club. After graduating from the course, they got a plaid red jacket at the Yankee Store on Richfield Road. Mom pinned the plastic holder for their hunting license on the back of their coats. Dad hunted with a Winchester .30-06 Springfield rifle, better known as a thirty-aught-six. For the boys he bought used .30-30s, lever-action Winchesters that were inexpensive yet fully capable of efficiently bringing down a deer.

I should note that Dad made a point never to take any of us kids to see *Bambi*.

My grandmother's house was perfectly situated for hunting. Cornfields surrounded the woods near Sanford, resulting in corn-fed venison. By winter, the deer would leave the stark fields and stagger around the woods looking for any kind of food, even bark, to survive. The resulting meat was tender and almost beefy, not like the deer Grandpa Charles and his friends bagged in the Upper Peninsula when they lived in Antrim. Those deer were fed mostly on acorns, and Mom says that venison was tough with an unappealing gamy flavor.

Deer hunting season lasted two weeks. My brothers, Sandy, and I could take the time off from school. This wasn't uncommon at the time. Schools allowed it as long as students had good enough grades and completed any schoolwork ahead of their absence.

At first, I'm sure my brothers thought: *Two weeks off school! To hang out in the woods!*

Hunting combined all the disagreeable qualities of ice fishing with a few additional unpleasantries. To start, everyone had to be in the woods and settled into position well before sunrise. This meant waking at five A.M. to dress in fifteen to eighteen pounds of heavy winter clothing. Next came a long, careful, and silent trek to the heart of the woods. Michigan temperatures in mid-November lean toward the brutal, sometimes as low as forty below zero with the wind chill factored in. Unlike the chatty camaraderie of fishing, men didn't sit with one another in the woods for fear they might be tempted to talk, scaring off prey. You had to sit still, usually on a stump or a log, from sunrise to midafternoon.

Just sitting, freezing in silence for hours, waiting to kill something.

Even as a young child, I felt fortunate to be a girl.

The women had their own ritual. Grandma would flee the man-infested house the first week to spend time with her daughters, Mom and Aunt Mel, in Davison. We'd start each day with a huge pancake breakfast. Then we'd get dressed up. Sandy would put makeup on Grandma Inez. We'd head into downtown Flint. We'd watch discount-priced movies in the middle of the day. I'd hang out looking at toys while they shopped at Kmart, Sears, or Smith Bridgeman's.

Smith Bridgeman's was the name my mother gave to the St. Vincent de Paul thrift store in town. She bought most of the family's clothes there, from the boys' underwear to the party dresses Sandy and I wore as little girls. Mom worried that if her chatty youngest daughter broadcast this information, the unkind people of the world might eventually make me feel bad that my parents bought so much secondhand. So Mom told me the place was called Smith Bridgeman's, the most expensive, ritzy department store in downtown Flint. When I finally went to the real department store at age eight, I was stunned by the three floors with an escalator.

"Wow, they really fixed this place up!" I kept exclaiming.

My mother, not missing a beat, agreed. "Yeah, they sure did."

In the evening, the adult women would drink Ernest & Julio Gallo jug wine while we played Scrabble and snacked on Cheez-Its. We'd all talk about how it was so much more fun than sitting freezing in the woods.

"Your grandfather has done all that sitting and all that freezing and still never gets a deer," Grandma Inez would pipe in to Sandy and me. "Maybe one day. Or maybe he'll get some sense and stay home."

Grandpa Charles hunted every year, yet never scored a deer. He liked being out in the woods, but he wasn't the most enthusiastic deer hunter. Imagine his surprise, then, when my dad showed him a huge buck hanging from a tree in their backyard the very first day he went hunting. Not only did Dad shoot a deer, he'd killed it with a single, precisely planted bullet to the heart. With that shot, the buck slumped with a thud to the ground.

"Well, I guess you got something out of Korea, son," Grandpa Charles said, slapping him on the back as they walked back into the house. "With all the bad, you got some good. Something you can feed your family with." The pair nodded knowingly at each other. Dad had been a marksman in the marines during the war. Grandpa knew he had a lot of experience sitting in the cold, silently waiting, gun in hand.

For a dozen years afterward, Dad shot a buck the first day of hunting season. Afterward, he acted as a guide for my brothers and cousins in the woods. He helped other hunters by teaching them how to stake spots or practice shooting. More than once, he was called into service to take care of a deer that had been shot and wounded. Ethically, hunters are bound to kill an animal that's been injured. Dad helped track suffering deer methodically and put them out of their misery.

But after the first day, he usually returned to the Sanford house by noon. If Grandpa Charles went hunting, he left late and came home early. The two would start to work on making a huge hearty lunch: kettles of beef stew or chili, roasting pans heavy with chicken and biscuits, steaming heaps of spaghetti and meatballs, or multiple chickens roasted with apples and cloves.

The men would arrive back from the woods in the afternoon. As they entered the house through the creaking kitchen door, they'd stomp their heavy hunting boots to shake free the snow and ease sore-from-sitting limbs from their heavy red-and-black jackets and immediately go into the kitchen to pile plates with food. Post-hunting lunch was about eating as much hot food as possible to restore your core temperature to a vaguely normal level. While you could sneak an olive loaf sandwich while sitting silently in the woods, you couldn't sit and snack. The crunch of a potato chip could ruin hours of waiting for a deer. Invariably the men returned ravenous.

After their first big feed, they'd head over to Jack's Log Cabin, a rustic bar that Grandpa Charles frequented. He wasn't a big drinker, but he liked the company. He'd nurse a beer while he played cards or hovered around an indoor shuffleboard. Once, a guy from out of town tried to pick a fight with him, an incredulous idea given Grandpa Charles's towering height. The owner, whose name wasn't Jack, stood between the two men.

"Hey, don't mess with my man Charles. He can crush your head with one hand. But never mind that, he's furniture here."

Hunters would gather with their sons and nephews at the Cabin in their hunting gear. Out front, the men who got deer left them strapped to their cars like trophies.

After a couple of beers at Jack's, the men would head back to the Sanford Farm, where they'd settle down for a second round of food. Then, as darkness descended, the apparent true point of deer hunting season got under way. They played poker. Hours of it. Too late for men who had to get up before dawn, but who could worry about curfews?

They'd drink cases of Old Milwaukee beer and plow through a mountain of snacks. We rarely had chips at the farmhouse; popcorn was the classic, economical treat. During hunting season, the boys had access to a veritable cornucopia of forbidden junk food: Fritos, Rold Gold pretzels, Lay's Potato Chips, Twinkies, and two Faygo pops a day. Such options were the stuff of dreams in my childhood, seemingly unattainable and apparently the reward for hours of boredom in the cold woods. Grandma Inez left Grandpa Charles five pounds of his favorite snack—fried chicken gizzards. My dad even got in on the action, splurging on mini Vienna sausages that he'd eat straight from the can.

They'd sit around Grandma Inez's big dining room table drinking beers, smoking cigarettes, and playing cards until two A.M. "We'd talk about how lucky we were to be boys," my brother Mike says. "Everyone would agree, 'Yeah, the girls are missing out.'"

Sometimes a younger hunter would fall asleep, head on hands on the table. As the first week wore on, they spent less and less time in the woods until some of them stopped going altogether. Then they'd just play cards, snack, and eat all day.

His first season, Dad went with Grandpa Charles out to the woods. When they returned after a couple of hours, Charles stomped the snow off his boots and took off his heavy red-and-black-checkered jacket. "Well, girls, no luck again," he reported as he came into the warm kitchen. "I'm going to take a hot shower."

Dad coughed in stifled laughter. He later explained why Grandpa Charles never got a deer. "He's the loudest person I've ever heard," he told Mom. "He shuffles his feet, he coughs, he talks, everything you're not supposed to do. At one point, he played his harmonica, for crying out loud!" No wonder the deer avoided him. Given that Charles was known for taking squirrels down with a precise bullet in the eye, he had his own reasons for avoiding that moment of truth when faced with killing a deer.

The first week of deer hunting tended to be clan-focused. My uncle Rich Fridline went hunting with his family that week. Dad had friends who came from families without a hunting tradition and he'd invite them along. One was his fishing buddy, Bill Wilson. Bill asked Dad if they could go up a day early so that he could "sight his rifle." Dad obliged. Although Bill had passed the requisite safety course to get his hunting license and had shot squirrels, he'd never hunted for deer. Mom suspected it was an excuse for an early start on poker playing.

Another friend was Frank, an Italian American with a bit of a Mafia air to him. Thanks to his job, Frank wielded extraordinary clout. Among other duties, he managed the delivery of cars from the Flint GM factories to dealers. When Dad ordered his first new car via the generous GM employee discount, he told Frank the order would take about two months. Frank scoffed. "No, it won't." The car showed up at the dealership the following week.

From the time I was two years old, Frank dressed up every year to play Santa Claus at our house. My folks would invite over Aunt Mel and Uncle Rich's four kids, the Fridlines. The year I turned six,

I noticed that Frank and Santa were both missing the same fingers on their left hands, and I confronted Mom about it. She tried to tell me that Frank was a helper of Santa, but I didn't buy it. So she confessed the truth, but then told me not to tell Dad.

"You see, you can't tell him because your dad still believes in Santa," Mom said gently. "Santa is very important to him."

For years, I pretended to believe. I sat on Frank's lap and asked him for presents. Mom and I would giggle at our secret when Dad would talk about Santa and his marvelous deeds.

Frank was a great guy, but he had terrible taste in wives. One ended up passing out drunk in our bathtub, a problem since we had only one bathroom at the farmhouse. One year, Dad patiently spent two full days with Frank and his son in the woods. His son got a deer. Frank proudly hooked it up to his fender, showed it off at Jack's Log Cabin, and then took it home. That wife refused to let him bring the deer into the house. She wouldn't even look at it. With a heavy heart, Frank drove the deer all the way to Ypsilanti and left it with another of his ex-wives.

The next hunting season, Frank was single.

Dad didn't believe in hunting simply for sport. We ate all the venison he shot. After letting it hang for a couple of days, Dad and at least one of the boys would strap the carcass onto the car and bring it to a place to have it "processed," a euphemistic way of saying that someone else would clean it, strip off its skin, and butcher it into packages of meat. More than once, I went with Dad to drop off a dead, glassy-eyed deer. A week later, Dad would pick up a big cardboard box filled with neatly labeled white-paper-wrapped packages of roasts, chops, steaks, and stew meat, the rest ground and seasoned into loose sausage.

By the second week of deer hunting, most of the men had either bagged a deer or given up and could relax. All the rest of the family would descend on the Sanford Farm for Thanksgiving. Cousins would sleep on any available spot of floor space at night. We played board games all day and late into the night. The whole place had a festive, celebratory air.

There was something primal about hunting season. The men

would tell stories of their experiences in the woods, while the women would sit transfixed and prepare the resulting feast, even though it featured a turkey.

We never ate venison during deer hunting season. It just wasn't something you did.

By high school, Sandy was a beautiful, smart girl who desperately wanted to be sophisticated. She felt confined to the provincial life of big land, tiny farmhouses, and small Midwest towns. Living hand to mouth for years had made her realize that other kids had things we didn't. The Wilsons routinely offered her Jell-O, for example, and pudding that came in cups. They bought cake mixes and frosting that came already made in a tub. They ate Sugar Corn Pops every morning for breakfast. Such a luxury was unknown to us.

Once Dad had splurged and purchased a variety pack of single-serving breakfast cereals. The eight-pack included Sugar Corn Pops, Sugar Smacks, Special K, Corn Flakes, Raisin Bran, Rice Krispies, Frosted Flakes, and Froot Loops. We kids had fought so aggressively—the Corn Pops and Froot Loops being the most sought after—that after forty-five minutes of fighting with one another, Dad scooped up all the boxes and threw them outside into the snow.

"And I don't want to see any of you kids go after them, either," he warned. "If you can't agree on how to share without fighting, then none of you deserves any." For the rest of that winter, we would cup our hands next to our faces on the living room's bay window and stare at the boxes. None of us dared to go after them.

The most amazing thing to Sandy was that when Bill and Bev Wilson went out for the evening, their two daughters each got to eat a TV dinner. They even showed them off to Sandy. Every time she went to their house, Sandy looked in the freezer just to marvel at the boxes. None of us had ever had a frozen meal, certainly not my sixtysomething Grandma Inez.

One hunting season, Sandy talked Mom and Grandma into trying some. "C'mon, the boys get chips!" she argued. We stood in the frozen-foods aisle of a Midland grocery store. We agonized over the choices for nearly a half hour. Mom and Grandma couldn't decide, so they went with Sandy's selection, an exotic-sounding medley called Mexican Fiesta.

"The flavors of Mexico can be quite spicy and bright," she said, selling them on it, sounding not accidentally like a passage from one of our encyclopedias. "Just look!" The glossy package showed a glorious assortment of beef enchiladas smothered in chili sauce and cheese, shocking yellow Mexican-style rice, and a side of less-than-photogenic refried beans. As a bonus, it included a caramel-flavored pudding.

I chose a Classic Turkey Celebration dinner. The cover was no less exciting: flat slabs of taupe-colored turkey, a mound of potatoes, the promise of "savory, traditional-style dressing," and the colorful, precise carrots cut in squares the exact same size of peas. Such uniformity didn't exist in my world.

Sandy tried to get me to also try the Mexican Fiesta. I wouldn't budge. Then she tried to talk me into a Classic French Beef Bourguignon.

"Come on, it's like Julia makes on her show," Sandy said.

"No, I want Thanksgiving."

"But we're going to eat Thanksgiving in two days," Sandy countered.

"I don't care." I stood firm.

Back at the Sanford Farm kitchen, we preheated the oven. Then we carefully prepared each TV dinner by tugging back the corners of the aluminum foil on the top of the compartmentalized aluminum tray. To our surprise, they took a *long* time. Somehow, we imagined they would appear magically, instantaneously. Wasn't it meant to be *convenience* food?

After a half hour, Grandma Inez, tired of waiting, stood up suddenly and threw down a kitchen towel in protest. "I could have made biscuits, mashed potatoes, and gravy in the time this is taking!" Mom poured her a fresh glass of Boone's Farm wine and settled her down.

Finally, forty-five minutes later, we pulled our precious,

lukewarm treasures from the oven. Mine definitely looked the most presentable, with distinguishable food items in each of the five tray compartments. In the main one, beige-ish lumps of turkey sat atop a pile of oddly white instant mashed potatoes. Another cubby held salty, soggy bread cubes meant to resemble stuffing. The cranberry sauce was a bright spot—it tasted like cranberries sliced directly from a can, the only kind I'd ever tasted. The vegetables were remarkable only for their flawless cuts.

The Fiesta turned out to be a party no one wanted to attend.

As they cooked, the Mexican-style dinners emitted a disturbing aroma. In retrospect, it didn't smell at all like *actual* Mexican food, but instead yielded an oddly spicy yet chemically sour odor. When they came out of the oven, Sandy peeled back the foil. Smell aside, the appearance was underwhelming. The Fiesta looked like a pile of mush in its aluminum container. It was almost impossible to distinguish the rice from the beans. The enchiladas resembled cardboard folded around an undetermined filling. Stains of tomato alluded to the chili sauce in which they were supposed to be "smothered."

Mom and Grandma looked dubious. Sandy, the eternal optimist, put our dinners on the table. They all dug in with various levels of enthusiasm for the first bite.

If memory serves, Grandma Inez spit hers out first.

"What's this wet bread stuff?" she asked, picking the remnants indelicately off her tongue.

"It's a tortilla, Grandma," Sandy said. After two heroic bites, she spit hers out, too.

In the end, everyone agreed that the bland turkey dinner had been the best choice. They kept trying to take bites from my hard-won TV dinner, so I encircled my tiny forearm around my aluminum tray like a prisoner in a dining hall. Grandma got up and made Farmer's Eggs, scrambled eggs with onions, potatoes, and crumbled bacon left over from breakfast.

The only upside of the entire episode was when Doug came back from the woods. He ate every last bite of the three Mexican Fiesta dinners. "It kind of tastes like corned beef hash," he said. Of course, that's probably the last thing enchiladas should taste like, but Doug was happy.

Days later, we had the genuine Thanksgiving feast. Grandma Inez was convinced that the best "modern" way to roast a bird involved a paper bag and two sticks of butter. The original recipe called for buttering the turkey and then slipping it into a large brown paper grocery bag. Grandpa Charles preferred to slather the bird with mayonnaise and then season it with salt, pepper, sage, and paprika. So then, Grandma Inez insisted, someone had to butter the *inside* of the bag for a perfectly roasted bird.

Buttering the bag was a horrendous job. There's simply no way to take a stick of soft butter and smear it around the inside of a grocery bag without ending up armpit-deep in the stuff. You couldn't easily shower off an armful of butter. The smell embedded itself in your pores. It took a good week before you didn't feel like a buttery slick. This task always went to one of the kids, usually a teen. My oldest brother, Miltie, was an obvious candidate, and so was Doug. Both had been raised to be respectful; they'd do whatever was asked. The key to the buttering-of-the-bag situation was to avoid being present when the task was being discussed.

As soon as the turkey came out of the fridge, my brothers would disappear deep into the woods. If they returned and the bag still wasn't buttered, they'd head outside to make forts with the neighbors. They'd attentively help Grandpa Charles with any car issues or hog feeding or absolutely any other possible chore that needed to be accomplished—anything to avoid buttering the bag.

But invariably one of them got snagged. They'd pass by just at the wrong moment and Mom would say, "Hey, Miltie, you're not busy. You don't mind buttering the bag, do you?"

The rest of dinner was as you'd expect. But that buttered-bag turkey was pretty amazing.

After a few years of being just "one of the girls," Mom decided to go out into the woods to see what hunting was all about. No gun, just to be a spectator. To join in on the *fun*.

A lot of men would have simply said no. Women just *didn't go deer hunting*. It was a male thing. Dad wasn't like that, though. If she wanted to go, he'd take her. They agreed that she'd head out with them the second week. For the first time, Dad had won a permit in the annual Antlerless Deer License lottery, also known as a doe permit. This allows a hunter to shoot a female deer or a young male with antlers less than three inches long, as young as two months old. The licenses were tough to get and couldn't be used the first week of the season.

Dad warned her that it would be cold in the woods. "Yeah, I know. Don't worry, I'll dress warm." After she struggled to get up at four A.M., she pulled on a pair of heavy wool socks under her new cute fur-lined boots. She tucked an extra sweater under her winter coat. A little before five, Dad, Mom, Milt, and Doug started their long, silent walk into the woods. They walked for a long, long time, much farther than Mom expected. She wondered if perhaps she should have dressed a little warmer.

They arrived at Dad's favorite spot while it was still dark. Dad had instructed her that once she was seated, she was not to move or talk. A slight shift of a foot can cause a crackling of dry leaves that can be heard for miles in the silent woods. Dad motioned for Mom to sit on a tree stump. The cold from the wood seeped immediately through her jeans up her spine. Within moments, she was shivering. Dad settled my brothers into other positions before sitting down himself. In the dark, Mom couldn't see any of them.

Sitting completely still turned out to be surprisingly difficult. As the first indistinct light of sunrise lifted darkness from the woods, her feet went completely numb.

"Milt . . ." she whispered hoarsely.

Just then, she heard the crack of a gunshot. Then another shot rang through the woods. A legion of wildlife scattered at the sounds.

"Milt . . . Milt, where are you?" Mom whispered frantically. In the dim light, she still couldn't see him.

"You're fine," he hissed back. "Be quiet."

"I need to go home," she whispered urgently.

"Why?" he whispered back.

"Because it's freezing and I'm not having any fun and I'll never go deer hunting again," she whispered quickly at the direction of his voice.

Silence.

"Doug, take your mother back to the house."

She heard Doug get up. Dad was right; the rustling leaves sounded a cacophony in the still forest. Doug put a heavy gloved hand in front of her. She took it, and they quietly walked the long trek out of the trees.

She wondered if Doug was happy to leave. After all, that morning, the cold was particularly intense. When they arrived at the house, Grandma Inez set him down at the table and made a huge stack of pancakes and a whole pan of homemade sausages. Doug looked quite content as Grandma refilled his cocoa and brought him fresh hot sugar syrup for his pancakes.

True to her word, Mom never went into the woods to hunt again.

Doug turned out to be a disciplined hunter. He headed back to the woods the next day. That season, though just seventeen and a high school senior, he shot his first deer. He was so proud of it that he had Dad hook it to the car to take it all the way to Davison to show it off.

No one was prouder than my mom. She finally understood what it took just to be in the woods. She took about twenty photos of the deer hanging from the metal pole of the clothesline. Then Dad slapped my brother on the back. I watched as the pair cut the deer down so it could be hauled off to be processed.

"So proud of you, son," Dad said. "Your first deer. The first of many, I'm sure."

That turned out to be Doug's only deer. None of them—Dad or my brothers—would ever go hunting again.

Grandpa Charles's Beef or Venison Stew

"The key is to get the meat good and brown," Mom says of Grandpa Charles's stew recipe. *"If it looks a bit charred, that's about right."* If desired, add 2 to 3

minced garlic cloves with the carrots and onions. If the meat is particularly tough, you'll need to simmer it longer. I like to serve this with hot buttered noodles; see Della's Homemade Noodles (page 250).

Makes about 10 servings

> 1½ teaspoons (7.5 ml) salt
> ½ teaspoon (2.5 ml) ground black pepper, plus more as needed
> ½ cup (70 g) all-purpose flour
> 2 pounds (900 g) beef or venison stew meat, cut into 1-inch (2.5-cm) cubes
> 2 tablespoons (30 ml) vegetable oil, plus more if needed
> 2 cups (500 ml) hot water
> ¼ teaspoon (1.25 ml) ground allspice
> 2 tablespoons (30 ml) apple cider vinegar
> 1 tablespoon (15 ml) light brown sugar
> 1 quart (1 L) water
> 5 tablespoons (70 g) tomato paste
> 5 carrots (285 g), diced (2 cups)
> 1 large onion (340 g), diced (about 2½ cups)
> 6 stalks celery (285 g), chopped (1 cup)
> 1 bay leaf
> 1 pound (450 g) potatoes, peeled and diced
> Handful of chopped fresh parsley

Mix together 1 teaspoon (5 ml) of the salt, the pepper, and the flour in a large bowl until well blended. Toss the meat with the flour mixture to coat well.

Add the oil to a 5-quart (4.5-L) or larger Dutch oven over medium-high heat. When hot, brown the meat well on all sides in batches; add a bit more oil if needed. Return all the meat to the pan. Add the hot water, allspice, vinegar, and sugar. Cover tightly and simmer for 1 hour, or until the meat is starting to get tender.

Add the water, tomato paste, carrots, onion, celery, and bay leaf. Put the remaining ½ teaspoon (2.5 ml) salt and a few more grinds of pepper on top. Bring to a boil and then lower the heat and simmer for another hour, or until the meat is tender. Then add the potatoes and simmer for another 30 minutes, or until they are softened.

Before serving, remove the bay leaf. Taste to see if it needs salt or pepper and stir in the parsley. Keep leftovers refrigerated for up to 5 days or freeze in an airtight container for up to 2 months.

CHAPTER 11

Lemon Pie

Fridline cousins with me (far right)
at the Sanford Farm, 1974

My mother's crafty decision to tack Inez on as my middle name
ensured I became one of Grandma's favorites. She never referred
to me by my loathed childhood moniker, "Kathy." Instead, she and
Grandpa Charles called me "Little Inez" or the full "Kathleen Inez."

The favoritism was blatant. She'd dish out cookies to me and my
cousins, saying, "One for you, one for you, and two for Kathleen
Inez." The others would wail at the injustice.

Feeling guilty, I'd divvy up my extra cookie among my cousins
once we went outside.

I loved Grandpa Charles the way only a tiny girl could love her
grandfather. To me, he was the tallest, most handsome old man in
the world. He treated kids as if they were important individuals.

He was the only adult who would listen to some of my ridiculous made-up stories and nod as if they were legitimate events.

Sometimes, if the mood struck, he'd spontaneously break out into song, usually old-time country tunes from the Opry, what he referred to as "cowboy music." As a young man, he'd had a great singing voice. But one night, Charles had been drinking a few beers with his best friend, a guy named Hank who worked as a train conductor, a good job in those days. On their way home, Hank slammed his truck into a post office with such force that it knocked the building six inches off its foundation. Both men were seriously injured. Grandpa Charles's lasting impact from the crash was the damage sustained to his larynx that left him with a ragged, hoarse voice for the rest of his life. Grandpa didn't care. He sang anyway.

Best of all, he was a natural storyteller. I'd spend hours on his lap listening to him talk about cooking at the army base or Saturday nights in San Antonio or the history of the Alamo.

One Saturday in October, Mom, Sandy, and I headed up to the Sanford Farm. On our way up, we stopped at Hamady's to pick up some groceries. As they came out the screen door from the kitchen that brisk afternoon, Grandpa seemed a little more frail than usual, yet he still picked me up and lifted me high in the air.

"Watch your back, Dad!" Inez clucked right behind him. "Little Inez is not a baby anymore, you know."

Grandpa Charles put me down and leaned over, his hands on his knees. "How old are you now, lovely?"

Proudly, I reported that I was almost four and a half. "I even go to school!" It was just Sunday school before service at the First Baptist Church in Davison, but it was "school" enough for me.

He slapped his knee with his hand. "You do! Well, come and tell me all about it." He reached for my tiny hand and led me into the house. We went to the living room and he sat in his favorite chair, a worn yellow plaid upholstered rocker. "I've got a surprise for you." He reached behind him to the credenza against the wall and grabbed a small box. He handed it to me.

It was one of his prized harmonicas. "Oh, Grandpa!" I exclaimed.

I threw my arms around his neck. "Really, can I have it?" He nodded and smiled.

"Here, let's teach you to play." He took the shiny harmonica out of the box and turned it around so I could see the holes. Each one had a number. I was to blow an even, solid breath through the numbered holes when instructed. To make some notes, you inhaled. Grandpa started my lesson by teaching me a scale. Then we progressed to a song, "Shortnin' Bread."

After the groceries were put away, Mom came into the living room to announce that we were all going bra shopping at Kmart, the most boring thing on earth. In the past, I might have been able to spend some time looking at the toys. But I knew that day I wouldn't be allowed.

A couple of weeks prior, when Dad took me to Sears to replace our car battery, he agreed to meet me in the toy department once he finished. I looked with great desire at all the Barbie merchandise. The reason my parents resisted buying me anything Barbie-related shifted week to week; either I was too young for Barbies or the whole concept was just too vapid. In reality, we couldn't afford the dolls, much less the expensive clothes and accessories, but my parents never told me that.

A woman started to talk to me. She seemed nice enough, even if her shoes didn't match and she had a faraway look in her eyes. She said she had some puppies in her car (or it might have been kittens), and asked if I wanted to go with her to look at them.

Hmmm. I liked puppies and kittens. But she was a stranger. I had a book featuring Patch the Pony, a do-gooder talking horse with a black patch on one eye from an unexplained injury who warned children about the dangers of unknown individuals. I'd learned his token catchphrase, "Nay, nay, from strangers stay away!" Dad, a former police officer, had taught me an additional step. If someone approached me and I sensed something was wrong, I should yell a certain phrase to get the attention of other adults. He'd made me stand outside in a field behind the farmhouse to practice it over and over again, so I'd be confident should the need arise.

"I'm not supposed to talk to strangers, but thank you," I politely replied and turned away. The woman persisted. They were especially cute puppies, she said. She reached for my shoulder. I remembered Dad's instructions.

I faced her directly and yelled, "YOU'RE NOT MY MOTHER!" with such force that it startled the woman and she instinctively backed away.

Other shoppers stopped and stared at her. As if waking up, she looked around at them. She turned and ran. Dad had been in the auto department, but showed up immediately. After that, I was on a tight leash no matter where we went.

I knew that shopping for intimates at Kmart meant hours trapped on the floor of the changing room. "Can't I stay here with Grandpa?" I asked.

"Little Inez can stay with me," Grandpa said, backing me up. "I gave her one of my old harmonicas, and we're learning to play it."

Grandma Inez appeared in the doorway, arms folded, wearing her baby blue down jacket. "Okay, but you remember what the doctor said. I left you a fresh pie on the counter for your lunch."

Grandpa Charles nodded. "Don't worry. Kathleen will keep an eye on me."

After they left, we took a break to have some pie. I didn't know then, but Grandpa Charles was sick. He suffered from a disease in which his body could no longer generate red blood cells. Mom and Aunt Mel took turns taking him for transfusions at the University of Michigan teaching hospital in Ann Arbor. The illness affected his appetite. The only thing that he wanted was lemon meringue pie. So Grandma Inez made him a fresh one every morning. It was all he had eaten for the past two months.

In addition to pie, Grandpa spooned me out some sweet salad. The dish was more of a slaw made with sliced apples, bananas, chopped celery, and a bit of shredded cabbage topped with a dressing made from mayonnaise laced with sugar. Grandma added walnuts to her recipe, since they had black walnut trees on their property. Invariably, I picked these out. It's unclear who developed the recipe, which was mainly intended to use up the deluge of apples that descended on both farms each autumn.

After lunch, we sat down with our harmonicas. The bird in the cage above their black-and-white Zenith kept trying to sing along. The little canary got so excited that it went from singing to making a genuine racket.

"Oh, that damn bird of your grandma's," he muttered. "I'll go fix it." Grandpa pulled an orange leatherette ottoman away from the couch and placed it under the birdcage. Then, as he reached for the embroidered cloth they put over the cage so the bird would go to sleep, Grandpa Charles fell backward and slammed to the ground.

"GRANDPA!" I yelled and jumped to his side. He was unconscious. "WAKE UP, GRANDPA! WAKE UP!" I sat there, unsure of what to do. I just kept asking him to wake up. Briefly, his eyes fluttered, but he didn't open them.

"Get me a pillow," he said hoarsely. I ran to their bed, stood on my tiptoes, and got a pillow. I kneeled next to my grandpa and put it under his head. He didn't say anything else, or open his eyes. It felt like an eternity before Mom, Sandy, and Grandma Inez returned. I don't remember crying, but my mother says I was sitting next to my grandfather, my face placid and tear-stained. They came in with their Kmart bags and stopped in their tracks at the sight.

"Grandpa fell and now he won't wake up," I said quietly.

Charles Eldridge Henderson died a week later on October 22, 1971. He was seventy-four years old.

We never found the harmonica he gave me that day.

🍓

Back in Davison a week later, I gave in to the one thing that could take my mind off Grandpa Charles: Halloween. For the first time, we were going to be allowed to go door-to-door trick-or-treating.

Aunt Mel had returned from California in 1965. She married a young German American named Richard Fridline. Mel and Rich settled into a ranch-style house less than a quarter mile down the road. The proximity in age to my cousins proved even more important, at least to me. Aunt Mel and Uncle Rich had four kids in five years, just like my parents. I was born in the "gap" year. So my two male cousins, Rich Jr. and Greg, were just a little older, while their two daughters, Julie and Pam, were just a little younger.

That first Halloween, only the boys and I went trick-or-treating. Mom fashioned a sort of princess outfit with a plastic tiara. Disappointingly, she made me wear my heavy winter coat over the ensemble and insisted that I also wear snow boots, which rather killed the effect. In a situation unfathomable today, our parents stayed at the Fridlines' house and unleashed six-year-old Richie, five-year-old Greg, and my four-year-old self onto the neighborhood. Trick-or-treating in a semirural community is radically different from doing it in a subdivision. The houses lie far apart. We trekked across the hardened ground in the dark. After an hour, we hit only a dozen homes. Wiped out, we called it a night.

Fortunately, the neighbors understood and were generous in their candy allotments, so we still took in a haul. We spent the rest of the night sitting in the living room, piling it into stacks. I put mine into A, B, and C groups. The A group represented the most desirable candy, which had to be carefully meted out over time: a small bag of pretzels, a few Tootsie Rolls, BB Bats taffy suckers, a Blow Pop, and a tiny pack of licorice. The B group included the lesser treats, such as butterscotch candies, gum, and cheap suckers, the kind they gave out at the dentist's. The C group was what we all agreed we'd be willing to give away. My C group included chocolate-heavy candy including snack-sized Hershey bars, M&M's, homemade popcorn balls, and anything sour. Early on, I decided that I wasn't crazy about most chocolate. This made it easy to barter. Everyone wanted chocolate; I wanted their pretzels, suckers, and licorice.

Halloween marked the beginning of tedious "indoor play." In the summer, it was easy to find things to do in the country. We'd build forts, explore the woods, pick blueberries or wildflowers, feed the chickens, play tag, and spy on neighbors. As night descended, we played kick the can for hours. This simple game involved a sentry in charge of minding a beer can; if the sentry spotted another player, he or she could run to the can, put their foot on it, and cry out, "I see so-and-so on the corner of the house." That player would voluntarily be imprisoned on the porch. The game's most glorious moments in-volved a player busting from the shadows to spiritedly kick the can, freeing everyone in captivity like an action-hero star. But generally, a round of the game ended when the sentry captured everyone. One August night with a bright harvest moon, we played kick the can until nearly 3:30 A.M., when the adults finished a drawn-out card game.

In winter, while the adults visited and played cards, we had two choices: play outside in the snow or play downstairs in the Fridlines' finished basement. I hated playing in the snow as a kid. I never got the point of it. Snow was cold, wet, and brought out a bullying ele-ment in other kids. More than once, I was pinned down and had snowballs rubbed in my face. It was not my thing. The Fridline kids knew this, so we spent a lot of time in their basement.

At home, my favorite game was restaurant. I had a small play table that I'd drape with a towel or fabric remnants. I'd pretend to prepare meals on the hand-me-down Easy-Bake oven that once be-longed to my sister. Dad, who had actually owned a restaurant, thought it was cute. Sometimes he'd sit on the floor and pretend to be a patron. More often, though, my customers were imaginary. Other than the Fridlines, I didn't have many friends as a small child; the neighbor kids were all too old, closer to my brothers' and sister's ages. The neighbor girl nearest my age, Shelley, was three years older. She convinced me to cut off my hair when I was a tod-dler, so Mom didn't encourage me to play with her much.

The Fridline kids were never interested in restaurant, so I re-signed to play house a lot. I was always the mom, Rich was always the dad, Greg was the boy, and Julie was the girl. Pam came up with some animal to play. "Let's pretend this family has a horse!" she'd say as we began. Invariably, I spent most of the game cooking meals.

"Okay, now the family is eating breakfast," I'd declare. They'd gather at the card table Uncle Rich had set up downstairs and pre-tend to eat. Then they'd disperse to gender-stereotype make-believe house activities. Pam would whinny or, if she were a dog that day, bark for attention. Rich would fix something or prepare to ready a rifle for hunting, prompted by the deer head mounted on a plaque in the basement, a souvenir shot by Uncle Rich years earlier. Julie would sit and brush her hair. Meanwhile, I'd panto-mime cooking. Minutes later, I'd declare it was lunchtime.

"But the family just ate!" someone would protest. But they'd converge on the card table and dutifully pretend to eat. Minutes later, I'd announce it was dinnertime to a collective groan.

When we got just a little older, house lost some of its allure. Our winter sport shifted to competitive gaming. The girls never liked poker, so we played mostly board games: Parcheesi, Yahtzee, and, ultimately, what we called ruthless Monopoly. Monopoly became a blood sport. You tried to break other players, not only to make them go out of the game but to be upset about it. The most prized way to win was to say, "Just give me all your money and the rest of your property."

Monopoly had two advantages. It was portable, so we could play it up at the Sanford Farm. Second, adults approved of the game, too, so they'd let us stay up until a game finished. Sometimes we didn't go to bed until two A.M. We'd shout and argue. One of the girls would always cry after losing.

"Julie, just give me all your money and your railroads," Richie would say gleefully.

"But that's all I've got left!" she'd protest. His sister would thrust the money at him angrily. "You're so mean! I don't like this game!" She'd get up and stomp up the stairs to the dining room, where our parents were playing cards. One of the adults would come down and suggest that we move on to something else.

So we'd go back to playing house for a while. I'd pretend to cook endless meals. Pam would be a horse, a cat, a dog, or another animal.

But after Grandpa Charles fell that one day, I never let her be a canary.

Lemon Meringue Pie

This is one of the lemon meringue pie recipes used by Grandma Inez. If you don't have shortening, you can use butter; the pastry will have a slightly different texture. Refrigerating the pastry allows the butter or shortening to firm up, result-ing in a flakier crust. If using stick shortening or butter, freeze it first and then grate it with a cheese grater. It makes it much easier to cut into the flour. Lemon meringue pie is best made and served the same day at room temperature.

Makes one 9-inch (23-cm) pie, about 8 servings

Pastry

    1 cup (140 g) all-purpose flour

    ½ teaspoon (2.5 ml) salt

    6 tablespoons plus 1 teaspoon (95 g) vegetable shortening or unsalted
        butter

    2 to 3 tablespoons (30 to 45 ml) cold water

Filling

    1 large egg yolk

    1½ cups (300 g) sugar

    ⅓ cup plus 1 tablespoon (40 g) cornstarch

    1½ cups (360 ml) water

    3 tablespoons (45 g) unsalted butter

    2 teaspoons (10 ml) grated lemon peel

    ½ cup (120 ml) lemon juice

    2 drops yellow food coloring (optional)

Meringue

    4 large egg whites

    ¼ teaspoon (1.25 ml) cream of tartar

    6 tablespoons (90 g) sugar

    ½ teaspoon (2.5 ml) vanilla extract

To make the pastry: Mix the flour and salt together in a medium bowl. Cut in the shortening using a pastry cutter or by pulling two table knives through the ingredients in opposite directions until the dough feels like thick corn-meal. You can also do this in a food processor, but take care not to overpro-cess. Sprinkle with cold water 1 tablespoon (15 ml) at a time, tossing with a fork or pulsing in the food processor just until all the flour is moistened. Press the pastry into a ball and flatten it into an oval. Wrap it in plastic wrap and refrigerate for about a half hour, until cold yet still pliable.

Preheat the oven to 450°F (232°C). On a lightly floured surface, roll the pastry into a circle about 2 inches (5 cm) larger than an upside-down 9-inch (23-cm) pie plate. Press the dough into the pan, trim the excess dough, and then press and pinch the edges into place. With a fork, thoroughly prick the bottom and sides. Bake for 8 to 10 minutes, until lightly browned. Let cool. Reduce the oven temperature to 400°F (204°C).

To make the filling: In a small bowl, beat the egg yolk with a fork. Set it near the stove. Combine the sugar and cornstarch in a 2-quart (2-L) saucepan and place over medium heat. Gradually add the water, stirring constantly, until the mixture boils and thickens.

Stir about half of the hot mixture into the beaten egg yolk. This will temper the yolk, bringing it up to a higher temperature without cooking it, and allowing it to properly thicken the custard. Pour everything back into the saucepan. Boil and stir for 2 minutes, or until thick. Remove from the heat and stir in the butter, lemon peel, lemon juice, and food coloring, if using. Pour into the cooled crust.

To make the meringue: In medium bowl with a handheld mixer or in a stand mixer bowl, beat the egg whites and cream of tartar on high speed until foamy. Beat in the sugar 1 tablespoon (15 ml) at a time. Continue beating the egg whites until they form stiff, glossy peaks. Quickly beat in the vanilla. Spoon onto the hot pie filling, carefully spreading over the lemon filling all the way to the edges. Bake 8 to 12 minutes, until the meringue is light brown.

Cool for about 2 hours at room temperature. Leftovers should be refrigerated and consumed within about 3 days.

CHAPTER 12

Paid in Eggs

Mary Stark and Della Stark Flinn, about 1924

The autumn after Grandpa Charles died, I finally started school. On the first day, Mom led me up the steps of an American icon: a classic red schoolhouse, complete with a bell at the top.

The Cottrell schoolhouse had been built in 1869, and at one time the school had taught grades one through eight. My brothers attended the school on their return from California, when one room was for kindergarten, the other for first grade.

I entered kindergarten in 1972, one of the last years the Cottrell School was open. A kind woman who genuinely loved children, Mrs. Cross told me that she could remember meeting my father on his first day of school in the mid-1930s. He had been one of her students her first year on the job. "Now it's my last year," she told me sweetly. "And I'm teaching his youngest daughter in the very same room. Isn't that nice?"

Meeting more kids my age at school confirmed something that I had long suspected. Most children had *two* sets of grandparents. I knew only about one set. With the loss of Grandpa Charles, I became obsessed with finding out what happened to my "lost" grandparents. At first, Dad just said, "Oh, they're in heaven. My mother died the year before you were born."

Then I started to quiz Dad. What were they like? Did his father play the harmonica and grow beans like Grandpa Charles? What was Grandma Flinn's name? Did she grow up on a farm like Mom? I flooded him incessantly with little kid questions, the kind that can drive a person crazy.

One Friday, he left work early and picked me up from the schoolhouse. "We're going to go on a little adventure," Dad said. Instead of walking back to our car, he took my hand. We went a little ways down the side of the road to a deserted two-room shack. We'd passed it loads of times driving back and forth to school.

The weathered structure wasn't big, perhaps twenty feet by fourteen feet. Anyone driving by would assume it was some kind of abandoned plow shed related to the overgrown field it anchored. The once white paint was deeply cracked. Several of the windows were broken. Dad lifted me up so that I could peer inside. The whole place looked dusty and forlorn. A couple of broken chairs sat discarded in a corner. A rusting pipe hung from the ceiling, the exhaust for a stove long removed from the premises. The roof—so damaged it had a shredded appearance—filtered in a patchwork of light on the sagging wood floor.

"I lived here when I was a little boy your age," he said quietly. I looked at him, surprised. "Your grandmother was named Della Stark Flinn. She was a wonderful woman. When I was your age, I honestly thought she was an angel from heaven."

"What about Grandpa Flinn?" I asked.

Dad's tone sobered. "Your grandfather was named James Flinn."

"Are they both in heaven?"

He hesitated before he spoke. "Yes," was all he said. Then he grabbed my hand. "We better get you home."

It was years before I knew the truth.

🍓

It turns out my grandfather wasn't in heaven. He was in Indiana.

My grandfather James was born in Alliance, Ohio. His dad was something of a scalawag who abandoned the family when James was a young boy. By his teens, James was a handsome, smooth-talking charmer, a natural-born showman and salesman. He ended up getting a job with a circus and traveled the Midwest entertaining crowds doing roller-skating stunts in the preshow parades and under the big top.

When the circus came to Flint in 1923, seventeen-year-old Della sat in the crowd, mesmerized. James saw her in the audience, and after his performance he asked her out. She fell hard for him. When they married a few months later, she was already pregnant.

Her father, Milton Stark, neither liked nor trusted James, and it wasn't just because he'd gotten his daughter in trouble. He was convinced James was some kind of con artist. There was just something about him.

James quit the circus. From then on, his erratic employment included random sales jobs, the oddest of which was a scheme he devised selling fresh fish door to door. He fell for a couple of get-rich-quick scams. Eventually, he took a job as a traveling salesman, which meant that he was away much of the time. Even with his absences, James and Della managed to have six children in rapid succession: Joyce, Clyde, Bob, Hazel, Doug, and my father, Milton.

As the years passed, Della's relationship with James turned increasingly unstable. When James was away for work, he rarely wrote. He'd turn up unexpectedly but with little cash. She'd quiz him about the income he should have had from his job. Smooth-talking James always had an explanation. By the time Dad was born in 1930, Della found herself alone most of the time, unsure if he'd ever return. When Della had their next child in 1932, James went missing again and wouldn't resurface for nearly three years.

It turned out that Della's father had been right about James.

🍓

James's last name wasn't Flinn.

It was Flint.

Before my grandparents met, James had gotten a girl in trouble in Ohio. At seventeen, he reportedly married her. Within a year, he'd left and joined the circus. He just *told* everyone his name was Flinn, even though he didn't have a lick of Irish in him. He married my grandmother without the hassle of a divorce, making him a bigamist.

Around the time my father was born, James started a relationship in eastern Michigan using yet a different name. He's thought to have married that woman and had another separate family. In the mid-1930s, he possibly married a fourth woman using yet another alias. It's impossible to know how many children he fathered. James took advantage of a world and a time in which a simple lie could change your entire identity.

"Back in those days, you could move to the next town, change your name, and you'd be missing," says Delynn Flinn, my sister-in-law and a certified genealogist.

No one had a social security number. Local police didn't fingerprint. Driver's licenses didn't exist in most states, and if they did, they didn't include a photo. Charismatic James Flint traveled the Midwest, wooing women and creating a complex web of deception.

Meanwhile, James left my grandmother to raise their eight children, including my father, alone during the Great Depression.

🍓

Della's life was tough from the beginning.

She was born to a striking young woman named Myrtle. With high cheekbones and pale eyes, she looked like a modern-day fashion model. Myrtle's parents arranged a lucrative marriage for her with a much older, wealthy businessman.

Predictably, she fell in love with someone else.

Milton Stark didn't have much. But he worshipped Myrtle. He took her for long carriage rides and wrote her tender love letters that she read again and again. Myrtle pleaded with her parents to let her marry him. Their response was to lock her in the house. Her father figured she would get over it.

On a moonlit winter's night just days before her arranged wedding, Milton and his father, Thaddeus, silently drew up in a horse-drawn sleigh. Myrtle threw a suitcase out her second-floor window into the snow. She hiked up her long skirt and climbed down a flower trellis. Milton bundled her in thick furs in the back of the sleigh and the trio slipped away. She had just turned fifteen.

The pair had four children; my grandmother Della was the oldest. In 1911, Myrtle caught whooping cough from her youngest child, then just a few weeks old. The infant recovered but her illness lingered, then worsened. Myrtle Stark died at just twenty-two years old.

Milton was devastated by the sudden loss of his beloved young wife. He struggled to raise the four children alone until he married his housekeeper. On the surface, she seemed a kind, even timid woman. In private, his second wife savagely beat my grandmother and her siblings.

When Milton finally clued in to the abuse, the youngest child was sent off to live with relatives. The others left home to work as young as fourteen.

Despite the horrific situation, they remained close to their father, especially Della.

From the beginning of her disastrous marriage to James, Della sought work cleaning houses, taking in laundry, and cooking for middle-class families. She'd do whatever it took to bring in a bit of money. They lived in a series of rental houses in Flint until she found the small ramshackle building in the countryside near the schoolhouse in Davison.

The place had no running water, a tiny outdoor privy, and only a small pot-bellied stove for heat. The little house was divided into two rooms with a crawl space above meant for storage. The girls slept on the floor in one room and Della and James (in the rare times he was around) slept in the main room. The boys slept in the attic, even though the owner had instructed that no one sleep there since the floor wasn't reinforced. They had no mattresses, just wool blankets and a couple of pillows the kids shared. But it was cheap and, more important, walking distance to the Cottrell School.

While they lived at the little house, James returned in early 1935 with promises to reform, a stint of good behavior that lasted two months. It was long enough for Della to get pregnant with their final child, my aunt Mary Jo. By the time Della's pregnancy started to show, James was long gone, this time for good.

Although Della worked as hard as she could, the family slipped into abject poverty. Her oldest daughter left to marry at age fourteen. Clyde and Bob worked after school helping out on farms nearby. Hazel stepped up to take responsibility for the care of the younger siblings, even though she was still a child herself.

All the kids went out to "pick coal." This routine chore involved walking along the railroad tracks searching for chunks that had fallen from the trains' coal cars. It was a dirty job, one that quickly covered their small hands with black soot. It could also be dangerous on lonesome stretches of track without a signal. Picking coal was something you did only if you were among the poorest of the poor. They'd tease one another and make a game of it, seeing who could gather coal the fastest.

While Dad had difficulty recalling what his father looked like, he clearly remembered years of going to bed hungry. He assumed this was normal.

Hunger was a real issue in many places during the Great Depression, but it hit Michigan especially hard. In the early 1930s, the unemployment rate in the state hit 34 percent. With so much competition for work, employers slashed pay rates, so even those fortunate to find and retain jobs earned little. Banks defaulted. At the area's largest, the Union Industrial in Flint, the 1929 stock market crash revealed bankers had embezzled $3.5 million from depositors that they'd bet on Wall Street—and lost all of it. When a bank went under in the era before federal deposit insurance, everyone simply lost their savings. Often that alone was enough to leave a family destitute. Local residents couldn't afford to pay their taxes, so Flint went into massive debt. In the fall of 1932, Buick shut down completely and it wasn't clear if it would ever reopen. It took years for the New Deal programs under Franklin Delano Roosevelt to take hold after he was elected in 1932. Meanwhile, the lucky lived paycheck to paycheck. The less fortunate lived meal to meal.

Della's primary focus was feeding her children the meager food-stuffs she could assemble. Their renter status meant they could rarely plant a garden of any significance. They subsisted on onions, dried beans, and potatoes, all foods she could buy cheap in bulk. Sometimes she got "paid in eggs," when farmers gave her eggs in place of wages. Fortunately, Della was a nimble, thrifty cook. She could make soup out of anything. Nettle soup is chic in culinary circles today, but back then, she made it because onions were cheap and nettles were free in the woods. She'd learned to make it while working as a cook for a Swedish employer who had a field of nettles on her property.

One of Dad's favorite dishes was Farmer's Eggs, a humble combination of onion and leftover potatoes that stretched to feed the eight kids with just four or five eggs. In the hardest times, they simply ate stale bread or single slices of stale bread folded over a little bit of sugar. They rarely had money for milk, and generally ate vegetables only in summer when Della could get them cheap or the kids could earn the food by picking in the fields.

In the autumn, Hazel taught Dad to climb so they could shimmy up the branches of apple and pear trees. They'd camp out under the clandestine cover of leaves and position themselves under clusters of fruit and eat a few. They'd jump down and run fast, in case a farmer saw them. But then they would be back to bread, onions, and beans. "My mother did her best, but we never had enough to eat," Dad said.

Most of the kids had various nutrition-related illnesses. A couple developed mild cases of scurvy, a result of not getting enough vitamin C. Dad developed rickets, a painful bone condition resulting from a lack of calcium and vitamin D, and had to be hospitalized for weeks.

Dad remembered his mother crying the Christmas he turned five when a neighbor gave them a chicken. Another generously donated a bucket of homemade corn syrup. That year, 1935, had been an especially tough one. Della was seven months pregnant with her last child but didn't want her kids to miss out on the holiday. She scrounged up enough work to earn a bit of money. On Christmas Eve day, she put cardboard in the bottom of her shoes—she didn't own any boots—and walked four miles through unpaved snowy roads to Main Street in Davison. There, she bought each child a candy cane, a naval orange, and a small gift. She packed them up, bought a five-pound bag of flour, and walked the four miles back in the snow.

On Christmas Day, the kids had picked enough coal to keep the drafty house toasty warm. Della made the kids pancakes on her cast-iron griddle atop the small stove and the kids lavished them with homemade syrup.

After breakfast, the kids helped her clean until the place was spotless. When every dish was done, the floor swept, and ashes tidied near the stove, they all sat down expectantly. She presented each child with their candy, fruit, and gifts.

"The gifts are from Santa," Della explained. "He gave them to me yesterday because we don't have a fireplace. Now, you all believe in Santa, right?" All the kids nodded eagerly.

Dad's gift was a sticker gun. When you pulled the trigger, it shot out a small arrow with a suction cup. The arrow would stick on anything you shot it at. He loved it. It was his favorite gift ever, in part because later he knew how much she'd sacrificed to give it to him.

For Christmas dinner, she crafted noodles from the flour she had bought and eggs she had been paid by a neighbor. She expertly rolled the dough out on the dining room table in a uniform, paper-thin sheet and then hand-cut the noodles by candlelight with a hunting blade that had belonged to her father. Afterward, she put them on top of newspaper spread with flour to dry. She pan-roasted the chicken in a cast-iron Dutch oven atop the stove and served the noodles with a simple gravy made from the drippings.

As they sat to say grace, Della reminded her children to be especially grateful because many families were so much worse off than they were.

In late 1936, Della's sister, Mary, landed a job working as a cook in the home of Charles Stewart Mott, then the president of General Motors. The Motts were fabulously wealthy. They lived in the Applewood Estate, a sprawling mansion on more than thirty acres. The Motts and their servants were good to Mary Stark.

When they learned about her sister, Della, and the poverty in which she lived with her children, the head cook insisted Mary take a bag of groceries with her on her regular visits. For Christmas in 1937, one of Mott's children gave Mary an Erector toy kit to take to the Flinn children. They had never owned such an expensive toy. They treated it with reverence.

Della and her children moved from the small house the following year, when the owner came by to talk to her about rumors that the boys slept in the prohibited attic. While he was visiting, one of the boys put a foot straight through the ceiling.

Sadly—and hastily—they left their beloved, shabby little house next to the only school my dad had ever attended.

Della moved back to Flint to be close to her friend Nell Wineman. Nell had recently been diagnosed with cancer. Della did everything she could for her friend. She took Nell to doctors, cared for her children, did the laundry, and fed her soup when she was weak.

After her death, Della stepped in to help out Roy, her widowed husband. She became distraught as Roy hired a series of housekeepers, each one more neglectful and abusive to her friend's four children than the last. Unexpectedly, one day Roy asked Della to marry him. Although she wasn't in love with Roy, she loved Nell's children and couldn't stand the thought of them possibly suffering at the hands of an uncaring stepmother, as she had. She told Roy she'd think about it.

Although Roy had completed only sixth grade, he owned his own house and had a good job as a press operator with Chevrolet. He earned enough to care for their combined brood of twelve children, ten of whom still lived at home.

Della's sons made a united plea to their mother not to marry Roy. All of them were working by late 1939. Even my nine-year-old dad contributed his earnings from a paper route to the family pot. Della had landed a position as a cook for a hospital kitchen so she had a steady income herself. But Della still had two small children to consider. Five-year-old Mary Jo was starting school. Myrtle had just turned eight. Roy's children ranged from nine to fourteen.

In 1940, Della sued James for divorce on the grounds of extreme cruelty and abandonment. A judge awarded her lifetime alimony of one dollar per week and ten dollars weekly toward child support, none of which he ever paid.

Della married Roy as soon as the paperwork was settled. While the youngest children had fond memories of her second husband, the boys did not. "Roy was tough on my brothers," Aunt Mary Jo admits. "While he was a good stepfather to me and Myrtle, for some reason he was a real bully to them."

As each got old enough, the boys left for the military to get away from their stepfather. Clyde was first, leaving in 1942 to join the marines to fight in Europe. The next year, Bob signed on as a marine and ended up in the Pacific theater.

Dad briefly lived with one of Della's sisters when he was in his teens. Two days after he turned seventeen, he joined the marines. They promptly shipped him to China to fight in what developed into the Korean War. Compared with the hardships he'd had as a kid, going to war didn't seem like a big deal, at least not at first.

While he was away, Della and Roy moved to Traverse City. She went to work at the upscale Park Place Hotel as a maid. Within a few years, she became the hotel's executive housekeeper, a job that typically required a college degree.

Back from Korea, Dad got past any issues he had with his stepfather so he could remain close to his mother for the rest of her life. He never forgot how hard she struggled to raise them all.

He also never forgot how cruel his father was to her.

In 1940, not long after their divorce, James, the grandfather I never knew, applied for a social security number using his real last name, Flint. Finally, his whereabouts could be tracked. In 1945, he married for the last time, to a woman named Beatrice, and they moved to Indiana, where they raised a family of four. Those children say that he was a good father to them even if he wasn't openly affectionate.

But time weighed on James. Shortly before his death in 1988, James told a daughter about his other marriages and the many children he'd abandoned over the years. He asked her to help him reach out to them.

When he contacted the Flinn family, the gesture was too little too late. Three of James's children were already dead. Those who remained wanted nothing to do with him.

Farmer's Eggs

Anyone who grew up poor anywhere near a farm in the Midwest in the 1930s or 1940s probably ate some variation on this dish. Modern restaurants call them skillets, but both my mother's and father's parents in Michigan referred to this as farmer's eggs. The reason? This humble combination of onion, potato, and a single egg offered a hearty breakfast from cheap staple ingredients, and could keep a man filled up until lunch, traditionally served around one P.M.

The key to this recipe is using cooked potatoes. You can cook them in the microwave and let them cool; just be sure to poke holes in the potatoes with a fork first, lest they explode. You can also use leftover potatoes of any sort: mashed, baked, boiled, or fried. If necessary, cut, shred, or smash the potato into bite-sized pieces.

Today, this remains a quick, budget-friendly dish that's endlessly versatile. You can add bacon or sausage, cheese, and cooked vegetables in any combination that suits, plus spices or herbs to generate the flavor you want. I've put a few variations on the initial recipe below. My maternal grandmother, Inez, invariably cooked this in bacon grease and my granddad Charles finished it with heaps of hot sauce. I make this with a bit of cheese stirred in, typically grated Cheddar or Parmigiano-Reggiano, so I've added it to the recipe.

Makes 4 cups, enough for 2 or 3 hungry farmhands

1½ tablespoons (22.5 ml) vegetable oil
1 large yellow onion, chopped (about 1 cup/200 g)
1 pound (450 g) potatoes, cooked, peeled, and cut into bite-sized pieces
    (about 2½ cups)
About ½ teaspoon (2.5 ml) coarse salt
A few grinds of black pepper
¼ teaspoon (1.25 ml) dried thyme, oregano, or paprika
2 eggs, lightly beaten
2 to 3 tablespoons (30 to 45 g) shredded cheese (optional)

Get the oil hot in a large skillet over medium-high heat. Add the onion and cook, stirring continuously, until brown and just opaque, about 3 minutes. (You want it to be a bit crunchy.) Add the potatoes, salt, pepper, and thyme, and cook, stirring occasionally, until the potatoes start to brown, about 2 minutes. Make a well in the center of the potatoes and add the lightly beaten eggs. Stir until they start to cook, then stir the eggs through the potatoes and onions until cooked through, about 2 minutes. Remove from the heat and stir in the cheese, if using. Serve hot.

Variations:

Tex-Mex: Add ¼ teaspoon (1.25 ml) each dried oregano and chili powder instead of the thyme, finish with Cheddar cheese and hot sauce; heck, you could add some drained red kidney beans with the potatoes and finish with a bit of salsa and chopped green onions (scallions).

French: Add ½ teaspoon (3 ml) herbes de Provence instead of the thyme, add 3 ounces (85 g) chopped ham and 1 cup (80 g) diced steamed green beans with the potatoes, and finish with Gruyère cheese.

Cajun/Creole: Chop half of a green pepper and 2 stalks of celery with the onion, then add 4 ounces (115 g) chopped cooked andouille-style sausage with the potatoes, and finish with hot sauce and chopped scallions.

Italian: Add 4 ounces (115 g) crumbled hot or mild Italian-style sausage and half of a green bell pepper (chopped) with the onion, use ½ teaspoon Italian seasoning instead of the thyme, and finish with mozzarella or Parmesan cheese.

"Loaded baked potato" eggs: Add 1 cup (150 g) coarsely chopped steamed broccoli with the potatoes and finish with Cheddar, sour cream, and crumbled cooked bacon.

Part III

"He who is transplanted still sustains."
—Motto for the state of Connecticut,
from the 1954 *World Book* encyclopedia

CHAPTER 13

Hill Street Blues

Me in front of Hill Street House, 1973

When Dad showed up one Thursday night after work with two dozen Coney Island hot dogs we should have been suspicious. My parents had never brought home takeout, much less *famously unhealthy* takeout.

Coney Island hot dogs are a variation on a chili dog topped with onions and mustard, something of a regional delicacy in Michigan. Their only relation to the amusement park in New York is that they originated from the sausages sold in buns there, first known as red hots, and later entering the American lexicon as hot dogs.

Dad came into the house with white bags full of the foil-wrapped Coney Island dogs and two six-packs of M&S soda pop, which stood for Michigan Supreme, six grape and six "red pop," a cherry-strawberry flavor combination. We never got pop, except at family reunion–type picnics, and then were limited to one each of the inexpensive local brand, Faygo, which could be had for ten cents a can. After everyone loaded their plates with chili dogs and picked out a pop, my parents called us in to a meeting in the living room.

"Big news!" Dad declared. "We're moving!" After all those years we'd be leaving the farm, just two months before the end of the school year.

"It's a great place," my dad started, trying to sell us on the spacious new ranch house they found on West Hill Street near downtown Davison. "We'll have so much more space, and hey, there are *two* bathrooms. Isn't this great? We'll be close to the high school, and there's an elementary school within walking distance for Kathleen."

My brothers and sister stared in disbelief. My parents had never even *mentioned* looking at houses in town, much less buying one.

My sister protested first. "But *this* is our house! We can't just *move*." The idea was unthinkable.

My brother Miltie would have none of it. He'd repeated first grade when they'd arrived from California since the curriculums from the two states varied so much. So although he was eighteen, he was just finishing his junior year alongside my brother Doug. "I'm an adult now. I don't *have* to move with you. I could stay here and live in the barn."

Doug stood up. "If Milt stays, I'm staying, too."

Mom and Dad exchanged glances. They weren't naïve enough to think that the new house would be a slam dunk, but they didn't expect flat-out revolt. After all, Mom says, they had endured years of complaints about the farmhouse. It had been cozy when the kids were little, but with two adults, four teens, and a seven-year-old sharing one bathroom, mornings were chaos. Afternoons and evenings didn't fare much better, as my four strong-willed and busy siblings required being shuttled back and forth to the high school, which was a half-hour drive away, for Mike's band rehearsals, Sandy's baton lessons, Milt's track practice, and Doug's football schedule.

Things might have been different if there was a public bus line that came anywhere near the farm, but there wasn't.

After nearly seven years of struggling, Mom and Dad had finally paid off the debts stemming from Century Products. At the same time, Dad got promoted to general foreman, a step up in the ultra-hierarchal GM management system. Suddenly, they felt flush. They wanted a place where the kids could be proud to invite their friends over. After all those lean years, Mom felt like she'd earned a dish-washer.

Dad stood up. The discussion portion of the evening was over. "We're all going to meet the Realtor at the new house on Saturday morning. Wait and see. You're going to love it."

As promised, Mom and the boys loaded into the station wagon and Sandy and I rode with Dad in his pickup truck. On the drive over, Sandy said she would go along with the whole new house idea if she could have a pony for her fifteenth birthday.

"There's a shed behind the house, we could probably keep a pony there," Dad said quickly. "We'll take a look."

The drive from the farm to the new house took about twenty minutes. Davison is often considered a bedroom community to Flint, one of the oldest continually inhabited areas in the state. It was Chippewa territory when a white man named Jacob Smith married into the tribe and started a trading post in Flint in 1819. The woods and fields of Davison were hunting grounds for the Chippewa and fur traders. In 1842, a man named Eleazer Thurston settled there, and Davison became an official village in 1889. Its pioneering roots are reflected in its downtown area; with a bit of work, it could pass for a Hollywood western set.

The new house was at the dead end of West Hill Street. Covered in white siding with black trim and faux shutters, it had a stately look for a modest ranch-style home. By comparison to the farm-house, though, the place felt huge, an oversized rectangle with an attached garage. We pulled up and parked in the driveway. Dad got out and waved to Milt, who pulled the station wagon up behind him. Sandy helped me down from the truck. "It looks like a rich person's house," she observed.

Once inside, it had a classic Midwest rancher layout. The first room we entered was the small living room that extended into a dining room with sedate avocado-colored carpeting. "This is the formal living room," Dad said enthusiastically. Then he led us to an oversized family room with blood-orange shag carpeting and wood-paneled walls with a door that shut it off from the rest of the house. It even had a window air conditioner. "Isn't this great? You kids can entertain your friends in here."

The kitchen was decked out in the latest fashion: bisque appliances and robin's egg blue cabinets with gold-speckled Formica counters. "Look, Sandy! A dishwasher!" Mom said, pulling down the creaking door. "Plus drawers! Six of them!"

The place had three bedrooms, including a generous master with its own bathroom. The kids looked on dubiously. Sandy had hoped to get her own room out of the situation.

"We thought the boys will have the master for now, and you girls can share," Dad said. "At least until the boys graduate next year, and then we'll move the arrangements around." The kids looked on without comment. Dad took it as agreement. "Okay! Let's look at the backyard!"

The backyard was big, about a half acre, but it felt tiny compared to the farm. "It's a good size for being in town," Dad explained. "There's still space for a garden."

"Where are we going to put the chickens?" Mike asked.

"Well, we've had chickens long enough," Dad said reassuringly. "We'll find good homes for them."

"Plus," Sandy interjected, "we're getting a pony." Mom and Dad didn't say anything.

After everyone had looked around, we piled back into the cars. Then we did something incredible. They took us out to dinner.

We *never* ate out. On the rare instances we got burgers at the A&W or fifteen-cent hamburgers at McDonald's in Flint, we all ate in the car. That day, Mom and Dad casually walked into a fish-and-chips place. We got *menus*. Dad told us we could get anything we wanted. Sandy ordered fried frog's legs. My brothers selected the fried whitefish with fries. I ordered the chopped steak, a dish in which a piece of cooked sirloin is chopped and tossed with onions and mushrooms. Mom and Dad both ordered surf and turf, steak with grilled shrimp. Mom ordered a glass of red wine.

It was as if we'd gone undercover to invade some enemy territory. Rich people bought new houses. Rich people ate in restaurants. If there was one thing we embraced about our collective identity growing up, it was that we were poor farm kids, the ones who sat in the brown bag lunch ghetto at school with the awkward sandwiches made from homemade bread and cheap olive loaf. My brothers still joke that they spent most of their school years wearing underwear with someone else's name written inside, the result of Mom's thrift store shopping. But we didn't mind. There was always plenty to eat and we never wanted for anything.

In the next month, more odd things happened. Dad came home one day in a new red Chevrolet Vega. Plastic-wrapped furniture showed up, including a faux leather La-Z-Boy recliner. Mom brought home a set of matching dinnerware—the first new set of dishes we'd ever had, aside from the collect-a-plate china she procured after years of shopping at Hamady's. The most startling acquisition: a twenty-two-inch Magnavox color television in its own massive wood cabinet that came with a heavy, black padded remote.

Dad packed up the last few chickens into a crate and sold them for cheap to a farmer in Lapeer, a thirty-minute drive away. No one around us kept chickens anymore. Mom left all of her canning jars in the cellar. I can still recall the smell, a musty mix of mildew, earth, and dust, as Sandy and I helped her carry the last few to store beneath the house. "We won't need these where we're going," she explained cheerily. I watched as she closed the cellar door the last time.

The kids took some adjusting to the new house. It was far from the friends they'd made over the years out at the farm. Aunt Mel and her family were now seven miles away, not far, but far enough that it felt like we rarely saw them.

A neighboring teen, a Cher-style hippie with waist-length shiny brown hair, showed my sister and brothers the bus stop just down the street for the high school. She barely spoke, and when she did, it was in a hushed, theatrical whisper.

When the bus arrived, to my siblings' horror, it was "the short bus."

There's no politically correct way to describe their reaction to the short bus. Simply put, the small buses were famously used to ferry special needs kids to schools. Whenever a short bus would show up at school, kids would crane their necks to see what souls would descend from the motorized lift.

In the case of the Hill Street bus, there was no need for such hysterics. The county had few students who lived in the small two-mile radius from school and hence put a smaller capacity bus on the route. Rationally, people should understand that. But teens are not rational people. Mike was a freshman, Sandy a sophomore, Milt and Doug juniors. When the bus pulled up in front of the high school, they'd flee from it as if it were on fire. Their teenage fears weren't completely unwarranted. After two weeks of trying to avoid letting anyone know they were short bus riders, my brother Milt saw a few students nodding their heads in their direction, smiling and obviously mocking them.

That weekend, Milt cashed in money from strawberry picking and lawn mowing and bought a used Ford Mustang—an act of independence against the bus and against my folks, knowing how much a Ford parked in the driveway would irk my GM loyalist father.

For reasons unknown, I thought the best way to get to know my new urban neighbors was to dress in my cowgirl outfit and wander the neighborhood ringing doorbells to disperse treats.

Mom had made a comment about "calling on" the neighbors. A week after we moved to Hill Street, my parents went out to dinner in Flint. Milt was off somewhere in his Mustang. My sister was at her friends' house, twin girls named Pam and Tam.

In theory, my brothers Mike and Doug were supposed to be

watching me. Instead, they were glued to the new color TV in the family room watching Karl Malden and a young Michael Douglas in *The Streets of San Francisco*. The new house came with an automatic antenna. You could turn a beige dial on a box and the antenna would automatically turn in the direction requested. We could hear the metal antenna pole lurching and screeching outside the window. Suddenly, TV viewing became something that the boys could do without fear of being sent outside for "pole duty."

I got dressed in my teal cowgirl vest and skirt, both attractively finished with a white leatherette fringe. I pulled on my matching white cowgirl boots and topped it all with my blue felt cowgirl hat. I set off into the neighborhood with a basket in hand, my mother's banana spice cookies inside.

The first neighbors I called on had a puzzling reaction. The man across the street operated a television repair shop out of his home. I knocked and, despite my hearing noise inside that would indicate they were there, they didn't come to the door.

I moved on to a tiny brick house with a young newlywed couple. "Who are you? What are you doing?" the husband asked. I tried to explain. "Honey, go get the camera," he yelled over his shoulder. They took my picture, then some cookies. I could hear them laughing behind the door. The Cher-style hippie girl's home was next. She was brushing her long hair when she answered the door. She took a cookie, whispered, "Thank you," and closed the door, all the while brushing her hair.

A sweet elderly couple explained that neither of them could eat sugar, but thanked me and welcomed us to the neighborhood. The woman gave me a dime. At another house, a woman answered, a baby in her arms. She chuckled as she helped herself to a cookie. "Okay, nice to meet you, candy girl."

The brown house on the corner looked run-down, the backyard enclosed by a sagging aluminum fence. The doorbell didn't work, so I knocked. A small girl with delicate features opened the door. She must have been three. I gave her several cookies. She never said a word, and just kept staring at me with big brown eyes as I made my retreat.

I left the biggest house on the block for last, a white two-story number with an immaculate yard. A flock of young girls answered the door. *Ah! Kids my age!* I thought. The dark-haired father pushed the girls aside. "Who are you? What are you selling? We don't want any." Before I could explain, he slammed the door in my face.

I turned away. I thought I might cry. But, then, how else would I meet the nice girls inside? I squared my shoulders. *Cowgirls don't cry*, I thought.

The next evening, I put my cowgirl outfit back on. That night, I emptied the cookie jar of Mom's oatmeal raisin cookies and repeated the endeavor of the previous night. The man across the street pulled aside the curtain but didn't open the door. The young couple took another photo of me. The old lady gave me another dime. The woman with the baby smiled broadly. "Hey, candy girl! What do you have tonight?" She took two cookies.

Steeling my little cowgirl will, I returned to the big white house and rang the doorbell. The front door was open, with only a screen door in place. The girls, all clad in long cotton nightgowns, clamored from up and down the split-level entry stairs to the front door. "Hey, it's you! Don't worry, our dad isn't home. You can come in."

That's how I met my closest childhood friends. Katie was the nearest in age to me and became my best friend. She starred in my first short stories. The oldest was Margaret, a dark-haired beauty who always got to wear new clothes before they were handed down to her sisters. Ann was younger, and could be a wicked tattletale. Carol was a toddler when I met her. Their mother gave birth to a fifth girl, Cindy, shortly after we arrived. They had Barbie dolls, including the three-story penthouse (with a pink elevator) and the pink Corvette, not to mention shoeboxes filled with clothes in various states of repair. I tasted my first Popsicle at their house—a cold, mouth-numbing, joyous moment. I watched in fascination as their mother unveiled the process of heating up a frozen supermarket pizza; given their restaurant history, my parents always made pizzas from scratch. Once baked, the frozen pie tasted both bland and sweetly spicy, like the soft, doughy pizza we had at the elementary school cafeteria. I marveled at the strangely synthetic nature of the cheese topping. As they were the only Catholic family I knew, I quickly assumed that everyone of that faith ate frozen fish sticks for dinner on Fridays. Baked until slightly crunchy, the fish itself tasted bland and mushy compared to the fresh variety we caught, yet the salty beige coating captivated my taste buds when combined with the sweet-and-sour tang of the store-bought tartar sauce. I begged my mother to buy fish sticks, but she would never give in.

In the summers, I spent most of my waking life with their family, at least until their father got home from work on the line at the Fisher Body assembly plant. Often, an awkward chill descended on the household when he gruffly announced his return by slamming the front door and pounding upstairs to his room. Their parents sometimes went days without talking to each other, an unthinkable scenario in my own household. I scurried away when he arrived home.

I learned that the residents of the brown house were a down-on-their-luck family with five kids. They were all older than me except for Anna, the sweet, tiny girl who answered the door. She'd run after my mother's car when she saw her coming home from work. Mom would feed her cookies and pamper her. "Aren't you just such a pretty little girl?" Mom would say. Sometimes she'd sit on our porch and brush Anna's hair until it gleamed. "Would you like a peanut butter and jelly sandwich?" Anna would nod. She always seemed hungry.

Other than Margaret, Katie and her sisters always complained about hand-me-downs. I didn't have anyone to give my clothes to when I outgrew them. By Hill Street, I knew that I'd never have a younger sibling, no matter how hard I prayed.

So every so often, I'd invite Anna over and doll her up in one of the dresses that I'd outgrown. I'd fix up her soft brown hair with bows and barrettes. One year, I did this every day before Vacation Bible School. A church member volunteering as a teacher remarked that doing such niceties was sure to get me into heaven.

"No, ma'am," I replied. "It's my sunshine work. You're not sup-posed to expect anything back in return, not even from God. That's what my grandma Inez says."

One positive about Hill Street was the arrival of a new family member: Dad's first powerboat. Now that we were no longer neigh-bors with Uncle Bert, it was unseemly to borrow his boat. But my parents were not the kind of people who would buy something on credit. So for six months, they set aside money from Dad's pay-check. When they started shopping, everything they found was too expensive.

One Saturday, Mom got up early to go to Hamady's. On her way home, she noticed a FOR SALE sign on a nice-looking blue boat in a front yard. It hadn't been there on her way to the grocery store. She stopped and took a look.

It had everything they were looking for: a walk-through wind-shield, a ladder in the back, enough seating for the family. Plus it was half the price of similar boats they'd seen. Just then, the owner emerged. He'd just put it out that morning after a fight with his wife.

"So, here's the deal," he started in a conspiratorial tone. "I'm selling it really cheap because I've bought this new boat, but I haven't sold this one yet and my wife is giving me all kinds of grief about it. How much I sell it to you for, she doesn't need to know. She just needs to know that it's not here anymore."

Mom bit her lip. It was just what they wanted and it was a fan-tastic deal. But it was a big purchase to make without Dad seeing it first. She gave the guy a check for one hundred dollars to hold it for her and said she'd be back with her husband to look at it.

"You tell him I'll throw in all the life jackets, the skis, every-thing," he said. "It's complete."

Mom rushed home. "Honey, there's this guy down the street who is selling his boat. I think we should go look at it," she said.

Dad was reading the paper. He was giving up hope of finding

anything they wanted at a reasonable price. Grudgingly, he got dressed. Eventually, they headed over to take a look.

As they pulled up, Dad got excited. He jumped out of the car immediately.

"Oh, my God! I love this boat, this looks perfect!" Dad exclaimed. He stepped up inside the immaculate interior. He hopped down as he saw the guy walking toward him from the house. "Hey, how much are you selling this for?" The guy told him the price. "Sold. I want it," Dad said quickly. "I can write you a check right now."

The guy scratched his head. "Well, here's the problem. I can't do that. It's been sold."

Dad had the look of someone who had a winning lotto ticket just snatched out of his hand by a gust of wind, lost forever. "Oh, no," he said, his voice weak with disappointment.

"Yeah, I sold it to that lady over there," the man said, pointing toward Mom, now just getting out of the car.

"That lady?" Dad said. Then it dawned on him. "That's my wife! That's my wife! That means it's our boat!" He jumped up and down. He went over, put his arms around Mom's waist, and lifted her up, spinning her around. "Why didn't you tell me?"

"Well, I just gave him one hundred dollars to hold it in case you didn't like it," she said.

"In case I didn't like it?" he said, surprised. "I love it! I've got the smartest wife in the world!"

Flint-Style Coney Islands

Despite the name, credit for this dish goes to immigrants arriving in Michigan in the early twentieth century who crossed hot dogs served at the iconic New York amusement park with variations of mild meat sauces from the Old Country. A Flint-style Coney Island employs a natural casing Koegel's Vienna-style hot dog topped with a mild, dry meat sauce, onions, and yellow mustard. In Detroit, the meat topping has more liquid, resulting in a wetter sauce.

Below is an adaptation of the recipe credited as the progenitor of Flint-style sauce developed by a Macedonian immigrant, Simeon O. "Sam" Brayan, who opened Flint's Original Coney Island restaurant in 1919. Brayan contracted with Koegel Meat Company to help engineer the hot dogs they still make today, and with Abbott's Meat to develop the sauce.

My uncle Rich Fridline wheedled the sauce recipe from a Flint's Original em-ployee in the late 1950s, years before it was published in the Flint Journal *after Brayan's death. That recipe made enough for 36-plus franks, so I halved it, and then halved it again. This version makes about 1½ cups (360 ml) of sauce, enough for 8 to 12 hot dogs. Be advised that each prepared Coney Island packs 380 calo-ries, with a high dose of saturated fat and sodium, so it's best to limit individual intake to one Coney, no matter how alluring a second might look.*

Makes 8 to 12 Coney Islands

8 to 12 beef hot dogs, preferably kosher reduced-fat
1½ teaspoons (7 g) butter
6 ounces (170 g) lean ground beef
½ medium yellow onion, minced (¾ cup/95 g)
1 garlic clove, minced
¼ teaspoon salt
¼ teaspoon ground black pepper
1½ teaspoons (22.5 ml) chili powder
1½ teaspoons (22.5 ml) yellow mustard, plus more for garnish
5 tablespoons (85 g) tomato paste (half of a 6-ounce can)
6 tablespoons (90 ml) water
2 hot dogs, minced
8 to 12 hot dog buns
Chopped raw onions, for garnish

Cook the hot dogs according to the package directions.

Melt the butter in a 3-quart (3-L) or larger skillet or saucepan over medium-high heat. Add the ground beef, onion, garlic, salt, pepper, chili powder, mustard, tomato paste, and water. Stir to combine well and simmer until it starts to thicken, 3 to 5 minutes. Add the minced hot dogs. Drop the heat to medium-low and simmer for about 15 minutes, stirring regularly, until cooked throughout.

To serve: Traditionally, the buns are steamed. At home, try microwaving the buns 4 at time, with a cup of water in the oven, for about 20 seconds to soften and warm. Nestle each hot dog in its bun. Plop 2 to 3 tablespoons (30 to 45 ml) of sauce on top of each dog, sprinkle with chopped onions, and squirt on a line or two of yellow mustard.

CHAPTER 14

Danke

Me, age nine, at a D.A.N.K. picnic, 1976

Life on Hill Street changed everything. My parents did strange things, like host parties. Mom made cheese balls, chicken liver pâté, and little appetizers with toothpicks in them. They would throw dinner parties with adults who were not relatives, serving main courses with names such as chicken Chardonnay.

Once I started first grade, Mom looked into possible part-time work. Instead, she landed an enviable full-time job as the executive assistant for the publisher of the *Flint Journal*. Even with an aggressive savings plan, with two salaries and no debt, they felt like they'd hit the lottery.

They stocked a bar and kept name-brand pops on hand, referred to as mix, for cocktails, which remained strictly off-limits for us kids. My brothers and sister were heavily invested in high school activities. Years earlier, my parents had scraped together enough money to buy Mike a trumpet, and now he was in every band at school and earned the rank of drum major of the marching band. Sandy landed a spot as one of five baton-twirling majorettes. Doug played football. Milt landed a summer job at AC Spark Plug. When he went back for his senior year, he stayed on at AC, working almost full time while maintaining his straight-A average. Proud, my dad taped his report card to the door of his office.

My parents went to dances at the Davison Country Club, and Mom joined a spa-style gym in Flint. With this shift came a major change to what we ate. For the first time, they bought some convenience foods: Swanson turkey pot pies, Dinty Moore beef stew, and Banquet frozen fried chicken—all items previously considered both too expensive and ridiculous when we lived at the farm. "Why would anyone buy *frozen fried chicken?*" I remembered Mom sniffing one time at Hamady's. Now we had boxes of it in our freezer.

Mom had little time to make cookies or bread from scratch, so now she bought gingersnaps. She drew the line at certain grocery items: no "white-white bread," as she called Wonder bread, or sugar cereal. But even the appearance of the relatively tame shredded wheat and Raisin Bran boxes on the table were greeted with raised eyebrows by my siblings.

I had longed for such foods when we lived on the farm. Now all I wanted was Mom's homemade fried chicken and bread. My siblings always complained about being brown baggers at school. Now that they could afford hot lunch, it didn't exactly live up to their expectations. Sandy got so fed up with the store-bought gingersnaps that she started making cookies on her own while my siblings watched TV. She even started to use this skill as leverage against my brother Doug, who would do just about anything in exchange for chocolate chip cookies.

Another strange thing happened. Mom and Dad went away for "second honeymoons." They'd pack up on a Friday and head off to Bayport, where they kept the boat in the summer months, and spend the night. After a night of dancing and a few drinks, they'd walk back to their motel. The next day, they'd fish in the morning and head home in the afternoon. Mom says, "It let us feel like we were Milt and Irene again, that couple that fell in love. Sometimes married people get so caught up in daily routine that you forget that you're in the biggest romance of your life."

When I was a child, my aunt Mary Jo was by far the most glamorous person I knew. The youngest of Dad's siblings, she was a beautiful woman with the high cheekbones and lovely, light-colored eyes of her grandmother Myrtle, and the jaunty joie de vivre of her ne'er-do-well father, James Flint.

Mary Jo had a man's job at the plant, but when she wasn't working, she dressed beautifully and smelled of *actual* perfume, not cheap dime-store cologne. She had a knack for interior decorating and lived in Grand Blanc, the classy part of Flint. Her four kids were roughly the same age as my brothers and sister so they were always at our house. They were so sophisticated that Joyce, the youngest, even took modeling lessons.

Aunt Mary Jo and her husband somehow got invited to a dance hosted by the Deutsch-Amerikanischer National Kongress, or the German American National Congress. Known by its initials, D.A.N.K., for short, it's pronounced with a soft *a* to sound like *danke*, the German word for "thanks." The group bills itself as "working to preserve German culture, heritage and language in the United States." D.A.N.K. was founded in 1959 as a way to ease post–World War II/cold war suspicions of German Americans and to promote pride in their own heritage and culture. Michigan had a couple of chapters then, including one based in Flint.

Mary Jo and Bill mentioned the German dance with inexpensive admission that included food to my parents. All four showed up, not quite knowing what to expect.

They arrived at the rented hall to find attendees decked in traditional German dress, the women in dirndls and the men in lederhosen. The Germans turned out to be great hosts, teaching the four interlopers how to polka as an accordion-driven trio pumped out rousing variations. Dad was impressed that the male members brought along their own steins to drink the free-flowing beer. The food was amazing: ham-stuffed schnitzel smothered with cheese and bratwurst cooked in dark beer served with sauerkraut slow-cooked with onions, apples, and bacon.

By the end of the night, a genial German couple from the Old Country suggested they join. "But my brother and I are mostly Irish and English," Mary Jo protested. Her husband's people were a mélange of Scottish, English, and Dutch with a wee token of Native American—also still *not* German. Mom admitted that her people were mostly Swedish.

The man waved his hand. "It's a German-*American* club," he insisted. "You're American, aren't you? We have lots of great parties just like this one, and picnics in the summer. It'll be fun."

They were sold. By their second party, Mary Jo had invested in a full-on dirndl.

At first, our membership was perplexing and a little odd. People would introduce themselves with names that sounded like characters out of *The Sound of Music*.

"I am Friedrich Moeller," a boy would say in introduction.

"And I am Britta Krause," a girl would add.

I'd meekly explain my name was Kathleen Flinn, so *not* German. Sometimes a person would say, "Oh, then your mother must be German." I'd explain she was Swedish American. They'd walk away, confused.

Mom and Dad were not the type to do anything by halves. They attended all the organizational meetings. They volunteered for fund-raising efforts. They worked in the trailer that the group took from fair to fair during the warmer months. These days, it would be known as a food truck. They called it the Krautwagon, not as a derogatory term for Germans but because of the vast amounts of sauerkraut they served.

Mom's sole experience with German food growing up was the sauerkraut that Grandma Inez made a couple of times. Utterly unfamiliar with the stuff, she took a jar of sauerkraut, dumped it ungraciously into a pan, and added chopped hot dogs or sausages to heat up in the liquid. Mom told one of the German women she worked with in the Krautwagon about it.

"She didn't drain it first?" the woman said, horror-stricken. "*Da wird ja der Hund in der Pfanne verrückt!* That's crazy! You're lucky you didn't get sick!"

She taught Mom how to prepare real sauerkraut. They'd start by thoroughly draining the fermented cabbage and then slowly simmering it to evaporate any leftover liquid. They'd add in diced onion, bacon, apples, and caraway seeds along with dark German beer and let it simmer slowly for an hour. Meanwhile, they grilled strongly seasoned bratwursts slowly and perfectly, until the skins grew dark and ready to burst. Just as the crowds were expected, they set up a small box fan in the trailer and blew the smell of the sauerkraut and brats outward.

The Krautwagon parked next to the usual fair offerings such as simple hot dogs and hamburgers. The German fare would crush such weak competition and they'd end up with long lines. In these situations, Mom heard many colorful German phrases:

"*Sich wie reife Kirschen verkaufen!*" one woman exclaimed during a rush as she piled sauerkraut onto platters as fast as she could.

"What does that mean?" Mom asked, working just as fast putting brats into buns.

"They're selling like ripe cherries!" she replied, handing two platters out the window of the trailer. "In English, you would say 'like hot pancakes!'"

Mom and Dad loved D.A.N.K. The members knew how to have fun. The dances were rollicking affairs. The beer flowed freely. Dad got a little green Bavarian-style hat that he wore while drinking from the massive stein my mom bought him as a gift. He looked completely at home, drinking his beer and wearing his hat as he chatted with the other members.

But honestly, it all came down to the food.

"When you went to a German potluck, it was like feasting in heaven. They'd have tables laden with the most amazing dishes," Mom says. "And then I'd bring something lame, like deviled eggs."

At the first party my parents took me to, the buffet had a variety of schnitzels. The members had made their families' versions of the traditional German dish made from pork or veal. Schnitzel begins with a piece of meat that's been pounded thin, then dredged in a mix of flour and cheese, before being fried to a golden crisp. There's a line in the song "My Favorite Things" from *The Sound of Music* about "schnitzel with noodles." I had never had schnitzel. For some reason, I had it confused in my mind with strudel, a dessert, and thus couldn't fathom why anyone would eat cake and noodles together.

With my first bite of *jägerschnitzel*, an entire world of possibilities opened. The pork schnitzel was layered with a silky, peppery mushroom cream sauce and served alongside homemade buttered spaetzle, a soft egg noodle resembling a small, squat dumpling. The tender pork, crisp coating, savory gravy, and supple noodles together yielded an intense flavor at once foreign yet comforting.

At picnics, they served huge, hot, Bavarian-style soft pretzels. One of the club's officers contributed his special pretzel sauce, a combination of strong mustard, white Cheddar, Worcestershire sauce, and dark beer simmered together and served warm in little bowls. Tasty, tangy, cheesy, it was absolutely everything you could want to have with a leathery, warm pretzel.

Sometimes our enthusiasm for the food got us into trouble.

At one fund-raising dinner, the hosting couple served their infamous *schweinshaxe*, a whole roasted pig knuckle, a specialty of Bavaria. Huge meaty knuckles arrived at our table with a knife sticking out from the middle of each. The hosts explained they'd made the *schweinshaxe* in the traditional fashion by marinating it for seven days, then roasting it atop a bed of sauerkraut. The result was fall-off-the-bone tender pork with a crackling hard crust. Everyone in my family—including me—ate one apiece. Later, we learned that one *schweinshaxe* is normally split between two to three people. That night we shivered in our beds from meat sweats.

Members took turns hosting a Christmas party at their house each year to serve the traditional dish *sauerbraten*, a beef roast that's marinated for days in a bath of red wine, vinegar, and juniper berries. One hostess explained that she added crumbled gingersnap cookies to thicken the sauce. She ended the night by handing each child a *pfeffernüsse*, a pepper nut cookie.

"Now, put that under your pillow and make a wish," she instructed. "Santa will grant it." Dad overheard. I was eight, and well beyond Santa. But I knew he still believed.

"Did you hear that, Daddy?" I asked him.

"Yes, so be careful with it," he said, as the hostess handed him his beer stein, now emptied and cleaned. "You don't want to waste a wish from Santa."

I handed him my cookie as I pulled on my wool mittens. "Of course, Daddy, I would never waste a wish from Santa."

Thanks to D.A.N.K., we spent time in Frankenmuth, a historical German settlement in lower central Michigan.

Frankenmuth is a bit of a curiosity. Called Michigan's "Little Bavaria," the entire town is built with alpine architecture. The restaurants, inns, shops, and even a couple of the banks look like ski chalets with their off-white exteriors, steep roofs, and half-timbered façades. Every other store's name seems to involve the word *Haus*.

In the mid-1800s, a popular German preacher decided to send members of his congregation to the American Midwest to offer spiritual guidance to Lutheran settlers in the region and, while they were at it, convert the Chippewa nation to Christianity. Through an acquaintance living in Ohio, the pastor discovered the lush Saginaw Valley and decided that's where he'd set up his colony of Franks, the name of people from the Franconia region where his church resided. He dubbed the whole effort *frankenmuth*, "the courage of the franks."

Today, more than three million visitors flood into Frankenmuth to partake in a seemingly endless string of festivals. They visit the quaint shops, drink freshly brewed beer at the brewery, and visit Bronner's Christmas Wonderland, which proclaims to be "the largest Christmas store on earth."

But like us with D.A.N.K., most people go for the food.

Frankenmuth restaurants offer the traditional schnitzel, sauerbraten, and bratwurst dishes, but most people flock there for the family-style fried chicken dinners. The dinners come with noodle soup, salad, creamy coleslaw, fruit preserves, and *stollen*, a fruit and nut bread. The chicken has a strong dose of paprika, not unlike Uncle Clarence's version. Best of all are the sides of hot German potato salad, studded with bacon and tossed in a vinegary dressing. Something about the tartness of the sour vinaigrette combined with the salt of the bacon hits just the right note in the back of the mouth.

The first of May took on a whole new importance as we became involved with the annual May Day weekend in Frankenmuth. Thanks to D.A.N.K., each of us had a role in the town's biggest parade. Dad carried the ceremonial Maypole, a canopy-like structure he held up with a holster while Joyce and I danced around it with other girls who were, in fact, at least part German. My brothers and my cousin Steve walked in the parade proudly holding German flags. As a kid, absolutely nothing was more exciting than being in a parade.

But none of us experienced D.A.N.K. quite like Sandy.

Every year as part of the May Day festivities, they held a Miss D.A.N.K. contest. To qualify, candidates had to take a test that covered German history and geography, and there was a section on the definition of German words. Sandy had never been to Germany, and aside from what she'd gleaned from our encyclopedia studies, she knew nothing about the country's heritage. In high school, she studied French. She didn't speak a word of German.

Sandy took the test but was convinced she had failed. Without revealing her score on the test, the president called to tell her that she had made it into the finals. At a pre–May Day dinner at a local dance hall, she performed the song "Willkommen" from the film *Cabaret* with the four other contenders for Miss D.A.N.K. Sandy had blossomed into a beautiful young woman. She had a certain poise from years of studying baton and performing as a majorette with the marching band.

When the moment came to announce the winner, no one was more stunned than she when they placed the crown on her head. Finally Sandy had an official excuse to wear a tiara.

The next day at the May Day parade, while I danced around the

Maypole, she sat in a convertible wearing a white dress, a blue sash across her chest declaring her "Miss D.A.N.K." She had practiced her wave.

Within a month, she was expected to go on to the national competition in Chicago, the home of D.A.N.K. headquarters. The Flint chapter would provide an all-expenses-paid weekend in the city with Mom as an escort.

Sandy refused to go.

"Mom, I'm not going to do it. They ask you questions in German. I don't even speak it, and all those girls are fluent."

"But we could go to Chicago," Mom said, making an appeal.

Sandy rolled her eyes. "Don't make me go. I only took the test to make you and Dad happy. I'm not going to embarrass myself. Plus, it wouldn't be right. I'm not even German."

Sandy manufactured an excuse. She gathered up the tiara and the sash and drove them the two hours to Frankenmuth to deliver them to the first runner-up.

"Oh, *danke*, Sandy, *danke*, for driving all the way here," the girl said as she answered the door. She cradled the tiara and the sash in her arm. "I wish you could go to Chicago. You're so pretty, you would surely win."

The girl's parents and grandparents had been members of the German club since its first year; she'd been crestfallen when she came in second place. At that moment, looking at the happy teen's face, Sandy knew she had done the right thing. Being Miss D.A.N.K. didn't mean as much to her as it did to the girl standing in the doorway.

"*Danke* to you," Sandy said. "My family loves being a part of D.A.N.K."

Hot German Potato Salad

This makes enough for a crowd, so halve it if desired. Cook the potatoes and fry the bacon a day in advance and it's a cinch to pull together. It might save time, but do not be lured into microwaving the potatoes, lest you end up with a gummy, unappetizing result. The leftovers can be refrigerated for up to 5 days and gently reheated in the oven, but do not freeze. You'll need a big baking dish for this, such as a 10-by-15-inch glass baker.

Makes 8 to 10 side servings

> 3 pounds (1.5 kg) Idaho or Yukon Gold potatoes (about 6 to 8 large
>   potatoes)
> 8 ounces (230 g) thick-sliced bacon
> 5 stalks celery, finely chopped (1¼ cups)
> 1 medium onion, finely chopped (1 cup)
> 1½ cups (360 ml) water
> ½ cup (120 ml) white wine vinegar or apple cider vinegar
> ½ teaspoon (2.5 ml) celery seed
> 1½ teaspoons (7.5 ml) coarse salt
> ½ teaspoon (2.5 ml) coarsely ground pepper

Scrub the potatoes well. Cut them into quarters with their peels still on. Put the potatoes into a 4-quart (4-L) or larger pot and cover with cold water. Bring to a boil over high heat, then drop the heat to medium-high and cook at a low boil until the potatoes are just barely tender when you pierce them with a paring knife, 15 to 20 minutes. Drain the potatoes and let them cool until you can handle them. While they're still warm, remove and discard the peels and cut them into bite-sized pieces. Put them in a large baking dish. This can be done a day ahead; let the potatoes cool completely, cover the dish with plastic, and refrigerate.

While the potatoes are cooking and cooling, fry the bacon in a large skillet until crispy. As it cooks, cover a plate with several layers of paper towels. Use a slotted spoon to remove the bacon to the plate and let the bacon cool. Pour the bacon grease into a heatproof container. If cooking the bacon ahead of time, transfer it to a separate container, cover, and refrigerate. If you're finishing the dish right then, don't bother to wash the skillet.

Preheat the oven to 375ºF (190ºC). If you cooked the potatoes and bacon ahead of time, take them out of the refrigerator to come to room temperature.

Measure out about 3 tablespoons (45 ml) of the bacon grease into the skillet. Add the celery and onion and cook over medium heat, stirring occasionally, until softened, about 7 minutes. Add the water, vinegar, celery seed, salt, and pepper and simmer for a minute or so. Pour everything over the potatoes, using a rubber spatula to get the last bit of it. Crumble the bacon into small pieces with your fingers as you add it to the potatoes. Stir gently but thoroughly to mix the sauce and bacon throughout the potatoes.

Bake for about 35 minutes or until the potatoes seem tender and falling apart. About halfway through, taste to see if it needs more salt; add some if it does, stirring again to distribute. Serve warm.

CHAPTER 15

Sunshine State

Dad on Anna Maria Island, Florida, 1976

The car is packed," Mom said, hands on hips. "Tomorrow at noon, it's leaving for Florida whether you're in it or not."

My dad wasn't opposed to vacations. He was just solidly against vacations that weren't in Michigan and didn't revolve around fishing. Friends at the *Flint Journal* had a second home in Florida and kept talking about their great times there. In dreary February, a week near a beach sounded great to Mom. Plus it would be their first weeklong vacation alone since they had children.

Dad fought the idea from the start. "C'mon, Florida isn't all that great," he'd say, an ineffective argument given he'd never been there. Mom can be intractable. After making one last plea to stay and go ice fishing, Dad relented and got in the car.

The drive from Michigan to Florida is essentially a straight shot south on I-75. If you drive nonstop it's about twenty hours from Flint to Tampa. Dad insisted on doing all the driving himself. They spent the first night in Kentucky. The next day, he stopped short of their final destination and they overnighted in Ocala, a couple of hours away.

At long last, they drove across the small bridge that leads from Bradenton to Anna Maria Island, a small barrier key about seven miles long in the Gulf of Mexico. In 1976, it was a sleepy place, its housing primarily sturdy low-slung cinder-block bungalows scattered amid swaying palms. The residents were mainly blue-collar or middle-class retirees. A portion of the island was set aside as a nature preserve thick with mangroves, the water teeming with waterfowl.

They found the small inn Mom's friends recommended and scored a room directly overlooking the gulf and its powdery white sand beach.

Coming from the snow-laden Midwest in February, the subtropical landscape of the island was such a dramatic shift, they could have landed on the moon. Sitting on their deck, they witnessed the slow descent of the sun and people walking back and forth on the sand, a beach otherwise populated with a handful of sunbathers. They sat there through the evening, nursing beers and cold wine procured from a local market, as they watched the crescent moon rise in the ink-dark sky. They left the windows open and fell asleep to the sound of the surf.

The next morning, they explored the island some more. The small local plaza had a store with the name Inez while the other was Irene's Resort Wear. Mom saw these as a good omen.

Finally they hit the Rod & Reel Pier at the north end. Dad walked out along the wood planks to the end. A dozen people sat

quietly fishing on the pier. Seagulls swooped by, pelicans splashed
into the gentle waves, and a boat drove past in the water.

"I want to live here the rest of my life," he declared to my mother.

🍓

They spread the *Islander* newspaper on a table at Duffy's, then located across from the public county beach.* The joint was a rustic
open-air beer and burger shack with chicken wire in place of windows and a polyurethane-encased wood bar that spanned the width
of the small building. Picnic tables and random beat-up tables and
chairs were crammed inside for communal seating. With the decor
an eclectic mix of old license plates and yellowing dollar bills signed
by the patrons and outdoor restrooms one step above a privy, it was
just the kind of place where Mom and Dad would feel at home.
They sold cheap beer in frosted mugs and burgers made from a mix
of ground sirloin and chuck that savvy patrons ordered "all the
way," with mayo, lettuce, pickles, and onion. The menu advertised
the navy bean soup was "made fresh daily with a new bone."

"Wow, listen to this," Mom said. Reading from the paper, she
began: "'If you like country living, come peek into the windows of
this house . . .'" She looked up. "How odd is that?" She went back
to the ad. The house was a duplex (which meant it had two units)
nestled on a generous double lot with fruit trees, room for a pool or
a generous garden, plus a boat dock in a canal across the street.
There was an address, but no phone number.

"There would be a place for the boat!" Dad said excitedly. "Let's
go look."

They finished their beers and rushed out. The house sat on a
corner lot across from the marina on a public canal. Orange and
mango trees dotted the property; the latter Mom and Dad had
neither seen nor eaten. As the ad suggested, they peered into all the

---

*Duffy's relocated to a different location in Holmes Beach, but still features the
same menu. A burger joint called Skinny's occupies its former space, where the
decor and feel are essentially the same as they were in the 1970s. No matter which
one you visit, tell them I sent you.

windows. Like most of the homes on the island in 1976, it was little more than a rectangular box made from concrete blocks, a requirement of strident local hurricane-minded building codes. From what they could make out, the larger unit had two small bedrooms, one bathroom, and a galley kitchen. In the rear was a generous porch, its walls comprised entirely of louvered windows.* The ad called it a Florida room. To my Michigan-born parents, it sounded exotic.

The smaller unit appeared to have one tiny bedroom and a minuscule bathroom accessed from the outside by a door. They puzzled on this until they figured that it was designed that way so you could go straight to the shower from the beach. They marveled at the fruit. Mom even plucked a heavy lemon right off one of the trees. "It's like the orchard on the farm, but with citrus!" she said.

Enchanted, they decided on the spot that they wanted to buy it—without even stepping inside. Why not? They decided to rent a farmhouse before they knew it had working heat and water pipes. But no one appeared at home. Maybe there had been a name of a real estate agent? They couldn't recall. They went back to their car and searched through the *Islander*. But they couldn't find the ad.

So they went by the newspaper's small office and asked for a couple of back copies, thinking perhaps they had somehow been looking at an older paper. The ad didn't turn up. Stumped, they went back to Duffy's for another burger and a beer to figure out what to do next. They had seen towels drying on a chair off the Florida room. It looked like someone lived there.

They went to the house the next morning. As they arrived, they noticed a car pasted with the magnetic placard for a real estate company. A woman in a beige polyester skirted suit struggled to plant a FOR SALE sign in the front yard. My parents hit the brakes, jumped from the car, and rushed to her.

"Oh, we're so glad we found you!" Mom blurted. "We loved your

---

*These were jalousie windows, featuring parallel glass panes set into a frame that open and shut in unison. They're typically controlled by a crank. They were common on homes built in the 1950s and 1960s in Florida and the Caribbean. They allow the windows to be open during rainstorms.

ad and we want to see the inside of the house. We think it could be perfect for us."

The woman, sweaty in the early morning Florida heat and flustered by the sudden appearance of such enthusiastic clients, balanced the sign against her hip. She swept a blond lock out of her eyes. "Ad?" she asked, wrinkling up her face. "We haven't done an ad for this house yet. It just went on the market this morning." My parents exchanged glances. They were both sure they had seen the now mysterious ad. "But I'll show you inside if you want."

They had guessed the interior correctly. The real estate agent explained that an elderly couple rented the larger unit. Dad nodded. "See, it already generates income," he told my mom. "We can keep the smaller unit for us when we spend time here." Mom stifled a laugh at the thought of how barely a week ago, Dad had been dead set against even *visiting* Florida. By the time they walked out of the house, they were discussing how they'd get the down payment together to buy it. After all, they had two kids in college and another two headed in the same direction. Buying a second home was just crazy.

"I'll do whatever it takes," my dad assured her. "I'll even sell my boat."

They shocked the agent by insisting they put an offer on paper right there. She'd never had an offer on a house within the first hour it went on sale. She rifled through her backseat for the paperwork and they filled it out on the hood of her car. The asking price was $54,000. Dad offered $48,000. He figured the owner would counter with $52,000. They gave her a $250 check as "earnest money." The agent said she'd give it to the owners. They told her they'd go to Duffy's and she could call them there with the news.

Mom and Dad sat nervously on the aging vinyl stools at the bar trying to ignore the black rotary phone hanging on the wall. They barely talked, instead focusing on their beers in frosty mugs.

Then the phone rang.

The proprietor, Pat Geyer, was a kind, heavy-set woman with gray hair pulled back in a bun. They'd visited the place every day that week and she knew them on sight now. She picked up the phone and yelled, "Duffy's!" Then she handed it to Dad. "Milt, it's for you."

Dad took the phone. "You've bought a house," the agent said. The owners hadn't counteroffered. They'd be closing in thirty days.

"By the way, I'm not sure how you found it," the agent said. "I checked. We never did put an ad in the paper."

Back in Michigan, my parents tried to explain how they bought a house on a whim. "It reminded us of the farm," they told everyone. How a concrete bungalow on a subtropical island could do such a thing, no one could figure out.

True to his word, Dad sold his beloved fishing boat. All of our family vacations now involved packing up the car and heading south on I-75. We'd drive at least ten hours the first day. "You can never stop before Knoxville," was Dad's mantra. "Otherwise, you can't get to the island the next day before sunset." Usually he'd press on to Chattanooga, perched on the edge of the Tennessee-Georgia border. On the drive from Michigan to Florida, Georgia's a mentally tough place to get through. Beyond a brief, exciting stint through Atlanta, if you stick to I-75, you're rewarded with three hundred charmless miles of six-lane traffic flanked by an endless string of massive billboards featuring cheap motels, fast food chains, strip joints, and the next Cracker Barrel location—a combination that ruins any possibility to admire the state's natural beauty. So invariably, we'd cheer when we saw the sign that declared WEL-COME TO THE SUNSHINE STATE. But even then, it took another five hours before we hit the turnoff to I-275 toward the Sunshine Skyway, heading toward Bradenton.

When they drove to and from California, they took a leisurely pace with plenty of stops to let the kids play. With just me in the backseat most of the time, the drive with Mom and Dad was nothing short of an endurance exercise. We packed up Mom's new Buick Regal and left by seven A.M. on the first day, by six A.M. on the second. Dad would stop three times a day for gas. Any feeding or peeing that needed to be done had to be completed in those three breaks.

On our first drive south, radio proved infuriating. They would find a decent country music station, but after a few hours it started to fade. Then Mom could tune in only rock- or disco-based stations playing standards by KISS, the Bee Gees, or KC and the Sunshine Band.

"That's not even real music," Dad scoffed, finally snapping off the radio in the middle of "Shake Your Booty." He reached under the seat to his limited supply of eight-track tapes. We listened to the same handful of eight-track tapes on every drive afterward, all the songs burned indelibly on our memories forever.

Their favorite was a two-tape country music collection. It had all my parents' old and new country favorites: "Sixteen Tons" by Tennessee Ernie Ford, "How Far Is Heaven" by Kitty Wells, and "Tennessee Waltz" by Patti Page. For variety, Dad played two other eight-tracks, Johnny Cash's *At Folsom Prison* and *John Denver's Great Hits*. Every so often, Dad put in Gordon Lightfoot's *Summertime Dream* and listened to the track with "The Wreck of the *Edmund Fitzgerald*" over and over again.

On one trip, after listening to the mysterious tale of the big tanker's sinking on the lake the Chippewa called Gitche Gumee more than fourteen times in a row, Mom declared, "Honey, that's enough" and snapped the tape from the player. When she fell asleep just north of Macon, he quietly popped the eight-track back in again and turned the volume down low.

To help pay the mortgage, they kept renting out the larger portion of the house, so all of us had to pile into the one-bedroom unit. On one of our first trips, Dad hauled down all our camping gear. Mom and Dad commandeered the small double bed in the tiny bedroom while we kids camped out in our sleeping bags on the floor or crawled into a tent set up in the backyard.

We brought down an inflatable yellow raft from Michigan that my brothers and sister had used in high school for outings at Holloway Dam. At low tide, we'd take it to our dock and all the kids would pile in, paddle down the canal, and then stop in a small bay on the Intercoastal Waterway. We'd get out of the raft and dig for clams under our feet. Then we'd load back into the raft with a bucket of clams and row slowly back home, where Milt and Mom would make a big pot of clam chowder.

We stocked up on supplies at the IGA on the north end of the island, which was then run by an old-timer named Ernie. An old-school grocery with limited selection, the deli and candy options were the best around. The short white-haired Ernie would stand at the antique register while chomping on a cigar. He'd share old vaudeville jokes.

"So a doctor gives a man six months to live," he'd say, then pause. "Man couldn't pay his bill. What does the doctor do?" Another pause, a chomp on his cigar. "He gave him another six months."

Dad loved learning about fishing in an entirely new climate. We all got outfitted for new poles at the Discount Fishing Tackle store on the island. Almost daily my dad would head to the Rod & Reel Pier. From there, you could see the dark blue outline of the old Sunshine Skyway Bridge crossing Tampa Bay. Barges would head in and out of the traffic lane to and from the Gulf of Mexico. Every day as we arrived, he'd say, "You know, the gulf was formed about three hundred million years ago by plate tectonics," or some other fact he'd learned from the *World Book* encyclopedia.

In Michigan, all of us had grown up putting slippery, slimy worms on our hooks. In Florida, we had to face a new bait reality: live shrimp. The sharp shells of the shrimp cut our hands at first, and they wriggled in the bait pail in a most disturbing fashion. You could see their eyes, their organs, and the fluid in their bodies through their translucent shells. The first time I hooked one, the ridges of its shell biting into my hand, I pulled it up for a look. It reminded me of the anatomical drawings in the encyclopedias. Its small eyes, stuck to antennae, sought me out.

The smart shrimp wriggled out of my novice grip and dropped into the water. Even in Florida, Dad's no-wimp policy remained intact.

"What's taking you so long to bait that hook?" Dad asked the first day we went fishing.

To cover my dread about impaling the shrimp, I asked, "What's the best way to put these on a hook?" He explained the idea was that you had to somehow ensnare the shrimp, hopefully not killing it, so that its frantic pained-by-a-hook-in-the-back movement would attract fish. I reached into our bucket, pulled out a sharp-shelled fluttering shrimp, and without engaging eye contact, stuck my hook in its crusty, clear backside. I felt terrible. Worse, I didn't catch anything. I pulled it up after hours of fishing to find it hanging limply, thoroughly dead, on my hook.

The other option was to buy frozen bricks of squid. These could be found next to the ice cream at the Foodway, the island's other grocery store. If that wasn't unsettling enough, the first time we opened a package we immediately saw the glaring, accusing eye of the squid, as if it knew our plan was to cut up its body into small strips and weave them onto our hooks.

For years, I couldn't bring myself to eat calamari or shrimp.

Dad was the kind of guy who could start up a conversation with anyone. He nursed draft beers in plastic cups and smoked Kent cigarettes and learned all about saltwater lures along with fishing for the elusive snook and prized groupers from the guys at the dock or at Bortell's, a casual pool joint not far from the pier. The men would share gory tales of late-night shark fishing and run-ins with barracudas.

Sometimes we ate breakfast *and* lunch at the pier. Dad never got sunburned, but instead developed a dark ruddy tan over the course of just a few days. Mom and I had a propensity to burn easily, so we'd hide our pasty Midwest skin under wide-brimmed hats and long sleeves.

My brothers got into the fishing action. Milt even learned to use a throw net for mullet, the fish that in many ways is responsible for people moving to that part of Florida. We learned this about mullet early on in a visit to Cortez, now the only working fishing village left in Florida and one of few fishing areas to earn a distinction on the National Register of Historic Places.

Cortez combined two of my father's favorite interests: fishing and history. Nestled on the coastline on the mainland just over the bridge from the island, Cortez is a rustic village that feels a bit like a living postcard from a bygone era, from the quaint clapboard houses, the boats up on blocks in front yards, to the rusting crab traps piled in side yards. Dad made friends with some of the locals there and sat enraptured by their stories. He'd buy beers and chat with rugged-faced fishermen as they told tales of how the plentiful supply of mullet drew the first settlers well before the Civil War. At first, they concentrated on drying mullet for shipment to Cuba. Later, the introduction of iced train cars allowed them to ship fresh fish up north.

The first year we visited the island, we went to the annual Cortez Fishing Festival. A local happily supplied me with a Cortez dog, a cornmeal-crusted deep-fried fillet of mullet placed in a hot dog bun with spicy tartar sauce. We were dazzled by the festival's signature dessert, "strawberry shortcake," featuring sliced berries suspended in red Jell-O. The star attraction was local oysters roasted over an open wood fire.

Elsewhere on the island, we became connoisseurs of grouper sandwiches, a local specialty in which the classic preparation fillets are dipped in buttermilk batter, topped with dill mayonnaise, and served with tomatoes and onion on a hamburger bun.

We'd hit the beach in the late afternoon. We built sand castles of ridiculous scale. Then we'd walk a mile or so down to the public beach, use the bathrooms, and walk back home at sunset. On one of these walks, we encountered a white egret standing motionless in the gentle surf as the sun dipped behind the waves against a crimson sky. We all stopped to marvel at the elegant, beautiful creature. It looked directly at us curiously, and then, with a noble turn of the head, looked back into the water. Dad quieted us.

"These are my favorite birds here on the island," he said. "You know, my friend Bill Wilson, the one who is part Chippewa, used to say that Native Americans revered herons. A lot of tribes and some African cultures believe that an egret has the ability to communicate with the heavens." The bird spread it enormous wings. Dad smiled. "He's a good fisherman," he said, motioning us to start walking. "He's trying to tell us we're scaring the fish."

The hardest part of a trip to Florida was the sad mood Dad

would get into the day before we had to leave. He loved Michigan, but the island was something else.

"Sometimes you just find the place where your soul lives," Dad told me once as we stood on the beach to say good-bye to the island before heading north. "I think mine lives here."

Clam Chowder

Hot chowder on a chilly day was a highlight of many family fishing expeditions. Mom served this with either hot buttered bread or oyster crackers. I add vinegar to provide a more complex flavor, but it's optional. Bacon and clams can be salty on their own, so go light on the salt early in the cooking process and add more at the very end if needed. Mom says, "I liked to finish it off with a lot of ground black pepper."

Makes about eight 1-cup (240-ml) servings

> Four 6.5-ounce (184-g) cans minced clams
> 6 thick-cut bacon slices (6 ounces/170 g)
> 1 large onion (340 g), diced (2½ cups)
> 1½ pounds (680 g) potatoes, peeled and diced
> 6 stalks celery (300 g), diced (1 cup/250 ml)
> 2 tablespoons (30 ml) flour
> 2 cups (500 ml) water, plus more if needed
> ½ teaspoon (2.5 ml) salt
> Several grinds of black pepper
> 4 tablespoons (60 g) unsalted butter
> 3 cups (750 ml) whole milk or half-and-half
> 1 tablespoon (15 ml) red wine vinegar (optional)
> 1 tablespoon (15 ml) chopped fresh dill or 1 teaspoon (5 ml) dried dill
>   (optional)

Open the cans of clams and drain the juice into a cup. Set aside the clams and juice separately.

In a 5-quart or larger stockpot or Dutch oven, cook the bacon until crisp. Remove the bacon from the pan and set aside. When cool, crumble it roughly.

Add the onion, potatoes, and celery to the bacon fat and cook until they begin to soften, about 5 minutes. Sprinkle the flour over the vegetables and stir to coat. Add the reserved clam juice, water, salt, and pepper. Scrape any brown bits off the bottom. Top off with additional water if needed to cover. Cook over medium heat, partially covered, until the vegetables are tender, about 15 minutes.

Using a spoon or masher, break up the potatoes until most are crumbling and some are mashed, to start to thicken the chowder. Add the butter and milk and bring just to a boil, then drop to a simmer. Cook, uncovered, for about 35 minutes, until thickened. If it gets too thick, add a bit of milk.

Just before serving, stir in the clams. Add the vinegar, if using, and let cook for a couple of minutes, until any obvious acidic taste mellows. Taste to see if it needs more salt. Finish with a generous dose of freshly ground pepper. Add the dill, if using. You can add the crumbled bacon atop each serving or stir directly into the pot of chowder.

CHAPTER 16

Veterans of Foreign Wars

Dad in Korea, about 1950

On Sunday nights after we moved to Hill Street, my dad and I had a standing date at the local VFW post in Davison. I looked forward to it all week. I could have Shirley Temples and eat all the free popcorn I wanted from the machine behind the bar in the post's basement. The decor was midcentury cheap fishing lodge with faux wood paneling and Miller Lite neon signs. Above the small wood dance floor in the corner, someone hastily erected a mirror ball, a nod to the emerging disco craze.

We sat on the worn orange vinyl chairs at a table at the edge of the dance floor. Dad smoked his Kent cigarettes and drank Miller drafts. The draw on Sunday nights was discounted beer and a live band led by a guy who tried to sound like Elvis and who had a shaggy haircut that Dad referred to as "hippie hair."

Sometimes my mom came and nursed a glass of Boone's Farm red wine in between dances with Dad, while other nights one or both of my oldest brothers would join in. By the time I was seven, Milt and Doug were of legal drinking age in Michigan. I could stay until nine P.M., when state law required that kids had to be out of the bar. I wondered, what happened after nine P.M.? Some secret, deviant behavior, perhaps? In retrospect, it was probably wise to get me out of there before watching veterans who didn't have day jobs get increasingly drunk.

My parents' favorite song to dance to was "Release Me," which made no sense when you listened to the lyrics, an impassioned plea to be allowed to leave a relationship to spend time with a true love. It was the theme song for lovers involved in an illicit tryst, not two longtime married types. Yet, they would dance to the song cheek to cheek, laughing and even kissing. Apparently, Dad just liked the melody, and thought the rhythmic beat perfect for their swaying kind of dancing. Sometimes he'd make up his own lyrics and softly sing them into my mother's ear:

"Please, my darling, never let me go,
for I couldn't love you any more.
My life with you is so much fun,
stay with me, my darling, till the end."

The hippie-haired Elvis sang a lot of the King's songs, invariably starting the first set with "Blue Suede Shoes." They also played more contemporary songs, such as "Bad, Bad Leroy Brown" by Jim Croce, "Turn the Page" by Bob Seger, and the full catalog of Charlie Rich. Invariably, the entire bar would sing along when they played "My Way" just before the nine o'clock break. Dad always considered it "his" song. A lot of other veterans felt the same way.

All of Dad's brothers had been in the military. While his own father never served, the other Flint men had fought in wars going back to Hiram Flint, my great-great-grandfather, who fought for the Union with the 19th Ohio Infantry during the Civil War.

One Sunday night, Dad and I were sitting alone when a guy with a weathered face in a worn blue plaid shirt came by and sat at our table.

"Heard your wife was the sister of Clarence Henderson," he said. Clarence was Mom's older brother. "I was stationed with him in Korea. I lost track of him after the war. What's he up to?"

Dad looked distressed. "Gosh, I hate to tell you, but he was hit by a car a few years ago," he said, genuinely saddened. "But really, if I'm going to be honest, he died in Korea."

The guy nodded thoughtfully. He didn't seem surprised. "So sorry to hear that," he replied solemnly. "He was a good guy." He lifted his can of Pabst Blue Ribbon in the air in a quiet salute. Dad nodded and held his draft mug of Miller aloft as well, and the man moved on.

When Clarence was finishing high school, my mother once watched him let a fly out of the house rather than kill it. Somehow, this guy who literally couldn't kill a fly ended up in the army infantry on the front lines in Korea, often referred to as the forgotten war.

The horrors of the war weighed heavily on Clarence. Mom, then in her teens, could see through his false bravado in his early letters home. When he wrote once that he felt lonely, she started to write him a letter every single day.

One of those letters saved his life.

Clarence was in a foxhole just south of the border with seven other soldiers when the mail call came. "Henderson! Mail!" a corporal snarled loudly.

The others in his foxhole looked up. It had been more than a week since anyone showered, and now they sat huddled in too-hot gear for the cool autumn weather. Another soldier yelled, "Anything for me?"

"No, only Henderson," the soldier replied, looking down into the hole. "Well, move it, soldier!"

As Clarence readied to exit the hole, the other soldiers made catcalls. "What, you got a girl back home? You never say who is writing you," one said.

Another said, "Aw, leave him alone. So what if he's got a girl?"

"I'll be right back," Clarence assured them.

The ranking officer kept scouring the horizon with binoculars. "You bet you will," he said without looking back. "Get going."

Clarence scooted from the hole and hopped through a labyrinth of camouflage-draped tents to get to the mailbag. Just as he started back, someone shouted, "INCOMING!" He heard the whistle of the mortar and instinctively hit the dirt. The bomb crashed directly into the foxhole with Clarence's squad. All seven men he'd left less than five minutes earlier had been blown apart. Clarence reported to my mother that there was nothing left of the men in his group, just blood and body parts.

After that incident, the tone of his letters changed. Clarence wrote to my mother about the difficulty of fighting an enemy that rarely wore uniforms. As in Vietnam, the bad guys looked identical to the "good" guys. Little children carried hand grenades that they would throw at the U.S. soldiers in public places. Clarence had seen more than a half dozen men blown apart by children with weapons. "But what do you do, shoot a kid?" he wrote to my mother.

When he returned from the war, Clarence was never the same. He suffered from posttraumatic stress disorder, but doctors didn't understand much about the condition in those days. He had flashbacks to scenes from the war. Clarence would go days without sleeping just to avoid bad dreams. He spent eight months at a Veterans Administration hospital to deal with stress-related ulcers that so severely damaged his stomach that doctors cut portions out.

Clarence tried to keep it together once he left the hospital. He got married, had children, and held a steady job until the Eisenhower recession hit in 1958. In 1960, he went to California to investigate whether he should consider moving his family out west, and worked briefly in my parents' start-up Italian restaurant. His wife decided she didn't want to leave Michigan so they stayed put.

Over the next few years, to combat his nightmares and flashbacks, Clarence started drinking and slid into alcoholism. By the late 1960s, he'd lost everything—his home, his wife and children— and was living at a Salvation Army homeless shelter. One evening, he was going up to visit his parents at the Sanford Farm.

Hitchhiking to the local train station, he crossed the street to reach someone who stopped to give him a ride. A young soldier home on leave from Vietnam didn't see my uncle until a split second too late. The GI hit him, killing him instantly.

The coroner reported that Clarence was completely sober when he died.

After his funeral, Mom and Dad sat up late talking. "Your brother died in the war, honey," Dad told her. "His body came home, but he wasn't himself anymore. I see guys like that at the VFW. It's a form of casualty no one counts."

Days after the service, Grandpa answered a knock at the Sanford Farm to find a young man in an army uniform. "You won't like me," the soldier started. "I'm the one who killed your son."

Grandpa responded by opening the door and embracing the stranger in his arms. The soldier cried on his shoulder. "I'm so sorry," he sobbed. "I really didn't see him."

They led him into the house, where Grandma Inez fed him some lemon meringue pie. She talked to him gently and assured him that they knew it was an accident. As he left, she hugged him. Then she held him by both shoulders and looked him in the eye.

"Don't carry this with you," Grandma Inez urged him. "There are things you can control in your life, and this isn't one of them."

My cousin Diane was Clarence's daughter. Mom took her in to live with us for a couple of years when Clarence was in the shelter and her mother couldn't manage her kids and work full time. She was living with her older sister when she learned her father died.

Based on Clarence's story and his own experiences in Korea, Dad was against any of his children signing up for the military. If any of his sons got drafted, Dad said he'd drive them over the border to Canada. One night, my eighteen-year-old brother Doug told my father that he was thinking of joining the marines after high school. It was 1974 and the war in Vietnam was still going on.

"Really? Well, that's an interesting idea," Dad said brightly. "Let's go and have a beer to discuss it, son." He grabbed Milt and Doug and they walked over to Madden's Lounge, an old-school bar around the corner. Hours later, after the bar closed, they walked home. All three were completely drunk. I woke up to find Mom in her robe in the living room, trying to get Doug to drink some water.

Weaving back and forth on his feet, Doug announced that he'd decided against going into the service. He was going to college after all. "Don't wanna be . . . not gonna end up . . . in a *straitjacket*," he slurred, nearly spitting out the last word. Then he put a hand over his mouth and ran for the bathroom. Dad followed. Milt slinked off to sleep on a couch in the family room.

"Straitjacket?" I asked Mom. "What does that mean?"

She looked at me with a blank face. "Go back to bed," was all she said.

When my dad was twenty-four, police arrived at a gas station and put him in a straitjacket. He thought the "gooks" were coming to get him. He spent three months in a military mental hospital.

Dad joined the 1st Marine Division in 1947. Just after World War II, it was a relatively peaceful period and Dad had little reason to think he'd see serious action.

He was immediately shipped to China, where battle continued after the war. He was among the marines who helped the last of the Allied refugees escape from China before it fell under Communist rule, perched atop a train car with his Browning Automatic Rifle.

In late June, he was among the first boots on the ground for the UN police action. When Seoul fell to North Korean forces, he was positioned again with his rifle on one of the last trains to leave the city.

On an unseasonably cold June day in 1951, Dad's platoon was ambushed by Communist Chinese soldiers fighting on the part of North Korea at Hangnyong. The enemy forces had the advantage of surprise and higher ground, shooting down on his team, who started to drop like flies around him. Dad was hit in his left side by shrapnel from a hand grenade that exploded near him. Knocked to the ground and disoriented, he heard the exchange of gunfire above him. He'd fallen next to a slight rock shelf. He dragged himself under it for protection from the gunfire.

He held still and listened as the barrage slowed and finally stopped. An eerie quiet blanketed the area. Moments later, mud-heavy footsteps trudged toward him. He hoped it was fellow marines.

But the voices that he heard were speaking Chinese.

Next came the sickening sound of what he assumed was a bayonet piercing through flesh. As he instinctively twisted to reach for any weapon he might have, a sharp flash of pain erupted in his side. His hand found a slick of warm liquid that he realized was his own blood. Dad held his breath as he listened helplessly to the enemy soldiers walk among his fallen unit. The worst pain was the thought that there was nothing he could do to help them.

Then his hand came upon something else. Somehow he managed to pull the pin and hurl the grenade over the ledge toward the voices before falling unconscious.

He awoke later shivering. He was in enemy territory and completely alone, as far as he knew. He had no access to food, water, or a weapon, plus he was injured. His legs went numb, then his arms.

Silently, he thought: *God, if I'm ever where it's warm and no one is trying to kill me, I promise to be happy and never want more than that.*

Then he heard the distant sound of a helicopter. It grew louder and landed not far away. A voice shouted out, "Marines!?"

Retrieving wounded comrades from the field of fire is a Marine Corps tradition more sacred than life. Dad yelled out, surprised to hear his voice crack. Marines from another unit in his platoon ran to him and lifted him out.

"We've got you, you're going home," a voice said.

Just then, he passed out.

He woke up in a field hospital. The shrapnel had been surgically removed from his side. Seriously injured, Dad had the option of being discharged early. Instead, once his wounds healed, he insisted on going back into combat. He was wounded once more before heading home.

When he came home from the war, Dad seemed well enough. He had bad dreams, but he accepted that they were a lasting souvenir of his time in Korea. His final injury was a head wound that left a soft area where a part of his skull had to be removed.

One day he stopped by a gas station and offered to help a friend fix a car up on a rack. Dad hit his head, prompting a complete sensory flashback to the war. He grabbed a long pry bar and held it like a gun, hiding behind the counter for cover. He kept talking about "the gooks," the derogatory slang the marines used for the Communist Korean soldiers. His friend tried talking to him. Dad called him David, the name of a friend killed that day he lay injured.

Someone called the police. Dad confused them with armed enemy soldiers. He held the pry bar like a rifle. A trained marksman, Dad couldn't figure out why they were still standing. "I shot you, gook!" he kept saying. "Why aren't you falling!"

After some plotting, the police called the local mental hospital. Six officers stormed the gas station where Dad was holding out. One sprayed him with pepper spray, while the others secured him in a straitjacket. He spent months in the mental hospital recovering. He never had another incident, but the worry over an episode like that reoccurring never faded.

Dad told my mother about the gas station incident after he proposed. He wanted her to know that it had happened, and said he'd understand if she didn't want to marry him once she knew. Mom had seen what the war did to Clarence. If anything, it drew her closer to my father.

"The only time I ever heard him talk about the war was when Uncle Clarence died," Mom says. He earned several medals, including two Purple Hearts, yet he never displayed or talked about them. The medals stayed in a box at the bottom of his dresser. "He would never say that he was a hero, but that he was just trying to stay alive."

In the end, I wonder if he thought a proverbial line in the sand was worth it. It's not like they knocked communism out of Korea; they just contained it. Apparently, he told Doug and Milt more stories about the horrors of war the night he took them out drinking.

He liked the VFW, in part because the guys never talked about the war. They would chat about fishing or hunting or football. Yet they all quietly knew what soldiers in foreign wars had gone through. They were brothers who had visited a certain kind of hell and lived to talk about it, but they never did. Instead, they sat at the bar, ate popcorn, told jokes, and listened to a hippie-haired kid sing "The Most Beautiful Girl in the World."

Dad loved one other thing about the VFW. He got to cook.

His primary contribution to the post harked back to his days working at That's Amore and, later, The Roman Knight in San Francisco. When the post would host spaghetti dinners as fundraisers in the post's parking lot, Dad would be the one to do all the shopping, chopping, prepping, and cooking. He'd stand over the rented portable stove in the summer heat stirring big pots of spaghetti sauce.

"That's some mighty fine spaghetti, Milt," the men would say in praise.

Dad would say thanks. It was warm, no one was shooting at him, and people liked his food. Life couldn't get any better.

Spaghetti Sauce à la That's Amore

This recipe takes a common tactic used in commercial kitchens and applies it to home cooking. Essentially, you make a "concentrate" using onions, carrots, celery, seasonings, and ground beef, cooked slowly to develop an earthy flavor of its own. This concentrate can then be used as the basis for numerous ready-in-20-minutes tomato-based sauces. For a Cajun-style concentrate, use minced green bell pepper in place of the carrots.

The prep for this goes quickly using a food processor, but if you don't have one, consider it a chance to practice your knife skills. If you want a higher ratio of vegetables to meat, use just a half pound (225 g) of ground beef. This recipe makes 5 to 6 cups (1.25 to 1.5 L) of the concentrate, which can then be frozen in individual airtight containers for up to 3 months. To use, just add 1½ cups (360 ml) of the thawed concentrate to each quart/liter or 28-ounce (794-g) can of tomatoes.

If you want to add other vegetables or seasonings, add them at the start of cooking. They may need additional time to cook until tender.

Makes 5 to 6 cups (1.25 to 1.5 L) concentrate; each 1½ cups yield about 6 servings of sauce for pasta

Concentrate

1 pound (450 g) lean ground beef
2 to 3 tablespoons (30 to 45 ml) olive oil
2 medium yellow onions, about 1½ pounds (675 g), minced
4 large carrots, about ¾ pound (340 g), chopped fine or grated
6 stalks celery, about ¾ pound (340 g), chopped fine
7 garlic cloves, minced
1 teaspoon (5 ml) coarse salt
1 teaspoon (5 ml) ground black pepper
1 cup (250 ml) water
½ cup (125 ml) red wine (leftover is fine)
6 tablespoons (85 g) tomato paste (half of a 6-ounce/170-g can)
½ teaspoon (2.5 ml) red chili flakes (optional)
2 teaspoons (10 ml) dried oregano

Sauce

One 28-ounce (794-g) can crushed tomatoes
5 tablespoons (85 g) tomato paste (half of a 6-ounce/170-g can)
1 cup (250 ml) water
1 bay leaf
1 teaspoon (5 ml) dried mixed Italian herbs or oregano
¾ to 1 teaspoon (3.75 to 5 ml) coarse salt
Few grinds of coarse black pepper
1 teaspoon (5 ml) red wine or balsamic vinegar (optional)
Optional sauce additions: diced green bell pepper, chopped zucchini, sautéed sliced mushrooms, chopped black olives, chopped green olives, diced roasted red pepper, pesto, chopped pepperoni, red chili flakes, hot or smoked paprika, chopped cooked Italian sausage

To make the concentrate: Brown the ground beef over medium heat in a 3-quart (3-L) or larger skillet, stirring to break it up. Remove the beef from the pan, drain out the extra fat, and wipe out the skillet with a paper towel, but leave behind any brown bits at the bottom. Add the olive oil and turn the heat up to high. Once hot, add the onions, carrots, and celery. It will look like a lot of stuff; fear not, it will reduce admirably as it cooks. Cook, stirring occasionally, until the vegetables begin to soften, about 5 minutes. Add the garlic, salt, pepper, water, and wine. Stir well, then turn the heat to medium. Simmer for about 10 minutes, stirring regularly, until the vegetables soften completely. Add the cooked beef, tomato paste, chili flakes (if using), and oregano. Cook for another 10 minutes over medium heat, stirring occasionally. Turn the heat to low and cook for another 30 minutes, occasionally stirring and adding water if needed to keep the vegetables and beef from sticking. Taste, and add additional salt if needed. At this point you can cool the concentrate and refrigerate for up to 5 days or freeze in 1½- to 2-cup (375- to 500-ml) batches.

To make the sauce: Use 1½ cups (375 ml) of the concentrate, thawed if frozen. If serving with pasta, start to boil the water before you start cooking the sauce. Combine the concentrate, crushed tomatoes, tomato paste, water, bay leaf, Italian herbs, salt, and pepper in a large saucepan. Bring just to the edge of a boil, then turn the heat to medium. Cook for about 15 minutes, stirring occasionally. Add the vinegar, if using, and cook another 5 minutes. Check the seasonings to see if it needs salt, pepper, or anything else.

CHAPTER 17

Don't Tell Our Parents

MooMal and Saydie, 1977

In 1974, my straight-A "top picker" oldest brother, Milton, plotted out what seemed like the perfect crime.

He pulled up outside the theater at Davison High School and placed a pair of jeans, underwear, and a sweater on the front seat of his red Mustang and left it running. He casually walked through the stage door as the first act of *Arsenic and Old Lace* got under way. After circling the darkened back area until he reached the other side of the stage, he dipped into the folds of the open curtains, stripped off his clothes, threw on a ski mask, and then streaked naked to the other side. He kept running, straight out the door, hopped in his car, and drove off.

Streaking was so popular that decade that the song "The Streak" hit number one on the Billboard charts in May 1974. The song was either apparent inspiration or simple acknowledgment; the Associated Press reported that more than a thousand episodes of streaking took place that year.

As Milton drove off, he sensed someone recognized him. Would the police come after him? He thought about where to go and headed to the one safe haven he knew: the Davison Hotline offices.

The hotline was started by Milton's high school classmate and friend Michael Moore. (Yes, *that* Michael Moore. His father worked with my dad at AC Spark Plug and they lived on East Hill Street, just a block away.) The hotline was a place that teens could call if they were depressed, thinking about suicide, or just wanted to talk. Sandy worked there part time after school, training to answer calls. Most were from teens sharing arguments they had with their parents or frustrations about school. Home pregnancy testing kits weren't available then, so the center also did pregnancy testing, which made the hotline controversial. Moore himself was already controversial. At eighteen, while still in high school, he had run for and was elected to the Davison school board.

Milton burst into the rental house that served as the hotline's office. "You have to hide me, I just streaked the high school play!" he frantically explained to Moore. "I can't go home. I think someone saw me." The strategy they settled on was to sit and eat chips and drink pop for two hours. When the cops didn't show, Milton went home.

Almost immediately, a stagehand identified my brother as the culprit. The next day, Mom got a call from the principal. Mortified, she sat with my brother in a small office furnished in atomic era institutional decor. After a stern talking to, the principal sent my brother to wait in the hallway. Mom pleaded his case.

"He's got less than a month to graduation," she started. "He's had straight As all through high school. Can't you cut him a break?"

The principal shook his head. "If we don't punish your son, we'll have kids running naked all over." He felt for his pocket protector, an absentminded habit. "No, I'm afraid the best I can do is a one-week suspension. But I've checked with his teachers. He has no major tests coming up, so it shouldn't affect his grades."

Mom stood up, smoothed her rayon floral-print skirt, and shook his hand. After all, it could have been worse. He could have been arrested or even expelled. Things like streaking didn't happen in Davison.

She found Milton slumped in a chair. "You're driving," she said brusquely and tossed him the keys. He followed her silently as she walked, her seventies-style sling-back heels clacking against the industrial marble floor and then across a black asphalt parking lot to her Buick Regal. She waited silently while Milton got in the car, unlocked the passenger door, then slipped into the camel-colored velour seat without saying a word.

Milt sat motionless behind the steering wheel. They sat silent for many moments. Then Milt said, "Promise me you won't tell Dad."

Mom kept staring out her window. "What's it worth to you?" she replied coolly, not looking at him.

"Anything," he said quickly. "I'll do *anything.*"

She turned to him and gave him a bright smile. "Great, I've got just the idea."

Along the northern edge of the house on Hill Street stood the base of what must have been an extraordinary oak. The ground rose up like a swell around the sad, blunt stump. Mom and Dad talked endlessly about what to do with the spot. Mom had long fancied building a big rock garden there. She'd seen one in *Better Homes and Gardens* and snipped out the page with a pair of scissors. The mound had flowers and rocks around a cascading waterfall that gently tumbled from one small pool down to another and finally into a pond filled with koi fish.

By odd luck (or not) Mom had this clipping in her purse. She made Milton a bargain. Build her this rock garden in a week or she'd tell Dad.

The next morning, she woke him at seven A.M. He got out of bed and headed over to the farm on Coldwater Road, now rented out to a couple with two young children. Far back on the property was a generous cache of granite rocks and small boulders. Using Dad's baby blue Chevy truck, Milt piled multiple loads of rocks into the truck, some two tons in all.

Dad came home the first night and saw the pile of rocks as he pulled into the driveway. Mom arrived immediately behind him. "What's this?" he asked Mom.

"Oh, Milton has the week off from school," she lied. "It's a special thing they do for seniors who have straight As. He asked if he could do a project in the backyard."

Dad looked at the pile of rocks. "Your rock garden?"

"Yeah, I told him about it," she said, careful not to look Dad directly in the eye. "He insisted on doing it. You know how he loves to work in the dirt," she added.

As they walked into the house, Milton was sprawled exhausted and filthy on the beige sofa. "Milton!" Dad said. "While I love that you want to do this for your mom, you should be out having a good time on your special week off!"

Milton looked up a bit dazed. He looked at Mom, then Dad. "Oh, right," he said slowly. "My special week . . ."

"You know, for getting straight As," Mom said, finishing his sentence.

"Right," Milton said, picking up the plot. "No, I'm happy to do it."

Dad seemed pleased. His son doing such a selfless thing on his special seniors' week! He'd raised that kid right, he thought.

All week Milton worked tirelessly on the rock garden. He hauled in hundreds of pounds of top soil and dozens of plants from a nursery. He stacked and set the stones in place like a complex jigsaw. He dug a pond at its base, then two cascading pools, and poured each with cement and installed a circulating water pump for the pond. Mom woke him at seven A.M. each morning and he worked right until dark every day. On Wednesday, Dad gave him twenty dollars and told him to go out with his friends. Mom made him give her the money.

In the end, Milton was proud of the garden. When people visited, it was the first thing my parents showed them.

At the end of that summer, when the garden was at the height of its bloom, Milton packed up his Mustang and headed off to college. He was the first of my siblings to leave home. Within three years of moving to Hill Street, my three brothers and my sister all moved out.

🍓

To ease overcrowding, Davison High School offered students with the best grades a chance to graduate early. Sandy qualified in January 1977. She still had her dreams of studying at the Sorbonne in Paris, but at seventeen, she was too young to apply as an international student. Some of her friends were taking a year off between high school and college and had moved to Holly, a picturesque small town about fifteen miles south of Flint that had become something of a hippie enclave. My parents helped her move there and even lent her some money to get set up in an apartment.

After all, they were glad she was alive.

In autumn 1976, Sandy was in a one-car accident that should have killed her.

She was driving to a party for the Davison Hotline. She had a jug of lemonade for the affair on the passenger seat of the car. She borrowed Dad's 1975 Nova, equipped with then-newfangled power steering. Driving out to the hotline's office, a car coming toward her seemed a bit too close to the center line, so Sandy turned the wheel a bit to the right and the car veered sharply off the road, skidding into the gravel on the edge of the pavement. She turned back onto the road and the car whipped across the line. Panicked, Sandy turned right, but ended up wildly overcorrecting, slamming into an embankment. The car bounced against it and somersaulted at least once, landing on the roof. The jar of lemonade punched violently through the passenger side window, shattering the glass.

The car was totaled, but aside from bruises and cuts on her face and hands from the shattered windows, miraculously, Sandy emerged uninjured.

A police officer who arrived at the scene with the ambulance told her that if she hadn't been using another newfangled device, a three-point seat belt, she wouldn't have survived.

Sandy nodded, understanding. She couldn't stop looking at the crumpled car. "Is there any way we can avoid telling my dad?" she asked. "This is his car. He's going to kill me."

The officer smirked and, without looking up from the clipboard where he was taking notes for his report, said, "Uh, I think he's going to be happy that you're okay."

When Mom and Dad arrived at the hospital, Sandy started to apologize. Her head and face boasted a smattering of bandages. "Dad, I'm so sorry about your car . . ."

Dad grabbed her and hugged her mightily. When he pulled away, Sandy saw the tears. She had never seen him cry before. "It's just a car, Sandy," he said, wiping his eyes. "You're the one I was worried about." With that, he grabbed and hugged her again, this time until she could barely breathe.

When Sandy moved to Holly a few months later, she worked as a cook making soups for a local vegetarian eatery. At night, she waited tables at a 1920s-themed restaurant at the historic Holly Hotel. Other nights, she worked as a bartender at a joint down the street.

Then she met some clown named Buffo.

Buffo wore a crazy mismatched thrift store getup with his shock wig and big shoes. His onstage gig consisted of sight gags and slapstick. In summers, he earned extra money working street fairs selling balloon animals. Sandy was intrigued. It seemed like an easier way to make money than waiting on tables or bartending.

She intimated her clown ambitions to Mike, who was all for trying it out, too. They found books on clowning at the Davison Library. Among their discoveries was the need not only to conjure up a clown name and costume but to develop a personality and general clowning aesthetic. They bought clown makeup at a magic shop in downtown Flint. They brought it back to Hill Street, where they practiced spreading the thick creamy "clown white" on each other and then trying out different looks with black, red, and blue greasepaint. Together they went to the St. Vincent de Paul thrift store and pulled together outfits.

Sandy chose the clown name "Saydie," a love-starved, socially awkward kind of clown. Saydie's costumes featured aggressively bad fashion choices that called to mind Diane Keaton's look in *Annie Hall* gone horribly wrong, plaid skirts topped with nubby wool vests matched with polka dot shirts, that sort of thing.

Mike chose "MooMal." We'd long had nicknames in our family. Mike's had been "MooMoo" from infanthood for his ability to drink vast quantities of milk. After Sandy started taking French, she called him MooMal, which loosely translates to "bad milk." MooMal was a once well-heeled, now down-on-his-luck yet fun-loving character with a quirky sense of humor.

Together they learned to juggle from a kit they bought at the magic shop. Via mail order, they purchased boxes of the long thin balloons needed to make animals plus a book detailing step by step how to make dogs, swans, monkeys, swords, and so on. Saydie and MooMal started working street fairs and discovered the money was pretty good. People would give them a buck or two to tie animals. Sometimes they earned as much as one hundred dollars in a day, a lot of money for a few hours' work in the seventies. Sandy's running joke when asked how many different balloon animals she could tie was, "I can do over two hundred, but they all look like dogs!"

Like Buffo, Sandy developed a one-woman clown show. My parents took me to see her opening night at the Holly Hotel. The first half of the show was a silent, mime-based Saydie extravaganza. Saydie had a "hopeless chest" instead of a hope chest. The show revolved around her readying for a date, but he never materialized. At the end of the act, to show she was down but not beaten, Saydie donned a tiara and presented a baton with a flurry of colorful ribbons on each end. She tried to twirl it, awkwardly at first, and then—thanks to Sandy's years as a majorette—wowed the crowd with her expert twirling.

After a break, Sandy returned to the stage dressed in costume as a tribute to Charlie Chaplin. She had borrowed copies of Chaplin's films from the University of Michigan, genuine films, in heavy round canisters. Fortunately, Dad had won a projector one night playing in a poker series at the VFW. She set it up at our house and she and I watched several of Chaplin's "tramp" series, including *City*

Lights, Modern Times, The Tramp, and *A Dog's Life.* I had never seen a silent film before.

A few minutes into the first one, I asked, "Why don't they talk?"

"Because they're silent films," she replied.

"So people didn't talk back then?"

"Of course people talked," she said. "The movies just couldn't play sound."

It was amazing to watch Sandy on the small stage. To replicate the frame-by-frame nature of the early films, she set up a light behind a moving box fan. As with Chaplin, in both her skits, she artfully showed well-meaning characters hungry for affection and doing their best to struggle against adversity. Mom and Dad were so proud. Dad even gave her roses after her performance.

She later enlisted me to come along on her gigs as a clown. At age nine, I became "Sissy the Clown." My clown persona mirrored my real-life one: I was the bookish, socially awkward younger sister of Saydie. I learned walkabout gigs from her at corporate picnics. She'd take a hot dog and put it on a leash and tell people she was "walking her dog." She taught me to make balloon animals, even teaching me to create a dog balloon in less than ten seconds.

Kids loved her. I loved her. All I wanted was to be like my big sister.

Dressed as a clown, I could see why she was drawn to it. There's a certain freedom in covering your identity with face paint. You can act silly or sad or outrageous. No one can question it. You're a *clown*. There's also an understanding that some people are fundamentally afraid of clowns. As a child who had routinely been mocked by other children for being too precocious or too small for my age, I relished the power of knowing that as a tiny, strange creature with a grotesque smile and a shocking burnt orange wig, I probably made a few adults uncomfortable.

Sandy ended up teaching a clowning workshop at Mott Community College. She taught the basics of makeup, development of a clown persona, and how to juggle. She truly embraced clowning, even applying for a spot in the famed Ringling Bros. and Barnum & Bailey Clown College, then in Venice, Florida. So many people wanted to be clowns that it was considered more difficult to get into than Harvard or Yale. She wasn't surprised when she got turned down, but that's how dedicated she was to clowning.

Sandy became involved with a musician twelve years her senior and soon announced plans to marry—dressed as clowns. The *Flint Journal* even ran a story about her with the headline SHE'S NOT JESTING, CLOWN TO WED, with a photo of Saydie and MooMal.

At first, my parents went along with it. Dad even offered to dress up as a clown, too. But then he got to know Sandy's fiancé. History repeating itself in a situation similar to that of his grandfather Milton Stark with his daughter Della, Dad told her that he didn't approve. While the guy was a talented artist, there was something about him Dad didn't like.

At first, he simply refused to pay for the wedding. Then he refused to take part.

For years, I assumed my nineteen-year-old sister eloped at a justice of the peace. But later I learned she did go through with her plans to marry as a clown in a ceremony held at a pinball arcade with walls painted like cotton candy. The minister and guests were all dressed in costume.

Later, Sandy realized Dad was right. The union lasted less than a year.

🍓

As eccentric as the other kids were turning out, my brother Doug was the epitome of a dutiful son.

One day after eating a pile of raw tomatoes from the garden, Doug lay down on the couch clutching his stomach. Mom asked him to pick up her dry cleaning from a shop around the corner. "I can't, Mom, I don't feel so good," Doug said.

Mom told him he just had indigestion. "You shouldn't have eaten so much," she told him. "C'mon, go get my cleaning."

Crumpled over and holding his side, he hobbled to the car. He returned white-faced. He handed over the plastic-covered dresses and then bolted to the bathroom, where he vomited everywhere.

Within two hours, he was in surgery for an emergency appendec-
tomy at St. Joseph Hospital in Flint.

"But what a good son," Mom kept saying in the waiting room to
the family, even strangers. "He was in all this pain and terribly sick
and he *still* went and got my clothes from the dry cleaner."

Once, when I was perhaps seven, Doug was pulling out of the
driveway. I stomped my little foot and yelled for him to come back.
He pulled back into the driveway. I went to the window and
counted out my pennies with instructions on candy to buy at the
store down the street. "Okay, three Tootsie Rolls, three banana-
flavored BB Bats, and two butterscotch-flavored hard candy sticks."
Doug obediently pulled out of the driveway and returned with my
candy.

While the other kids became too busy with their own social
lives, Doug made a point to spend time with me. As long as it
wasn't a chick flick, he took me to any movie I wanted to see, from
awful movies such as *Herbie Rides Again* to genuinely good films
such as *Blazing Saddles* and *Young Frankenstein*.

But Doug hit his strident point, too. After one year in college,
he debated whether or not he needed to go back. He could always
get a job in a GM shop, for instance, or he could start his own business. Doug also wanted to strike out on his own and move to
Florida.

Dad listened to his reasoning and said he understood. "I've got
an idea, Doug. Why don't you go spend the summer at the house
in Florida working?" Dad offered to pay for gas both ways in exchange for some work on the house that needed to be done. "You
know, that way you could see what kind of work you could get
there, just check it out."

Doug thought this seemed like a great opportunity. He corralled
our brother Mike into the scheme. They had it all worked out.
They'd earn a bunch of money and spend their free time hanging
out on the beach.

Just before they left, Dad explained that, of course, he'd be
charging them rent and utilities for their stay. After all, this was

their chance to see how they would make it in the "real world." Doug and Mike agreed. How hard could it be to make the reasonable rent that Dad had set? They weren't even quite sure what "utilities" meant, but they figured whatever they were couldn't be that expensive.

Reality proved a bit different. Without anything more than a high school diploma, Doug found he was eligible only for blue collar or manual work. His first job was working as an orange picker for a contractor that supplied Tropicana with citrus for its juices. If he thought picking strawberries in the heat of a Michigan summer day was tough, it was nothing compared to late-harvest Valencia oranges in the searing Florida heat in June. The oranges were first reaped via a shake-and-catch system, in which a mechanical arm shook the branches of the tree to release some of the fruit, which were then caught in the bed of a truck. But the shake-and-catch system captured about 20 percent of the fruit. The rest was hand-picked.

Doug, a seasoned picker thanks to his days in the strawberry field, showed up for work alongside a whole group of migrant workers, a motley mix of immigrants and general day laborers. They took a bumpy ride deep into the grove in the back of a filthy truck thickly plastered with bird droppings that reeked of fresh manure and the sour scent of spoiled fruit. A supervisor assigned each a few trees, a pole picker, and a bag.

The work was hot, exhausting, and every so often, Doug would find snakes woven around branches of trees or encounter a hornet's nest. He collected his cash at the end of each day. Valencia season ended in late June, so he hunted up other work, eventually getting hired on a crew for Florida Power & Light digging ditches to bury power lines. If he thought picking oranges in a green grove was bad, standing on asphalt in the middle of a Florida summer wearing an orange vest breaking up concrete wasn't exactly a dream job, either.

Meanwhile, Mike, then between his junior and senior years of high school, got hired on in the bakery department of a supermarket in town. Since they had only one car, Mike bought a cheap bike to pedal the nine miles into town along the causeway and back in the Florida heat for each shift. Since he was new and had the least seniority, sometimes he worked the late shift, until four A.M., baking cakes for the next day, and then had to get up to work a second shift starting at noon. He earned $2.10 an hour, the minimum wage.

Meanwhile, they learned that utilities included air conditioning, something they ran a *lot* when they weren't working. Dad called to let them know that one of their electricity bills equaled a full week of their pay combined.

My brothers' dreams of living a languid life at the beach quickly evaporated. Doug says that during that summer, he spent exactly three afternoons at the beach. The rest of the time, they both worked as many hours as they could just to make ends meet.

When September rolled around, Doug went to college. Mike went back to high school. When Doug had to take out student loans, he never complained.

※

"By the time you get this, I'll be in boot camp," the note from Mike started.

When we lived on the farm, my parents scraped together enough money to buy Mike a trumpet when he turned ten. One of the first songs he learned to play was the marines' theme song. Dad would sit outside under a tree at the farm listening to Mike play, sometimes singing along.

> *From the Halls of Montezuma,*
> *To the Shores of Tripoli;*
> *We fight our country's battles*
> *In the air, on land, and sea;*
> *First to fight for right and freedom*
> *And to keep our honor clean;*
> *We are proud to claim the title*
> *OF UNITED STATES MARINE.*

Mike had a natural gift for music as well as a talent for art. He could pick up virtually any instrument and learn to play it within a half an hour. By his teens, he could sketch anything. He began painting canvases as a freshman. Mike learned to play the piano by ear. When he first put on his marching band uniform, Dad hugged him so hard with pride that Mike couldn't breathe. When he rose to the rank of drum major at Davison High School, Dad would dart alongside parades, taking his picture over and over. It embarrassed Mike to no end, but Dad couldn't help it. He was so proud of him.

Like Sandy, Mike also graduated early, finishing his requirements in the fall of his senior year. He was torn between pursuing music, art, or his emerging interest in electronics and computing. One day, a recruiter from a local electronics program made a visit to the house. Dad threw the guy out. "My son is going to art school!"

So at seventeen, Mike packed his bags and left for Kendall College School of Design with a fifteen-hundred-dollar student loan and money he'd earned over the years mowing lawns. He shared a sixty-dollars-a-month apartment with a roommate and walked the two miles to school and back. He learned he was in the top 25 percent, but only the top 1 percent of graduates ever made a living in the art world. As he puts it, "Back then, the rest ended up pasting ads in newspapers."

His friends in Grand Rapids were all older, among them a Vietnam vet, an adrenaline-addict sports freak, and a navy veteran, a dangerous combination for a disenchanted art student. After eating liverwurst for two weeks and hearing all the stories of his friends, he decided this was the one chance in his life to see the world by joining the military. But he knew if he mentioned this to our parents, Dad would talk him out of it.

At the end of the second semester, he packed up all of his belongings. He sent Sandy a box of his most valuable art tools along with a key to a friend's long-term storage place with the address. Then he left for Naval Training Service Command in Great Lakes, Illinois, just outside Chicago.

Sandy was stunned. She immediately drove to Davison. When

no one answered at the house on Hill Street, she called Aunt Mel. Mom and I were there. She came through the door crying. "Mike joined the navy!" she wailed. She and Mike were close. After all, they were *clowns* together. "He didn't even tell me! I could see him not telling Dad, but not *me?*"

Mike's recruiter had signed him up for the naval engineering school. Mike's idea of engineering was its most classic definition: "the application of scientific, economic, social, and practical knowledge in order to design, build, and maintain structures, machines and devices." Only later did he learn that *engineering* in the navy meant working in the boiler room.

He was eventually assigned to the USS *Bigelow*. His first day at sea, he ran to the top of the ship to see the waves breaking over the bow for hours. Then he was seasick for days. When he got his sea legs, though, it was great. They went to Spain, Egypt, Palma de Mallorca, and Yemen before being called to the Persian Gulf, where they went around in circles for months.

It took Sandy a long time to collect herself enough to retrieve Mike's belongings. I sat in the backseat while she and a friend drove late into the night to Grand Rapids. Among his boxes were canvases of works that he'd painted. One of them was a landscape of the farm on Coldwater Road.

With my siblings gone and my mother working full time, at nine years old, I was the only latchkey kid in the neighborhood.

The week before Mike left home for winter classes at art school, Mom did something unusual: she took me to lunch. We lived near Four Corners, the intersection of Davison and State roads, the epicenter of what was euphemistically referred to as downtown Davison. On one corner sat Archie's, an old-school diner, the kind featuring only booths and counter seating and waitresses in orange poly/cotton uniforms with small aprons and cheap name tags. The roof had a high arch, reminiscent of a faux Swiss chalet. We had never been inside, even though it was only a couple of blocks from our house.

I felt quite grown-up as I perused the oversized laminated menu. I had never heard of some of the items on offer. "What's a Monte Cristo?" I asked my mother. Since we were Midwest WASPs, I followed up with "What's *rye* bread?" In the end, I selected the soup and sandwich special with a glass of milk. I daintily nibbled at my grilled cheese sandwich and quietly slurped chicken noodle soup. Mom looked around the place and chatted with the wait staff. Then she casually dropped this idea.

"Hey, you know, your dad and I have been trying to figure out where you might go after school now," she started. "What do you think of coming here?" For $1.99, she could be assured I'd get soup, half a sandwich, and adult supervision for the two and half hours between the time class ended at Hill Elementary School and they typically arrived home from work. This also solved a dilemma; we ate "lunch" at my school at eleven A.M., and invariably I was hungry again when school let out at three P.M.

I burst with pride at the suggestion. *I must be nearly an adult now for her to think something like this*, I thought!

At first, this arrangement worked fine. As the school bell rang, I put on my mittens and purple parka, collected my books and homework, and then walked the few minutes to the diner, snow crunching under my small boots. On my first day, I requested a table for one, and the amused waitress led me to a corner table. I tried to eat slowly, savoring the hot yet bland chicken noodle soup and my warm wedge of grilled cheese sandwich. Once she cleared my plate, I worked on my homework. Then I opened a book and read until it was time to go home. Time goes more slowly when you're a child. To me, the afternoon felt pleasant, yet endless. At precisely 5:30 P.M., I bundled up and walked home, arriving just as my mom's Buick Regal pulled into the driveway.

The next day, the waitress seemed surprised to see me. She led me to the same corner table. Within two hours, I finished my soup, sandwich, homework, and a short book. Bored, I took out paper. I started to write down notes about the people at the other booths in the diner. That night at dinner, I told my parents about the grizzled man with one eye at the counter, the giggling teen girls who split a stack of pancakes, and the couple at another table arguing about a lost library book. Dad congratulated me on my ability to notice details.

"Maybe you should start to just make up stories about the people you see and write them down," Dad suggested. "That's what a lot of writers do."

So every day after that, I spent my posthomework time writing stories. The red-haired waitress who appeared to have been crying on her break? I wrote she was being tormented by a ghost whom only she could see. He would taunt her and call her names, but she couldn't make him go away. A pair of pretty teenage girls came in late one afternoon dressed in long, formal gowns. They carefully folded their elbow-length gloves on the table. In my story, they were princesses who wanted, just for one day, to be treated like average people. Neither of them had ever eaten "normal" food, so all they wanted was to taste a waffle and a grilled tuna melt—just once—before being forced back to their elaborate fairy tale–style castle somewhere in Europe.

For two months, I went to the diner. The waitresses knew that I always had the same soup and sandwich, so they just brought me lunch without an order. One let me have milky hot tea, even though the other waitresses debated whether the caffeine could stunt my growth.

One day, a new woman named Edith began working there. She was a little unusual. She wore black tights with her orange outfit. You could not ignore the large silver cross she kept on a piece of white yarn around her neck. While the other waitresses thought little about my unusual postschool lunch visit, she found it unsettling.

Edith insisted on waiting on me. She asked me a lot of questions, some quite odd. How often did we go to church? Why didn't my parents hire someone to watch me? How often was I left home alone? How did I feel about Jesus? Had I ever wanted anything from Santa that he didn't bring? Raised to be polite to adults, I answered her questions, even as I wrote stories about her. In one, she had been rejected from a witch's training program for being too odd.

Then one day, as I finished my lunch, she sat down across from me. She asked if I wanted to live with her. She had prayed to God about it, and he said that I should go home and live with her and her boyfriend. I could go with her after her shift the next day.

I told her that I would think about it. I paid my bill, left her a nice tip, and never went back there again.

I decided that it was time I learned to manage my own lunch. On my way home from school the next afternoon, I stopped at a small grocery. With my daily diner budget, I purchased a trio of forbidden gastronomic treasures: a can of premade vanilla cake frosting, a small bag of Fritos, and Hostess Ho Hos. I ate them straight from the package when I got home. I was so sick that my mother didn't ask about the diner.

I shunned the Ho Hos and decided to make a real lunch the next day. My parents had recently bought a box of bulk steaks from the VFW. On one of his visits home from college, I watched Milt thaw one in cold water and cook it in a skillet. It seemed quite straightforward. I submerged the plastic-wrapped brick of a steak into a bowl of cool water in the sink.

Just to be sure I cooked it correctly, I pulled out a stool and selected my mom's copy of *Mastering the Art of French Cooking* from the kitchen shelf.

While the meat softened, I explored the fridge for something to go with it. I found a package of fresh green beans with a small label noting they had been "shipped from the Sunshine State." I'd watched Julia make green beans on her PBS show several times in reruns. I flipped through her book and found the directions. I dropped the beans in a pan of boiling water for a few minutes and then shocked them in a bowl of ice water. I pulled out a skillet from the cupboard next to the stove and then . . . I realized something was missing.

Music. My mother listened to music while she cooked. She'd learned that from Grandpa Charles. We had a stereo in the other room, a fancy multicomponent affair with an eight-track player, the latest in home audio. I pushed in Johnny Cash's live album *At Folsom Prison* and turned up the volume.

With Johnny's twangy music in the background and the cookbook open on the counter, I went forward with my maiden voyage in the kitchen as I pan-seared the thawed steak. Using the step stool, I retrieved from the pantry the Montreal steak seasoning my dad always used on grilled meat. When it seemed cooked—or as it turned out, overcooked—I wiped the pan with a paper towel. Then I added butter, waited for it to sizzle, and cooked the green beans.

I moved the stool over to retrieve a paper plate from the cupboard. I sat in the baby blue kitchen at the gold-speckled Formica counter and ate my lunch, thinking. Recipes were like homework. If you read the directions and did what they said, your food turned out. Maybe not perfect, but that was also the point of homework. It took practice. I ate my tough steak and my slightly oversalted green beans with an overwhelming sense of pride as Johnny Cash went on to sing about the "Orange Blossom Special."

I made my own afternoon lunches afterward, sometimes just a grilled cheese sandwich, sometimes a steak, and occasionally scrambled eggs. Eventually, when Mom asked about the diner, I truthfully informed her that now that it was warm and nearly summer, I preferred to make my own lunch and then go out to play with my friends until they came home.

"But don't tell Dad, okay?" Mom agreed.

One sunny May afternoon, I had my first "dinner party." I invited Katie and her sisters over for lunch. I set the table with my mother's matching dishes. I served what Mom called Flinn burgers, hamburgers seasoned with Montreal steak seasoning served on bread with a thick slather of mayonnaise and slices of store-bought tomatoes and onions. Aided by Julia's recipe, I made a side salad with vinaigrette. As I watched them happily gobble up their burgers and poke at their iceberg salad, I thought nothing was better than feeding people. It was like my old game of restaurant, but better. The food was real and so were my friends.

Panfried Steak à la Julia Child

"Diet food is what one eats while waiting for the steak to cook," was a famous quip by the late Julia. She recommended T-bone, porterhouse, Spencer cut, or sirloin steaks as these cuts are more flavorful than the more expensive tenderloin. Season both sides of the steak with salt and pepper or a rub such as Montreal Steak Seasoning (recipe follows). Melt butter with a bit of oil over medium-high heat. After the foam from the butter subsides, add the steak. Depending on the thickness, cook it 3 to 4 minutes per side. I prefer to use tongs when turning steaks as they are easier to maneuver but a humble fork works perfectly well.

Many people aren't sure how long to sear a steak without overcooking. For a precise measure, use an instant-read meat thermometer inserted into the center of the steak. Aim to hit an internal temperature around the following for your desired doneness: rare, 125°F (52°C); medium-rare, 135°F (57°C); medium, 145°F (63°C); and medium-well, 155°F (68°C). It's always best to let a steak rest for a few minutes before eating, to allow the juices to redistribute evenly throughout.

The chefs at Le Cordon Bleu taught us a trick for determining by touch whether a steak is done: Relaxing your hand, hold thumb to forefinger, as if making the okay sign, and touch the soft pad under the thumb with your other forefinger. That's bleu, or extra rare. Touch the thumb to the middle finger, the bump gets a bit taut. That's the way rare meat feels. The thumb to ring finger equals medium-rare. The thumb to pinkie? That's well done—or "Américain," as one chef quipped. In other words, the more done the steak, the stiffer it feels to the touch.

Homemade Montreal Steak Seasoning

Making seasoning blends at home allows you to control the amount and the kind of salt, to use organic spices, and in this case, to decide whether you want to use hot or mild paprika. This terrific recipe is adapted from Aliza Green's Field Guide to Herbs & Spices. To her recipe, I also add fennel, so I've included it here.

Makes about ⅔ cup (160 ml) of seasoning

2 tablespoons (30 ml) paprika
2 tablespoons (30 ml) crushed black pepper
1½ tablespoons (22.5 ml) coarse salt
1 tablespoon (15 ml) granulated garlic
1 tablespoon (15 ml) granulated onion
1 tablespoon (15 ml) crushed coriander
1 tablespoon (15 ml) fennel seed
2 teaspoons (10 ml) dried dill weed
2 teaspoons (10 ml) red chili flakes

Mix together the paprika, pepper, salt, garlic, onion, coriander, fennel seed, dill weed, and red chili flakes. Store tightly capped in an airtight container, away from heat and light, for up to 1 year.

CHAPTER 18

Dollhouse

The Flinn family at Milton Jr.'s wedding to Delynn, August 1980

No one ever told me that my father had cancer.

I can't say that I blame anyone. I was only eleven years old. Besides, my parents were optimists. They figured it was just a speed bump in their otherwise happy, productive lives.

In the late summer of 1978, Dad was diagnosed with malignant melanoma. It originated in his left side, exactly at the site where he'd been wounded in the war. My parents told me that he was going in for a different, more routine surgery and sent me to stay with my cousins, the Fridlines.

Afterward, Dad didn't go to work as usual. He went to the

doctor often while I was at school. Then, one night, I heard my mother's alarmed cries from our family room, where they were watching TV on the Magnavox. Dad was on the floor, clutching his chest. An ambulance came and took him away.

He'd had a heart attack from the strain of the surgery, chemotherapy, and radiation treatments, but no one told me that. Over the course of two months, his skin turned a disturbing gray color. His hair started to fall out. He had another surgery. This time I stayed with Katie and her family across the street. Her mother had a frightened look on her face when I showed up with my small round pink suitcase clutching a handful of books.

When he came home from the second surgery, I overheard Mom talking on the phone to an acquaintance. That's the first time I heard the word *cancer*.

In late November, Mom announced that Dad was going to go live in Florida. He was leaving on a flight the next day. We'd spend Christmas there, but then he would stay and we'd come back. "The warm weather will be better for his health," she explained. It was vague, but enough.

Two weeks later, I overheard a hushed conversation with my brothers, now home from college for their winter break. My parents had just had an offer on the house on Hill Street. We'd move to Florida in June. In the meantime, she rented an apartment near Central Elementary, where I was attending the sixth grade.

No one told me anything.

On the entire two-day drive down to Florida for Christmas, I itched to ask my brothers Milton or Doug what was going on, but for some reason, I didn't feel like I should.

Dad looked good when we arrived. His color was better. On the advice of his doctor, he'd been walking the beach every day. At first, he could walk only a few minutes before he had to sit down and put a nitro pill under his tongue.

"The heart is a muscle," his doctor told him. "Muscles can be built back up."

Every day he walked more. In two weeks, he was up to a half mile. By the time Christmas came around, he was able to walk the length of the public beach again, as if nothing had happened. Over the course of the holiday break, no one mentioned his illness. I assumed he was cured of whatever he'd had.

When we returned to icy Michigan, Mom accumulated boxes. Sandy came from Holly to help her. They had ten days before the new owners took possession, and Sandy assured her the two of them could get it all done.

Then the phone rang.

For years, Grandma Inez had complained about stomach pains. Her country doctor kept suggesting she take Maalox. Everyone thought she had the flu when she went into the hospital in Midland. She had collapsed in the middle of making herself a big pot of chicken soup.

"She's bad off," reported her younger brother, Rich. "But no one knows what's wrong with her."

By the time Mom arrived two hours later, Grandma Inez had slipped into a coma.

The boys were back in college. Mom left me with Sandy so I wouldn't miss school. Sandy started packing. She called and placed ads for all the furniture in the *Flint Journal*. She loaded dozens of boxes to donate to the St. Vincent de Paul thrift store, where my mother had shopped for so many years. The first night, Sandy came out of my parents' bedroom with a half dozen small pillows from their bed. Some of them had once adorned our shared room at the farmhouse.

"I remember when Mom bought these at the thrift store, and then spent a full day re-covering them with matching fabric when we lived on the farm," she said wistfully, fingering the edge of a pillow. Then she shoved them into a box. Her eyes misted. "I guess by going back to the thrift store, they're sort of going home."

Mom stayed in Sanford for three days. She and her siblings took shifts to be with their mother around the clock. Surely, Grandma Inez was going to wake up. The doctors couldn't figure out what had happened to her.

Mom took a break and went to the Sanford Farm to take a shower. She was driving over to Uncle Rich's house in her Buick Regal to pick him up to head back to the hospital when a song came into her head. She could hear it so clearly that she checked to see if the radio had switched on somehow. The song was an old turn-of-the-century country tune that Grandpa Charles liked to sing, "Lightning Express." The chorus goes like this:

Please mister conductor,
Don't put me off of your train.
The best friend I have in this whole wide world,
Is waiting for me in pain,
Expected to die any moment sir,
She may not live through the day.
I want to kiss Mother good-bye,
Before God takes her away.

Just then, sunshine broke through the dark snow clouds. Mom pulled into the driveway at her brother's house. Rich walked out and hugged her.

"Mom's gone," was all he said.

Inez Monk Henderson died on January 21, 1979.

An autopsy showed she had uterine fibroids that had become cancerous—a rarity. The stomach pains she felt had resulted from massive tumors. A timely ultrasound might have saved her life.

After an exhausting day making funeral arrangements, Mom spent the night at the Sanford Farm. She fell asleep on the couch in the living room. Around three A.M., she awoke to see a big figure of a man standing over her. The next day, she asked her brother Rich why he'd come by the house in the middle of the night.

"What are you talkin' about?" he asked, surprised. "I was home sleeping."

The only other person staying at the farm that night was my aunt Mel. She said she'd been so exhausted that she'd never left her room.

"I wonder if it was my dad," Mom muses. "Maybe it was his way of letting me know that he and Mom were okay. He always loved her so much."

🍓

Mom headed home the next day, and stunned with grief, she tried to pack. After a couple of hours, she sat overwhelmed in the kitchen and sobbed. Her husband was sick, her mother was dead, and money was tight once again. Inflation was rampant. They couldn't keep up with two sons in college, medical costs not covered by insurance, and two residences with only Mom's paycheck now that Dad was no longer working.

I didn't know then, but Dad's diagnosis came just as Sandy had started the application process to the Sorbonne in France. The heavy packet arrived *par avion* the day after our father was diagnosed with terminal cancer. She never sent the application back. "It wasn't just money, although there wasn't any," Sandy says. "I couldn't leave the family at a time like that."

The closing on the house was scheduled for the day after Grandma Inez's funeral. Mom panicked. There was no way she could get it done. Sandy walked into the room to find Mom crying, her face in her hands.

"Leave it to me," Sandy said gently. She got on the phone, and within three hours, my brothers Milton and Doug were at the house, ready to work.

Mom and I left to attend the funeral in Sanford. She left Sandy money to buy the boys beers and pizza. Sandy bought the pizzas, but after twelve hours of labor each day, she allowed them only a single beer apiece. "I don't want you drunk and unable to get up and work the next day," Sandy explained to my frustrated brothers.

Tougher than any drill sergeant, she started them at dawn. The boys carried furniture through the snow to the waiting trucks of people who bought it via the newspaper ads. They packed up all my parents' clothes, the kitchenware, my toys, and Dad's books. After three days, they had sold most of the furniture and packed what remained into the eight-by-ten storage space in the basement of the building where Mom had rented a one-bedroom apartment. They then cleaned and scrubbed every inch of the house.

On their final walk-through, they found Dad's 1954 *World Book* encyclopedias in a closet of the family room. None of them could face packing them up. They shut the door and left them with the house for the new owners.

In those days, Michigan funerals were curious affairs. A visitation was set up for three full days so that people could drop by and pay respects at their convenience. Families had to be sure that at least one but preferably two family members were on hand at the funeral home at all times during the visitation. They'd rotate shifts. After the funeral service itself, the family would host a massive potluck buffet. These had to be dishes that could be served at room temperature and could withstand travel and a long wait on a table. The food was different from what you'd take to a family picnic, typically referred to as cold dishes. A respectful dish was served warm. A wry cousin once referred to these as "casket-friendly casseroles."

It was disorienting to come back from the Sanford Farm and not go home. Instead, we went to the nondescript one-bedroom apartment Mom had rented across from my school in downtown Davison. Mom would sit next to an egg timer while talking to Dad long distance. They kept each conversation to fewer than ten minutes to avoid racking up the phone bill.

Briefly, Sandy moved in. She had just started to date a local TV newscaster named Frank Klim. The first time Katie and I met him, we asked him for his autograph. After all, he was on TV! He was *famous*! I wanted to impress him. So every time he visited, I wore my "roller disco" outfit, a pair of red satin shorts with a matching red satin jacket. Mom didn't mean to, but apparently wore the same dress every time he visited. Frank didn't know what to make of us. The three of us lived in an odd apartment with too much furniture while Mom and I always wore the same clothes.

Mom worked at the *Flint Journal* and for a time also took on a second job helping a friend start a restaurant. Sandy held a glamorous position as an administrator at the United Way in Flint. She spent most of her evenings out with Frank. But I was used to spending time alone. I could walk across the busy street to a big Hamady's grocery store. I watched various Julia Child shows on TV. She was one of the few constants in my life, and watching her make coq au vin and omelets somehow made my upside-down world feel normal. For my Girl Scout badge in cooking, I made Julia's beef bourguignon.

I had a lot of time on my hands after finishing my homework. I decided to start writing. I finished a full-length novel and three plays. Bored at school, I began skipping whole days to spend time reading in the library. I concocted a plan to read all the books in the world by reading a book a day based on the false assumption that the small Davison Library contained every volume ever published.

When we visited Dad on my spring break, he reported the doctors thought he'd gone into remission. He had a boat at the dock across the street. It wasn't as nice as the one they'd sold to buy the house, but he'd gotten it at an estate sale for next to nothing. Sure, we had the crummy furniture that came with the house, a mismatch of an uncomfortable gold sofa set, a wobbly kitchen table, and wicker dressers with drawers that didn't work. But Dad was getting better and that was all that mattered.

In June, Mom sent me to Florida for a two-week vacation. I never went back to Davison. Mom stayed in the apartment and worked since she could earn double in Michigan what she could make in Florida. Dad, knowing the hours she worked and keen on his own sense of mortality, prevailed on my mother to let me stay with him for the next school year. So it was just me and my father alone as I faced the horror of entering junior high.

Anna Maria Island is a retiree destination. If you're a kid looking for playmates, it's not a target-rich environment. The only other child who lived in our area was a girl four years younger who was obsessed with pretending to perform surgery on a distressing collection of worn, bald baby dolls. Seeking something to do that summer, I joined the Island Baptist Church, misled by the idea that they might have a youth group. Only later did I learn that a church "youth group" in Florida consists of thirtysomethings. Quickly, I learned that Southern Baptists aren't the same as their northern cousins. The initial pastor clearly considered drinking and dancing mortal sins that would commit a soul to hell. The church didn't go so far as to forbid either activity, but it made get-togethers mighty boring, even for a kid. Almost immediately, I got corralled into the choir, an amiable group of twenty-two. The choir was led by a woman named Grace, a sweet sixtyish woman with a prominent gold tooth and a tight blue-haired perm. The first night, she took me aside from the choir and coached me through some simple vocal drills. She sat back, impressed.

"Where'd you get that voice?" she asked, sitting on the bench behind the church organ. "You sing very well, my dear."

I answered as honestly as I could. "My grandmother told me as a kid that if I ate burnt toast, I'd be able to sing good."

"Well, I guess she was right," Grace said, sitting up to organize some sheet music. "You've got some set of pipes for a kid your age."

Grace was good to me. She gave me private voice lessons and always made sure I got a solo at the holiday cantatas. I might not have found friends my age at church, but I found the choir. It gave me something to belong to when I genuinely needed to feel that I belonged somewhere. I learned the standard Baptist hymnal so well that I can still sing the opening lines to about forty hymns. A few, I still know by the number.

Meanwhile, Dad seemed better. He wasn't quite his robust self, but he was well enough to go fishing, do the grocery shopping, and frequent a small bar called the Purple Porpoise on the island with friends at night. We ate hamburgers at Duffy's near the beach. He got permits for eight crab traps and set them out. We rose early every morning to check them. It was like Christmas, seeing what the traps held. Sometimes an irritated blue crab, sometimes a fish, and other times nothing. If we got a crab or two, we took them home to the house in a five-gallon bucket of water and then Dad would fix up a big boiling pot with Old Bay spices. We'd drop the crabs into the pot until their pale blue shells turned sunburned red.

Dad would spread newspapers on the counter and he'd set out two sets of crackers and tiny forks. We ate the still-warm crab, dipping the sweet meat into small bowls of melted butter laced with lemons right off a tree in our yard.

When I complained one morning that the wet ropes from the traps were hard on my hands, Dad came home that afternoon with a special present: a set of waterproof gloves.

Sometimes we'd walk the beach and just talk. As the sun set, he told me stories about his years at the little two-room house near my first school, about meeting my mother, about everything. He clearly thought he'd dodged a bullet with the cancer.

Mom came down for a visit just before I started school that autumn. Once again, she started to shop for my clothes at thrift stores. "Why, look, these barely have any wear on them!" she remarked as she picked out a pair of pure-white off-brand tennis shoes.

When I showed up the first day of school, a gaggle of popular girls stood in a corner looking at me. Finally, a dark-haired girl with a poufy perm called out, "Hey, nice shoes!"

I was naïve enough to think it was an invitation to talk to them. "Hi!" I said brightly, walking toward them. "I just moved here from Michigan."

The girls looked at one another with exaggerated eye rolls. "Like, we're *so interested* in that," said the dark-haired gang leader. "You must be poor. The rest of us have Nikes." I had never heard of the brand, but I knew the name.

"Nike was the winged goddess of victory in Greek mythology," was my catchy, encyclopedic comeback. The girls burst out in hysteric laughing.

"Why would your parents let you leave the house dressed that way?" a placid blond girl asked coolly. She was clad in an expensive pink miniskirt ensemble.

Startled by the unexpected taunting, I didn't know what to say. "Why do yours?" was all I said, immediately wishing I could have come up with something better.

She trilled a light laugh that made her small nose crinkle just so.

"Because I'm rich and I can have any clothes that I want. You dress like you work at the Salvation Army."

The dark-haired girl stood clutching her notebooks to her chest in judgment. "It's not even that, you're just a total weirdo," she said. "I don't think any of us like you and we're certainly not going to waste any time even *talking* to you." In unison, they turned on their heels and walked away to a pair of other girls, pointing and laughing at me.

Humiliated, I just stood there, unsure of what to do. Aside from the church choir, I was desperately lonely and painfully eager to make friends. I slumped away in an effort to put the girls' mocking laughter behind me. I'd unwittingly caught the attention of the most powerful clique of mean girls in the seventh grade my first week of school and they'd deemed me a social clod. Over the next couple of years, the girls ruthlessly ridiculed me.

As an upshot, my outcast status meant I had a lot of time to spend with my father. We made dinner together every night. He taught me to make all the old farm favorites: chicken and biscuits, oven-fried chicken with paprika, spaghetti, and Grandpa Charles's "Mich-Mex" chili. I would come home to find loaves of homemade bread cooling on towels in the kitchen.

We went fishing often, and when we caught anything, he'd clean it and I'd help him fry it coated in almonds. We'd eat the hot fish with the warm homemade bread slathered with salted butter, just like old times.

Mom finally moved down to Florida in January 1980. She found work as an administrative assistant with the development company that owned the posh Longboat Key Club on an island south of us. She earned $5.50 an hour, easily less than half of her previous salary. But her new role had its perks. Where her commute had been snowy highways into the gritty urban landscape of downtown Flint, she now had a slow drive south through the small beach towns on the island along the Gulf of Mexico. Every day, Dad would put together a plate of chopped vegetables and cheese for her to nibble on when she got home, along with a glass of wine. They went dancing at a small bar called Trader Jack's on the weekend. Fresh out of college, my brothers Milton and Doug moved nearby. All of us would go fishing in Dad's small motorboat.

Life felt back on track. Except that it wasn't.

Late that summer, I started to notice Dad had a lot of doctors' appointments again. He became winded walking the beach. His skin took on an ashen gray color. Dad had developed lung cancer. It was unclear whether his melanoma went systemic or he had developed it separately, the result of years of smoking.

No one told me; I overheard my mother telling someone in Michigan about the diagnosis on the phone. But still, Dad persisted with everyday life as if nothing were wrong.

Since our days at the apartment, I'd become obsessed with dollhouses. I wanted one so badly that I made my own by taping together shoeboxes with duct tape into a series of rooms. At first, I crafted furniture from household items. I glued small pebbles onto a box cut into the shape of a hearth to make a fireplace. Small spools of thread made up the seating for the dining table fashioned from a metal jar lid with matchstick legs to hold it up. Then Mom said I could sign up for a subscription to the House of Miniatures dollhouse furniture kits advertised in the back of the *National Enquirer*, a scheme not unlike the Columbia Record House arrangements of the day. For a dollar, they shipped an introductory kit to make a Colonial-style dresser complete with the required balsa, tiny hinges, and tubes of stain. Each month, they forwarded a new kit at an increased fee. I made the dresser, then moved on to a grandfather clock, a Chippendale-era writing desk, a nightstand, a three-piece dining set, and a floral-covered canopy bed circa 1750. Dad watched me forge together the tiny furniture with the tinted glue with amusement. "You really want a real dollhouse, don't you?" he remarked.

One day while he was getting the car serviced at the Sears in a nearby mall, I found the *perfect* one in a country crafts store situated in one of the storefronts. I dragged Dad there to take a look.

Made from unvarnished cedar, pine, and heavy balsa, it was supposed to resemble a Victorian-era farmhouse with five rooms, a generous attic, and a wrap-around porch. Crafted with remarkable detail, the exterior even boasted tiny wood shingles.

"What do you think, Daddy?"

He noted the sturdy construction and the fine craftsmanship. Then he asked how much it cost. At about $450 in today's dollars, I knew even before I took him there that the price tag made it wildly unlikely I'd ever own it. Cancer was expensive.

"Maybe Santa will bring it for you," was all he said.

Dad took me to visit "my house" at least once a week for about three months. I would sometimes sit in the store for more than an hour, imagining the magnificent house was mine. The visits stopped in early November when my father got too sick to take me.

Mike came home for a leave from the navy. My sister, Sandy, Aunt Mary Jo, and her husband flew in for a visit from Michigan. Mike wouldn't be home through Thanksgiving, so they decided to make a big turkey dinner one Saturday instead. Dad was weak, and for once didn't help cook. He sat back in his recliner and watched the action in the kitchen. Sandy and I worked on the turkey and, with Aunt Mary Jo, made the side dishes. He seemed so pleased.

"I love watching my daughters cook," Dad told Mom. "It just amazes me how good those girls are in the kitchen."

Mike found a log in the yard. Ever the artist, he spent his break whittling it and carving it into a boat as a gift for Dad. He erected the masts, crafted small sails from a discarded pillow case, and painstakingly arranged lines for rigging. Dad marveled at his skill. "Isn't that Mike so talented," he told Mom, gazing at the ship. "He knows how much I love boats."

Doug secured work as a manager at Walgreen's while Milton was working at Tropicana in human resources. Both worked long hours, yet still came home and took care of all the maintenance on the house. They took turns taking Dad to various doctors' appointments, mowing the lawn, weeding the garden, and even taking Mom's car to be washed. Dad was touched at their thoughtfulness. "How did we raise such hardworking boys?" Dad asked my mother.

On Sunday, Dad started having trouble breathing. Mom called

my brothers and they came to the house and drove him to the hospital. A doctor explained that Dad needed oxygen to get his breathing regulated. Sitting in his bed, a line of oxygen strung from a machine by his side, he seemed all right. On Monday night, my mother took me up to see him. I told him about my day at school. He assured me he'd be home before Thanksgiving.

When I prepared to leave, he gave me a long hug. "Always remember how much I love you," he said. Then he pulled back and studied my face. "Gosh, you look just like me."

"Well, of course I do! I'm your daughter!" I replied.

Dad's condition declined overnight. His breathing became shallower as he gasped for air, struggling to breathe. Alarmed, Mom called Doug and Milton. They rushed to the hospital. As the day wore on, things got worse. He panicked occasionally, unable to take solid breaths. Mom fetched a nurse. "We have to turn the oxygen machine up higher," Mom urged.

The young nurse gave her a sad look and put a hand on her shoulder. "I'm sorry, it's as high as it will go. But let me take a look." She went in to check on Dad and take his temperature. "Is there anything I can get you, Mr. Flinn?"

He smiled at her. Through his wheezing, he asked, "You wouldn't happen to have a spare lung in your back pocket, would you?" She smiled back and shook her head. "Well, then I guess I've got everything I need."

At eight P.M., a doctor suggested they give Dad a light sedative to help him sleep. The same nurse pulled Mom outside the door. "I think you may want to consider saying your good-byes now," she told my mother gently.

Mom went in and spent a half hour talking to Dad. As she caressed his hand in hers, she thought of the night he'd extended it to pick her up off the floor of the skating rink.

"I'm so glad that I ran into you at the rink," he said, reading her thoughts. He looked sweetly in her eyes and added, "I will love you always and forever."

Tears welled up in Mom's eyes. "I will love you always and forever, too."

"Don't cry," Dad said, his breathing sharp and shallow. "We've done good, haven't we? Look at what good kids we raised. I'm so proud of every one of them. We had so much fun together. California, the restaurant, the farm, fishing, cooking. I'm so glad that I've spent this life with you."

Milton came in to let Mom know the nurse was ready to give Dad his shot. As she finished, Dad asked Doug to open the window so he could look outside. It reminded Mom of her final day with Hazel those many years earlier.

"It's going to be a long night," was all Dad said. With that, he drifted to sleep.

Mom went to a pay phone and called Aunt Mary Jo. She told her what was happening. Mary Jo said she'd take care of flying Sandy back down first thing in the morning. They'd come together.

My brothers and mother stayed at the hospital all night, taking shifts so someone would always be in Dad's room. Around five A.M., Milton slowly walked to the waiting lounge where Mom and Doug were dozing in the hard chairs. His steps echoed in the empty hallway. He shook my mother awake.

"He's gone."

Milton Gale Flinn Sr. died on November 19, 1980. He was only fifty years old.

🍓

My brother Milton's new wife, Delynn, had come to stay with me overnight. I'd made a fire and we ate popcorn and watched old movies. Back from the hospital, Mom, Doug, and Milton wearily sat around the counter.

No one woke me for school the next morning. When I rushed from my room, concerned I'd be late, Doug broke the news. Mom came into my bedroom.

I sat on my bed, stunned. "I didn't know he was that sick," I said to Mom. No one ever told me he might not make it.

"Oh, honey, he's been so sick for such a long time," Mom said, her face softening. "The doctors gave him two weeks to live months ago." Then she wrapped me in a hug and started to cry.

"Mama, don't worry," I said, hugging her back. "I'll always take care of you."

Dad had been sick enough that Mary Jo and Mom had made funeral arrangements a month before he died.

Since they didn't know many people, the three-day Michigan-style visitation didn't make any sense. They had a simple viewing, then a funeral. Mike flew back in from his station in the Middle East to attend the service. When members of the local VFW post placed the American flag over my father's casket, Mike stood and saluted in his uniform.

By Thanksgiving, Mary Jo and Sandy were back in Michigan, Doug was working, and Milt celebrated Thanksgiving with his new wife's relatives. Mom and I decided to go shopping at the mall. For lunch, we sat in the empty Piccadilly Cafeteria eating tepid turkey entrées. As we finished, I insisted that we go visit my dollhouse. Though she'd heard about it in exquisite detail, Mom had never seen it. I'd always gone with my father.

She didn't want to go. I stood firm. Finally, I dragged her through the mall and into the store. I was confident that once she saw it, she'd understand.

But it wasn't there. The saleswoman told us it had been sold.

My mother offered to help me find another dollhouse. It wouldn't be the same, I told her. That was *our* house. It belonged to Dad and me. Now they were both gone.

The weeks drifted by until Christmas. Everyone tried to act happy, as if nothing were missing. My father's absence was overwhelming.

I woke late on Christmas morning. My oldest brothers and Sandy were there, along with my mom. They had all finished at least one cup of coffee. I rubbed my sleepy eyes and saw the tree my brother Doug had hastily erected and decorated when my mother couldn't bring herself to unearth the Christmas decorations she'd put up the year before with Dad.

Underneath the branches was a large, bulky object covered with a white sheet. A red bow and a small card were awkwardly taped to the top.

I went over and read the card: "For Kathleen," clearly written in my father's careful hand. Slowly, I pulled back the sheet. It was my dollhouse.

I turned to look around. My family was looking at me with quiet expectation.

"How . . . ?" I whispered.

My father had bought it just before he died. He gave my mother only one instruction.

"Tell her it's from Santa."

CHAPTER 19

How Far Is Heaven

White egret in our Florida yard

On New Year's Day, a white egret, Dad's favorite bird, flew into our yard—unusual behavior for the statuesque birds, as they prefer to perch at water's edge seeking out prey. Mom and I marveled as the stately bird awkwardly poked around the greenery. Why was he in our yard? I asked Mom.

"This will sound crazy," she began. Dad said that Native Americans believed egrets hold the ability to communicate with the heavens. "Maybe it's a sign from your father? Maybe the bird is watching over you on his behalf?"

I rolled my eyes. "You're right, that *does* sound crazy, Mom."

Every day afterward, the bird returned to our yard when I came home from school. It would stay for hours. Often I'd catch it staring directly at me.

In the wake of my father's death, I listlessly attended classes. I barely talked to anyone, losing myself in books instead. I even brought paperbacks to math class rather than pay attention to the pre-algebra taught by Mrs. Sicard on the overhead projector. In March, the shipment for Scholastic Books arrived. I'd ordered more than twenty titles, but one was missing—a novelization of the film *The Swarm*. In its place was another one that hadn't even been on the list, *A Tree Grows in Brooklyn* by Betty Smith. I looked dubious. It sounded like some old boring book.

"It's wonderful," stressed my English teacher, a kind woman named Mrs. Sally Baggett. "It's about a girl your age who loses her father. They're very close. I had actually been meaning to recommend this book to you so it's very strange that it showed up here like this."

The cover showed a pretty young girl with long brown hair reading a book in a window. She reminded me of my friend Margaret back on Hill Street.

"Maybe you could write a report on it?"

My ears perked up. Quite possibly, I was the only kid in the world who loved to write book reports. "You mean, for extra credit?"

Mrs. Baggett knew me better than any of my other teachers. "No," she said quietly. "For you. But I'll give you extra credit if you want."

It was Friday. I took my books home on the bus. I walked into our empty house, my mother still at work for at least another couple of hours. I went outside into our yard and sat down to read on the porch in the shade of the mango tree. The scent of orange blossoms drifted on the light gulf breeze.

> The one tree in Francie's yard was neither a pine nor a hemlock. . . . Some people called it the Tree of Heaven. No matter where its seed fell, it made a tree which struggled to reach the sky. . . .

After I finished the first chapter, I looked up. The white egret stood silently studying me just a few feet away. Unnerved, I got up and headed back inside to my room.

By the time my mother came home, I was so engrossed I barely heard her enter. As became her habit after work, she wearily asked me about my day and if I was hungry. Often I had already eaten, so she'd head into her room "to close her eyes for a moment." Sometimes she slept for more than ten hours. I didn't know her fatigue was a sign of grief and lingering depression.

At 528 pages, *A Tree Grows in Brooklyn* is a long book, even for a thirteen-year-old with a voracious appetite for reading. I was awake reading when my brother Doug came home from work around one A.M. I kept at it until after he went to bed: Katie falling in love with Johnny Nolan, Francie's love for her romantic father who died tragically when she was a preteen. When I got to a passage in which she and her brother, Neely, sat on a curb crying after the loss of their father, I put the book down and cried—long, hard, ugly, gulping sobs, and the first tears I'd shed since he'd died. I cried myself into an exhausted sleep and woke with the book open on my chest.

I identified with Francie, the main character, in a way I hadn't connected to anyone real or fictional. She was a constant reader and a devoted Daddy's girl. She grew up in poverty, and somehow Brooklyn in the early 1900s didn't seem that much different from 1970s Michigan. I finished the book on Saturday, and, as promised, took my report to Mrs. Baggett after school on Monday.

> Francie Nolan's father died. My father died. She grew up with little, and yet felt that she had so much in her colorful world that she wrote stories, just like me. She loved books, even once making an attempt to read all the books in the world just as I had done when I turned eleven.
>
> She was the sum total of her romantic father, her practical mother, her brutal grandfather, her angelic grandmother, fun-loving aunt and handsome brother. I

am my father, my mother, my brothers, my sister, my aunts, my uncles and my grandparents, even the ones I never met.

The most important message of the book to me was that Francie somehow gets over the loss of her father, she emerges stronger somehow. I will, too.

It reminds me of the saying my grandmother had, that "burnt toast makes you sing good." You suffer through something to come out on the other side better for it. . . .

I stood by Mrs. Baggett's county-issued steel desk as she read my two-page report. When she finished, she stood up, hugged me, and we both cried.

Heading home on the county bus, I thought of the foods the Nolans ate: fried dough balls made from stale bread, simple soups, potatoes. It reminded me of the foods that my dad said he subsisted on as a kid. As the bus headed toward the island, it occurred to me that I was hungry and we had no food in the house. The past week-end, Mom had resorted to opening a can of tomato soup and toast-ing a heel of bread for Sunday dinner.

I looked in my small purse. Doug had left me a ten-dollar bill that morning. I pulled the cord for the stop at the Island Foodway. I wandered the store picking up what I could remember from the recipe for beef stew that Mom used to make when we went ice fish-ing: a package of stew meat, a couple of onions, carrots, celery, potatoes, and wide noodles. I hopped back on the bus, and once home, I pulled down Mom's copy of *Mastering the Art of French Cooking* and flipped to her recipe for beef bourguignon. I found a half-empty jug of Ernest & Julio Gallo red table wine in the fridge and a frozen tub of chicken stock in the freezer.

As I had done at the house on Hill Street, I cranked up some Johnny Cash on the eight-track. I browned the meat and chopped up the vegetables as Dad had shown me so many times. While the stew cooked, I slid another tape into the eight-track, the country music collection we had listened to on so many drives to and from Florida. I sang along to "Sixteen Tons," "Orange Blossom Special," and then a tune came on by Kitty Wells. I'd heard it for what felt like a thousand times from the age of eight, but this time, I put down my wooden spoon and sat on the couch as she sang "How Far Is Heaven."

> *"How Far Is Heaven? When can I go?*
> *To see my daddy, he's there, I know;*
> *How Far Is Heaven? Let's go tonight.*
> *I want my daddy to hold me tight. . . ."*

I looked out in the yard. Once again, the white egret was staring right at me through the windows. I looked around the house. It was a mess. I heard my grandma Inez's voice. "You have time to feel sorry for yourself, Kathleen Inez? You have time to clean the house."

So I pulled the country music collection from the eight-track. I put in ABBA instead. They were Swedish, after all. Great-grandmother Anna would approve. I danced around as I picked up the house, belting "Dancing Queen" at the top of my lungs.

Mom came home, looking tired as usual as she made her way through the front door. As she put her purse down on the couch, she asked, "What do I smell? Did you cook something?" Then she looked around and smiled. "Well, the house sure looks good!"

I turned down the music as we sat down to eat stew at the counter. I poured Mom a glass of the red wine from the fridge and set down a simple iceberg salad. Mom took a sip and placed a napkin on her lap. "Well, isn't this nice?"

The next day, I made Dad's spaghetti from That's Amore. Then chicken and biscuits, followed by Uncle Clarence's paprika chicken. The following weekend, Mom drove me to the store with my list in hand, entrusted with our weekly grocery budget.

Feeding my grieving mother fed me, too. My father was gone, but I had not lost the flavors of my childhood, nor the lessons that he left me. When everything else seemed so unsettled, the simple act of cooking saved me somehow.

Epilogue

B ut I can't afford to go," I stammered into the phone.
"How long have you wanted to study in Paris?" he replied.
"You may never get another chance. Your dad would have wanted
you to go."

Mike, my boyfriend of less than three months, lived in Seattle.
I lived more than four thousand miles away in London. I had just
lost my corporate job, one I had been longing to quit. I woke him
up at five A.M. his time to make the case to move to the Pacific
Northwest so we could be together.

My sister's dream was to study at the Sorbonne. Mine was to
attend Le Cordon Bleu, the alma mater of Julia Child and the most
famous culinary school in the world. I'd come up with the idea
when I was in my early twenties, working as an obituary writer at
a Florida newspaper.

Writing obituaries in southwest Florida is a *busy* job. After a
year on the desk, I estimated that I had marked the passing of more
than five thousand people. They ranged from a 6-year-old musical
prodigy to a 101-year-old World War I veteran. One day, the short-
est obituary I had ever seen came across the fax machine. It simply

stated the woman's name, age, and the identity of her late spouse. No services, no survivors, no memberships in any organization, no education, no employment history, not even a place to send donations in lieu of flowers. The funeral home confirmed on the phone that that was all they had to say about the 84 year-old.

I hung up and sat back in my chair. How does a person get to such an age yet leave no apparent trace, at least where documented achievements are concerned? Could that happen to me? Just then, I looked down at my desk. An issue of *Gourmet* magazine lay open. An ad caught my eye. "Study French cuisine in Paris," it read. The walls of the farmhouse bedroom flashed before my eyes.

How many times had I talked about Paris with my sister? Yet Sandy never did study at the Sorbonne. My father didn't live to see me graduate high school. He never knew any of his grandchildren.

At that split second, I decided that I wanted my own obituary to read, "She also earned a degree from Le Cordon Bleu in Paris." I pulled a pair of scissors from a drawer. I cut out the ad and pinned it to the wall of my beige cubicle. The next day, when the short obit ran, I cut it out and put it up next to the ad. I took both with me to every desk I occupied for the next fourteen years.

Mike knew about the obituary. I rarely told people the whole story, the same way you can't tell people you plan to run a marathon and not follow through. But as much as I longed for Paris, I knew one thing for certain: I was crazy in love with him. So why would he use this dream of mine to go to Paris against me? I thought. Was this his way of dissuading me from moving to Seattle? Maybe he wasn't as into our relationship as I thought.

I kept up my protests, finally ending with: "But I won't know anyone in Paris."

Mike paused for a moment. "Well, you'll know me," he said quietly. "Because if you want me to, I'll go with you."

Within a week, I had been accepted into the last spot open in the Basic Cuisine course and cashed in a 401(k) to pay my tuition. Mike quit his job in Seattle. Three weeks after the last official day with my company, I was in the kitchens of the famous school. Every day I passed a photo of Julia Child in the hallway.

"We just decided to go," my mom says of their trip to California all those years ago. I imagine her holding my sister, Sandy, then a toddler, against her pregnant lap as they doggedly sang "Route 66" over and over again.

My great-grandmother arrived in America with a single suitcase, barely able to ask directions in English. My whiskey-running grandfather packed up for a chance to cook for the troops in San Antonio when he was deemed ineligible to fight. These are my people.

Like Francie from *A Tree Grows in Brooklyn*, I'm pieces of my parents, siblings, grandparents, and great-grandparents. Like so many of them, I love to cook—enough to drive me to another country. I learned endless lessons in generosity from Grandma Inez and Grandpa Charles. I inherited the thin steel that ran through Della Stark and the salesmanship of her scoundrel husband, James. I'm the daughter of a marine, a cop, and a man who would rather go without than go back on his word. I'm my mother's daughter, who was tough enough to kill chickens, yet kind enough to tell me that a church thrift shop was a posh department store so that I wouldn't feel ashamed of wearing secondhand clothes.

Burnt toast makes you sing good. Be thankful; no matter how little you've got, someone's always worse off than you. You can't give anything away, it always comes back. They handed down these simple life lessons to me as surely as they did their recipes.

I'm a mutt. But as they say with dogs, mixed breeds prove the most resilient. The people in my past helped make me tough, passionate, and endlessly optimistic. That's what I want to talk about even if it happens that my grandfather wasn't Irish after all. But a distant grandmother was from County Kerry. So I'm still Irish, at least a wee bit.

All of this, ignited by a short obituary and cheap posters in a farmhouse bedroom, led this Midwest girl to don kitchen whites as I embarked on a love affair in the most romantic city in the world.

But that's another story.

Extra Recipes

Grandma Inez's Pancakes

Once I asked my grandmother if she loved me. It was in the middle of a hectic weekend morning when she was acting as short-order cook for a flock of kids and six adults. With a bit of exasperation, she replied quickly, "I don't have to tell you I love you. I made you pancakes." I was then handed my plate and told to sit down. She was right. I could taste her love in every bite.

I consider these Swedish American–style pancakes; the extra egg yields something more akin to a crepe. Try to use at least 2 percent milk if using reduced-fat milk; nonfat milk will thin the batter.

If you don't have self-rising flour, add 2½ teaspoons of baking powder and ½ teaspoon of salt to 1 cup of all-purpose flour. No buttermilk? Put 1 table-spoon of vinegar or lemon juice in a 1-cup measure, add milk to fill, and let sit for 5 minutes.

To make fruit-flavored pancakes, gently fold in about a handful (about 1 cup or 225 g) after the batter has rested.

Makes 12 to 14 pancakes

4 tablespoons (60 g) unsalted butter
2 tablespoons (60 ml) sugar
4 large eggs

1¾ cups (420 ml) buttermilk or whole milk, plus more if needed
1 teaspoon (5 ml) vanilla extract
2 cups (250 g) self-rising flour
Nonstick cooking spray or vegetable oil, for cooking

To make the batter: Melt the butter in a small saucepan or in the microwave; let it cool to room temperature. In a large bowl, beat the sugar, eggs, milk, and vanilla with a large spoon, whisk, or electric beater, then stir in the melted butter. Beat in the flour until the batter is mostly smooth. The batter should be a little thicker than heavy cream. If it's too thick, thin it with a bit of extra milk. Let the batter rest for about 5 minutes.

To make the pancakes: Get a small skillet hot over medium-high heat. (If using a cast-iron skillet, you want to keep the heat at medium.) Cover the bottom with a thin coating of nonstick cooking spray or a little bit of oil. Test the pan's temperature by spooning a large tablespoon of batter into it, adjusting the heat as needed so that it takes about 2 to 3 minutes to cook per side without coming out too light or dark. When the pan is ready, use a ladle or measuring cup to pour about ¼ cup of batter into the pan. Cook until the top of the pancake is mostly dotted with air holes, 2 to 3 minutes, then flip. Let cook about 1 minute more, until the bottom, when lifted with a spatula, appears golden brown. Keep pancakes in a 200°F (93°C) oven loosely covered with foil. If needed, add a bit more cooking spray between pancakes.

Della's Homemade Noodles

My grandmother used to dry her noodles on newspaper, but you're better off using a wire cooling rack or adding flour to a shallow baking pan or cookie sheet and enveloping the noodles in the flour. The dough can be prepared a day ahead of time (see note for storage information).

    Be sure you've got additional flour on hand to roll out the dough. If you have a pasta machine, put the dough through its widest setting—it's easier than rolling it out—but hand-cut the flattened dough.

These can be served with a main course such as my Grandpa Charles's Beef or Venison Stew (page 129) or Sauerbraten (page 260), or mixed with a bit of butter and cheese and served alone as a side dish.

Makes enough for about 4 side servings but is easily doubled

1 cup (140 g) all-purpose flour, plus more for kneading and rolling
½ teaspoon (2.5 ml) salt
2 large eggs

Combine the flour and salt in a large bowl. Make a well in the center. Crack the eggs into the well. With a fork, beat the eggs and gradually incorporate the flour until it forms a sticky dough.

Turn the dough out onto a well-floured surface. With floured hands, knead the dough until it is smooth and not sticky, 4 to 5 minutes. Mold it lightly into a ball and then flatten it into a disk. Cover the disk with plastic wrap and chill for at least 30 minutes or as long as overnight.

When you're ready to roll it out, divide the dough into 2 pieces. On a floured surface, roll each piece to about ⅛ inch (3 mm) thick, turning the rolled out dough by a quarter turn after each roll to keep it from sticking. If using a pasta machine, insert the dough at the widest setting and run through 2 or 3 times, until smooth and flat.

Place the dough on the counter or atop a large cutting board or cookie sheet. Using a sharp knife or a pizza cutter, cut the dough into thin or wide noodles as desired, but try to cut them evenly so they have a consistent cooking time. Lay the noodles on a wire cooling rack or on a cookie sheet smothered in flour and let sit until you're ready to cook them. Cook the noodles in boiling salted water until tender to the bite, about 4 minutes, but this will depend on thickness.

Note: To store the cut noodles for later use, let them rest for about 1 hour or until completely dry. Place in an airtight container, plastic freezer bag, or freezer container. Store the dried noodles for up to 3 days in the refrigerator or freeze for up to 6 months.

Grandpa Charles's Secret Chili Powder

Grandpa made his own chili powder for years. This is the closest I've been able to come to re-creating it. Adjust the cayenne to your preferred level of heat.

Makes about 4 ounces (113 g) of spice mixture

    4 tablespoons (60 g) Hungarian paprika
    1 tablespoon (15 g) oregano
    1 tablespoon (15 g) cumin
    2 to 3 teaspoons (10 to 15 g) cayenne
    2 teaspoons (10 g) unsweetened cocoa powder
    2 teaspoons (10 g) garlic powder
    2 teaspoons (10 g) onion powder
    ¼ teaspoon cinnamon
    ¼ teaspoon nutmeg

Combine the paprika, oregano, cumin, cayenne, cocoa powder, garlic powder, onion powder, cinnamon, and nutmeg in a pint-sized jar. Shake well. Store in an airtight container away from heat and light for up to a year or so.

Homemade Salt-Free Poultry Seasoning

You could argue that the first step in this recipe is to find a place that sells herbs and spices in bulk. Many supermarkets now offer DIY bulk options. If you've never explored buying spices in bulk, it's worthy of investigation.

I set aside a coffee grinder for milling whole spices and mixing blends such as this one. If you want to use a coffee grinder that's been employed for coffee beans, you can clean it by grinding rice and salt together thoroughly, then wiping it clean with a paper towel.

Makes about 3½ tablespoons (52.5 ml)

    1 tablespoon (15 ml) crumbled dried sage
    2 teaspoons (10 ml) dried thyme
    2 teaspoons (10 ml) dried marjoram
    2 teaspoons (10 ml) dried rosemary
    ½ teaspoon (2.5 ml) celery seed
    ½ teaspoon (2.5 ml) freshly grated nutmeg
    ½ teaspoon (2.5 ml) ground black pepper

Combine the sage, thyme, marjoram, rosemary, celery seed, nutmeg, and pepper and grind together with a mortar and pestle or in a small coffee grinder. Store in an airtight container shielded from heat and light. It's best used within about a year.

Shortnin' Bread

Grandpa Charles loved the song "Shortnin' Bread," made famous by the Andrews Sisters but covered dozens of times since. The origins of the lyrics are thought to be a combination of an old plantation song and a 1910 poem by James Whit-comb Riley. This recipe is adapted from a newspaper clipping in Grandma Inez's old recipe box. I don't know what paper it appeared in or when, but it was most likely the Midland Daily News. *If you don't have buttermilk, you can make it by adding 1 tablespoon (15 ml) of vinegar to 1 cup (240 ml) of whole milk. Let it sit for 5 minutes to thicken. If you don't have a 10-inch cast-iron skillet, you can use a similarly sized baking dish.*

Makes one 10-inch (25-cm) round loaf, about 8 servings

    Nonstick cooking spray, vegetable oil, or unsalted butter for the skillet
    2 cups (280 g) all-purpose flour, plus more for the skillet
    ½ teaspoon (2.5 ml) ground cinnamon
    ¼ teaspoon (1.25 ml) ground nutmeg
    1½ teaspoons (7.5 ml) baking soda

½ cup (120 ml) buttermilk
6 tablespoons (90 g) unsalted butter
1 cup (240 g) molasses
1 large egg, slightly beaten

Preheat the oven to 350°F (177°C). Prepare a 10-inch (25-cm) cast-iron skillet by coating it with cooking spray, then with a light coating of flour.

Combine the flour, cinnamon, and nutmeg in a large bowl, mixing well. Dissolve the baking soda in the buttermilk.

Combine the butter and molasses in a heavy saucepan over high heat. Bring to a boil, stirring constantly. Reduce the heat to low and whisk in the flour mixture. Remove from the heat and let the mixture cool slightly, allowing the flour to absorb the butter and molasses. Stir in the buttermilk and egg. Pour into the prepared skillet.

Bake for 20 to 25 minutes, until it's firm to the touch and golden. Cool for 10 minutes in the skillet, then invert onto a plate and cut into wedges.

Aunt Myrtle's No-Knead Yeast Rolls

The greatest thing about these rolls is that the dough is made ahead of time and refrigerated. Thus they're an easy addition to any meal, since you just plop them into a muffin pan, brush the tops with butter, and pop them into the oven.

Makes 2 dozen rolls

One ¼-ounce (7-g) package active dry yeast (2¼ teaspoons)
¼ cup (60 ml) warm water (90°F to 110°F/32°C to 43°C)
¼ cup (60 g) vegetable shortening
1½ teaspoons (7.5 ml) salt
2 tablespoons (30 ml) sugar
1 cup (250 ml) boiling water
1 large egg

3½ cups (450 g) all-purpose flour
Nonstick cooking spray for the pan
3 tablespoons (45 g) unsalted butter, melted

Dissolve the yeast in the warm water and let sit for about 10 minutes.

In a different bowl, combine the shortening, salt, sugar, and boiling water. Let cool slightly. Add the dissolved yeast, egg, and flour and mix well; the dough will be slightly sticky. Cover the bowl with plastic wrap and chill the dough for least 2 hours and up to 24 hours.

Coat a muffin pan with cooking spray. Pinch off dough and fill each muffin slot about ⅓ full. Brush the tops with melted butter. Let rise for about 2 hours in a warm place, until doubled.

Preheat the oven to 425°F (218°C). Bake the rolls for 20 minutes, or until they rise up firmly and are slightly browned. Let cool slightly before removing from the pan. Store leftovers in an airtight container.

Blueberry Jam

"This tastes just like my dad's jam," Mom said at breakfast at the Tupelo Honey Café in Asheville, North Carolina. As no one in the family could find one of Grandpa Charles's recipes, I adapted this recipe from the Tupelo Honey Cafe cookbook.

Makes about 2½ cups, or 5 half-pint jars

¾ cup (150 g) sugar
1½ teaspoons pectin
1½ pounds (680 g) fresh blueberries (4 cups)
1 tablespoon (15 ml) freshly squeezed lemon juice

Combine the sugar and pectin in a large bowl until thoroughly blended. Place the blueberries in a medium saucepan and stir in the sugar mixture and lemon juice.

Bring to a boil, reduce the heat to medium, and cook, stirring occasionally, for about 10 minutes, until the mixture falls in a sheet off the back of a spoon.

Allow to cool to room temperature before serving. Store in an airtight container for up to 30 days.

"Candy Girl" Moist Oatmeal Cookies

These are cheap to make, so they were among the most common variety Mom had in our cookie jar at the farm. Cooking the raisins before adding them to the dough makes them tender.

Makes 1 dozen large cookies or 20 smaller ones, depending on how you shape them

2 cups (360 g) raisins
1 cup (250 ml) water
½ pound (225 g) unsalted butter
2 cups (400 g) sugar
2 teaspoons (10 ml) ground cinnamon
1 teaspoon (5 ml) salt
4 large eggs, beaten
3 cups (285 g) old-fashioned oatmeal
3 cups (420 g) all-purpose flour
2 teaspoons (10 ml) baking soda
1 cup (100 g) chopped walnuts (optional)

Put the raisins and water in a large skillet. Cook slowly over low heat until tender, about 15 minutes.

Remove the raisins from the heat. Add the butter and let it melt through. Add the sugar, cinnamon, and salt and mix thoroughly. It will be a thick liquid. Cool to lukewarm.

While the raisin mixture is cooling, preheat the oven to 350°F (177°C). Line a cookie sheet with parchment paper or a nonstick silicone liner. (If you make large cookies, you may need to do 2 batches.)

Add the eggs to the raisin mixture. Mix the oatmeal, flour, and baking soda in a large bowl until well blended. Add to the raisin mixture. Blend well. Stir in the walnuts if using.

Drop by teaspoonfuls for small cookies or use a tablespoon for larger cookies, leaving about ½ inch between spoonfuls as the cookies will spread during baking.

Bake according to cookie size, about 10 minutes for small ones and up to 18 minutes for larger ones. Let cool briefly before serving. Store in an airtight container.

German Buttermilk Coffee Cake

Need a quick, simple cake for a potluck? Here's my mother's go-to dish. If you don't have buttermilk, you can make it by adding 1 tablespoon (15 ml) of vinegar to 1 cup (240 ml) of milk. Let it sit for 5 minutes to thicken.

A bit of orange extract or vanilla-scented sugar adds some extra aroma to the cake. For variation, add 1 tablespoon (15 ml) of crushed nuts and ¼ teaspoon (1.25 ml) of ground nutmeg to the topping. If you're not a nutmeg fan, use cinnamon.

Makes about 10 servings

Butter or nonstick cooking spray for the pan
3 cups (450 g) all-purpose flour, plus more for the pan
1 teaspoon (5 ml) baking soda
1 cup (250 ml) buttermilk
2 cups (400 g) sugar
½ pound (225 g) unsalted butter, frozen and grated, or cut into 1-inch
    (2.5-cm) pieces

½ teaspoon (2.5 ml) freshly grated nutmeg, plus more for sprinkling

2 large eggs, beaten

Preheat the oven to 350°F (175°C). Grease a 9 x 13-inch (23 x 33-cm) baking pan and dust lightly with flour.

In a small bowl, add the baking soda to the buttermilk. In a large bowl, mix the flour, sugar, butter, and nutmeg together with your fingertips until well blended into crumbs; it should feel like coarse cornmeal. Reserve 1 cup (250 ml) of these crumbs for the topping.

Add the eggs and buttermilk to the remaining crumbs. Mix with a spoon until just blended. Pour the batter into the prepared baking pan. Sprinkle the reserved crumbs evenly over the top. Sprinkle with a bit of additional nutmeg. Bake for 30 to 35 minutes, until it sets firm and the topping browns slightly. Let rest briefly before serving. Can be served warm or at room temperature.

Midwest-Style "Goulash"

When paprika hit the Hungarian culinary scene in the early 1800s, locals loved it. One of their favorite dishes for entertaining involved searing meat spiked with the seasoning. Over time, Hungarians' foreign guests incorporated meat and paprika into a variety of dishes, often including a starch (such as pasta) and other vegetables (such as tomatoes) to stretch the meat further, and descendants of those immigrants brought those dishes to America, where they continued to fiddle with them. Growing up in Michigan, seemingly every family had its own version of goulash. This one is adapted from my dad's recipe. Given that this is a hearty dish meant to serve a crowd, you'll want to start it in a 6- to 8-quart (5.5- to 7.25-L) pot or Dutch oven with a cover.

    If you prefer some extra kick or flavor, add additional cayenne, minced garlic, or dried oregano. To finish, Mom notes: "Some people would cover the goulash with slices of Cheddar or Velveeta cheese and put it into the oven until the cheese melts. I didn't do this as it made the macaroni too soft. Sometimes we put grated cheese on top when it was served but it is delicious without it." This keeps well in the fridge for up to 5 days.

Makes about 12 cups (3 L), about 8 to 10 servings, but can easily be halved

  2 tablespoons (30 ml) vegetable oil
  1 large yellow onion, chopped into ½-inch (13-mm) pieces (2½ cups/340 g)
  5 stalks celery (285 g), chopped (about 1 cup)
  1 green bell pepper, seeded and chopped
  2 teaspoons (10 ml) salt
  2 teaspoons (10 ml) dried oregano or thyme
  2 teaspoons (10 ml) paprika
  ½ to 1 teaspoon (2.5 to 5 ml) red chili flakes or cayenne pepper
  2 pounds (900 g) very lean ground beef
  ¼ cup (60 g) tomato paste
  One 28-ounce (794-g) can diced tomatoes
  2 bay leaves
  6 garlic cloves, minced
  ½ teaspoon (2.5 ml) or more coarsely ground pepper
  1 pound (450 g) elbow macaroni
  8 ounces (225 g) cheese, such as Cheddar, Parmesan, or mozzarella,
     grated (optional)

Add the oil to a large pot or Dutch oven over medium-high heat. Once hot, add the onion, celery, green pepper, 1 teaspoon (5 ml) of the salt, the oregano, paprika, and chili flakes and cook until the onions soften, about 5 minutes. Add the ground beef and cook, breaking the beef into small pieces with a spoon as it cooks, until browned, about 8 minutes. If the ground beef gives up a lot of grease, skim or drain it off.

Stir in the tomato paste, tomatoes with their liquid, the rest of the salt, the bay leaves, and the garlic, plus several grinds of pepper. Cover, reduce the heat to simmer, and cook for another 35 minutes. Stir occasionally.

Meanwhile, boil generously salted water in a separate pot. Cook the macaroni according to package directions. Drain and set aside.

Taste to see if the dish needs more salt, pepper, herbs, or chili flakes. Add the cooked macaroni and simmer for about 5 minutes, until the macaroni is heated through. If desired, top portions with cheese and broil, or add cheese to individual servings.

·· ⤳ ··

Sauerbraten

Legend has it that sauerbraten evolved more than five centuries ago as a way to preserve meat so it could be served on Christmas, one of the few times German hunters took a day off.

This recipe is a variation on the one included in the famous Time-Life series Foods of the World *from the late 1960s and early 1970s. The meat sits in a marinade for 2 to 3 days, and is then braised with vegetables along with a secret ingredient: gingersnaps. The instructions look long, but this is a straightforward dish that's great for entertaining. The meat can be put into its marinade well ahead of the gathering and the vegetables can be chopped and prepped the day before braising. I marinate in the same Dutch oven that I'm going to cook it in, covering it with two layers of plastic wrap and then the lid.*

Traditionally, sauerbraten is served with dumplings, boiled potatoes, or noodles. I serve this with Della's Homemade Noodles (page 250). Roast some Brussels sprouts while you're at it and you've got a full meal.

Makes 8 to 10 servings when served with a side of noodles or potatoes

Marinade

    1 cup (250 ml) dry red wine, plus more if needed
    1 cup (250 ml) red wine vinegar
    2 cups (500 ml) cold water
    1 large white onion, thinly sliced (12 ounces/340 g)
    1 tablespoon (15 ml) black peppercorns, coarsely crushed
    1 tablespoon (15 ml) juniper berries, coarsely crushed
    2 bay leaves
    1 teaspoon (5 ml) salt
    4 pounds (1.8 kg) boneless beef roast, preferably bottom round

Braising and Sauce

   3 tablespoons (45 g) unsalted butter

   I large yellow onion, chopped (2½ cups/340 g)

   8 carrots (450 g), chopped (2½ cups)

   6 stalks celery (325 g), chopped (1¼ cups)

   2 tablespoons (30 ml) all-purpose flour

   ½ cup (125 ml) water

   ¾ cup (100 g) crumbled gingersnaps (about 15 cookies)

To make the marinade: Combine the red wine, vinegar, water, onion, peppercorns, juniper berries, bay leaves, and salt in a 2-quart (2-L) or larger saucepan. Bring to a boil over high heat. Remove from the heat and let cool to room temperature.

Place the beef in a deep glass or ceramic bowl or a nonreactive pot just large enough to hold it and cover it with the cooled marinade. The liquid should be at least halfway up the sides of the roast. If necessary, add more wine. Cover tightly with foil or plastic wrap and refrigerate for 2 to 3 days, turning the meat in the marinade at least twice each day.

To braise the beef: When ready to cook, preheat the oven to 350°F (177°C). Remove the meat from the marinade. Pat it completely dry with paper towels. Strain the marinade through a fine sieve and reserve the liquid. Discard the spices and onions.

In 6-quart (5.5-L) or larger Dutch oven or heavy-bottomed pot with a tight-fitting lid, heat the butter until it bubbles. Brown the meat well on each side over medium-high heat. Transfer to a plate.

Lower the heat to medium. Add the onion, carrots, and celery to the pot and cook until the carrots soften and the onions turn translucent, about 8 minutes. Sprinkle with the flour and cook for 2 minutes, stirring constantly. Turn the heat to high, add 2 cups (500 ml) of the reserved marinade and the water, and bring to a boil. Return the beef to the pot, cover tightly, and place in the oven. Cook for 2½ hours, or until the meat begins to flake off with a fork. Transfer the cooked meat to a plate and cover with foil to rest while you make the sauce.

Pour everything from the pot into a bowl or large measuring cup and skim off the fat. Pour the remaining juices and solids back into the pot. Add the gingersnaps. Cook over medium heat, stirring regularly, for about 10 minutes, adding more water or additional crumbs, until it reaches the consistency of thick gravy.

Strain the sauce through a fine-mesh sieve, pressing with a wooden spoon to push as much of the soft vegetables and crumbs through as possible. Return the sauce to the pan, and taste to see if it needs salt or pepper. Simmer gently until ready to serve.

Slice the roast into thick pieces. Pour a small amount of the sauce over the meat and serve the rest separately.

Acknowledgments

This book wouldn't exist without the work of my mother, Irene Flinn, who set down so many stories to paper. Then again, I wouldn't exist either, so I guess I should thank her for that, too. I'd like to recognize my sister-in-law Delynn Flinn, a certified genealogist, for her exhaustive work in the past twenty years researching the family history.

I'm grateful for all the support of my Viking Penguin family for this project, including Patrick Nolan, Emily Murdock Baker, Clare Ferraro, Maxwell J. Reid, Lindsey Prevette, Bennett Petrone, Randee Marullo, and the entire sales and marketing team. This would have been one long, meandering trip down memory lane without the story editing talents of Mike Klozar. I'm delighted to have my agent Andy McNichol at William Morris Endeavor in my corner. Suzanne Fass did a bang-up job copyediting the recipes.

Numerous family members gave their memories and photos to the project, among them Mary Jo Greendwood, Melvina Fridline, Richard Henderson, Steve Wilson, Joyce Wilson, and Ron Newcombe. I want to thank my brothers, Milton, Doug, and Mike, for allowing me to share their stories and being great older brothers. I'm grateful to my sister, Sandy, for inspiring me to dream about Paris and just for being there for me when I need her. My brother Mike shifted crumbling vintage photos and others taken with cheap Instamatic cameras into images good enough to use in this book, so here's an extra nod to you, big brother.

A group of tireless testers contributed to assuring all the recipes in the book work. The most active include Clare Sanborne, Maria Hawkins, Jodi Moriarty, Karen Levin, David St. Clair, Pascale Poitras, Georgia Connell, Sonia Kap, Nazila Merati, Lori Rice, Deborah Schapiro, and Lee Mohr.

I spent a lot of time digging into the past. Thanks to the Davison Historical Society, the Mancelona Historical Society, the Anna Maria Island Historical Society, the City of Frankenmuth, the Chippewa Tribe, and The Ellis Island Project for making available invaluable resources. The members of the Facebook group Growing Up in Davison offered terrific links and memories. As always, I rely heavily on feedback from readers. The most active for this manuscript include Monica Bhide, Jacqueline Donnelly Baisa, Sandra Klim, Cherie Jacobs Featheringill, Rebecca Dawson, Jamie Schler, Nena Price, Sheri Wetherall, Stephanie Gieseke, and my longtime friend Laura Evelev. A tip of the hat goes to my plucky assistant, Marianne Hale, who worked with me from the first word of this manuscript and contributed endless hours of support and feedback.

I turned to some experts for specialized knowledge: Edward Golder at the Michigan Department of Natural Resources for hunting and fishing information, Cpl. Walter Beddoe for information on the U.S. Marines, Matt Crawford for hunting rifle information, Sven Frietag for checking my nonexistent German, and Jefferson Colt for background on moonshine in Carter County. Thanks to food writer Aliza Green for allowing me to use her excellent Montreal steak seasoning recipe. I relied on research done by my cousin, author, and historian Gary Flinn on the history of Flint. Michael Moore reminded me of all the culinary wonders of the state of Michigan along with details of my brother's streaking incident.

A nod to neighbors Vincent Hsieth and Susan Wong in Seattle and Stephanie Gemperline on Anna Maria Island for contributing to our care and feeding during this project.

Finally, I'd like to add a separate and final thanks to my husband, Mike, for finding adventure in the everyday and the extraordinary in the ordinary. Dad would have loved you.

Selected Bibliography

Bosanko, Dave. *Fish of Michigan Field Guide*. Cambridge, MN: Adventure Publications, 2007.

Child, Julia, Simone Beck, and Louise Bertholle. *Mastering the Art of French Cooking*. New York: Knopf, 1961.

"Cold Cuts." *Modern Marvels*. The History Channel. December 17, 2007. Television.

Cowles, Walter. "The Antrim Iron Company." *Antrim Review*, May 9, 2006. http://news.google.com/newspapers?nid=2486&dat=20060509&id=Yk-wzAAAAIBAJ&sjid=shEGAAAAIBAJ&pg=839,848192

Fallone, Margaret. "Mancelona—1180 and Beyond." Antrim County, n.d. (accessed April 28, 2013). http://www.ole.net/~maggie/antrim/mancy2.htm.

Flinn, Gary. *Remembering Flint*. Charleston, SC: The History Press, 2010.

Frankenmuth Historical Association, Heritage Cookbook. Frankenmuth, MI: Frankenmuth Historical Association, 1983.

Genesee County Historical Society. *Genesee County: 1900–1960*. Mount Pleasant, SC: Arcadia Publishing, 2006.

Green, Archie. *Railroad Songs & Ballads: From the Archive of Folk Song*. Washington, DC: Library of Congress, 1968.

Gustin, Lawrence. *Billy Durant: Creator of General Motors*. Ann Arbor, MI: University of Michigan Press/Regional, 1973.

Haber, Barbara. *From Hardtack to Home Fries*. New York: Free Press, 2002.

Hemingway, Ernest. "Up in Michigan." *Three Stories and Ten Poems*. Paris: Contact, 1923.

Hesser, Amanda. *The Essential New York Times Cookbook*. New York: W. W. Norton & Company, 2010.

Johnson, Myrna. *Better Homes and Gardens New Cook Book*. Des Moines, IA: Meredith Publishing, 1965.

Kalish, Mildred Armstrong. *Little Heathens: Hard Times and High Spirits on an Iowa Farm During the Great Depression*. New York: Bantam Dell, 2007.

Kamp, David. *The United States of Arugula*. New York: Clarkson Potter, 2006.

"The Making of Frankenmuth." Frankenmuth Chamber of Commerce and Convention and Visitors Bureau, n.d. (accessed April 28, 2013). http://www.frankenmuth.org/aboutus/history.

Mead, Rebecca. *Swedes in Michigan*. East Lansing, MI: Michigan State University Press, 2012.

Michigan Department of National Resources Wildlife Division. "A History of Deer Hunting in Michigan." Report 2868, September 1980.

Moore, Michael. *Here Comes Trouble*. New York: Grand Central Publishing, 2011.

Morgan, Diane. *Roots*. San Francisco: Chronicle Books, 2012.

Ritsema, Nancy. "Antrim County Helped Supply Nation with Iron." *Antrim Review*, February 28, 2013. http://www.antrimreview.net/local_news/article_992f52e8-810a-11e2-8346-0019bb30f31a.html?TNNoMobile.

Roger & Me. Directed by Michael Moore. Warner Bros., 1989. Film.

Rombauer, Irma. *The Joy of Cooking*. Indianapolis, IN: Bobbs-Merrill Company, 1964.

Smith, Betty. *A Tree Grows in Brooklyn*. New York: Harper & Brothers, 1943.

Thompson, Charles D., Jr. *Spirits of Just Men: Mountaineers, Liquor Bosses, and Lawmen in the Moonshine Capital of the World*. Champaign, IL: University of Illinois Press, 2011.

Time-Life. *Recipes: The Cooking of Germany*. Foods of the World series. New York: Time-Life, Inc., 1969.

Turley, James. *Automobile Sales in Perspective*. Federal Reserve Bank of Michigan, June 1976 (accessed April 28, 2013). http://research.stlouisfed.org/publications/review/76/06/Automobile_Jun1976.pdf.

Zehnder, John. *The Flavors of Frankenmuth*. Frankenmuth, MI: Zehnders, 2000.

Index of Recipes